DATE DUE

OCT 3 0 1998	
Justice Institute	
due May 20/01	
JAN 2 3 2002	

BRODART   Cat. No. 23-221

CULTURE AND PSYCHOPATHOLOGY

A Guide to Clinical Assessment

Edited by
Wen-Shing Tseng, M.D.
and
Jon Streltzer, M.D.

BRUNNER/MAZEL, *Publishers* • NEW YORK
A member of the Taylor & Francis Group

Library of Congress Cataloging-in-Publication Data

Culture and psychopathology : a guide to clinical assessment / edited
by Wen-Shing Tseng and Jon Streltzer.
   p. cm.
   Includes bibliographical references and indexes.
   ISBN 0-87630-839-6 (hard cover)
   1. Psychology, Pathological—Cross-cultural studies. 2. Mental
illness—Diagnosis. I. Tseng, Wen-Shing. II. Streltzer,
Jon.
   [DNLM: 1. Mental Disorders—diagnosis—case studies. 2. Cros
-Cultural Comparison. 3. Psychopathology—cases studies. WM
C968 1997]
RC455.4.E8C787   1997
616.89′075—dc21
DNLM/DLC   97–22
for Library of Congress   CI

Copyright © 1997 by Brunner/Mazel, Inc.

Published by
BRUNNER/MAZEL, INC.
19 Union Square West
New York, New York 10003

Manufactured in the United States of America
10 9 8 7 6 5 4 3 2 1

CONTENTS

CONTRIBUTORS

Iqbal Ahmed, M.D. Associate Professor, Department of Psychiatry, University of Hawaii School of Medicine

David M. Bernstein, M.D. Assistant Professor, Department of Psychiatry, University of Hawaii School of Medicine

Alan Buffenstein, M.D. Assistant Professor, Department of Psychiatry, University of Hawaii School of Medicine

Richard J. Castillo, Ph.D. Associate Professor, Department of Psychology, University of Hawaii at West Oahu

Steven L. Chaplin, M.D. Clinical Assistant Professor, Department of Psychiatry, University of Hawaii School of Medicine

Gary H. Cohen, M.D. Professor, Department of Psychiatry, University of Hawaii School of Medicine

Patricia Harrison, M.D. Assistant Professor, Department of Psychiatry, University of Hawaii School of Medicine

Danilo E. Ponce, M.D. Professor, Department of Psychiatry, University of Hawaii School of Medicine

R. Andrew Schultz-Ross, M.D. Associate Professor, Department of Psychiatry, University of Hawaii School of Medicine

Jon Streltzer, M.D. Professor, Department of Psychiatry, University of Hawaii School of Medicine

Junji Takeshita, M.D. Assistant Professor, Department of Psychiatry, University of Hawaii School of Medicine

Wen-Shing Tseng, M.D. Professor, Department of Psychiatry, University of Hawaii School of Medicine

Dykes M. Young, M.D. Assistant Professor, Department of Psychiatry, University of Hawaii School of Medicine

PREFACE

The emergence of cultural psychiatry over the past half-century coincides with the increasing recognition of the powerful influence of culture upon psychopathology. Yet, the impact of culture in clinical conditions is still poorly understood, even though it affects the daily practice of mental health professionals. Ethnic and cultural heterogeneity *and* inclusion of minority and refugee populations has become the norm for many societies due to enhanced global communication and transportation. Clinicians must inevitably assess and treat patients of widely varying backgrounds. In 1994, the American Psychiatric Association formally acknowledged the importance of cultural factors in the *Diagnostic and Statistical Manual of Mental Disorders—Fourth Edition* (DSM-IV). This manual points out the potential for ethnocentric bias, briefly notes cultural correlates and variations of symptoms and disorders, suggests a format for cultural formulation, and provides a glossary of culture-bound syndromes and idioms of distress. It whets our appetite to learn more about the extent of and the manner in which culture influences psychopathology. This book aims to provide such knowledge, and, at the same time, provide guidelines for translating the current state of knowledge into clinical practice.

The focus of this book is on *assessment*, in the broad sense of understanding a patient sufficiently to formulate a treatment approach, rather than *diagnosis* in the narrow meaning of a descriptive categorization. Assessment is taken to include the conduct of the evaluation, as well as the interpretation of the information obtained. Treatment issues are mentioned only peripherally, if at all, in order to concentrate our efforts on the cultural aspects of clinical assessment. The topic of culture and psychotherapy is deserving of a book in itself.

In contrast to many books on cultural and mental health issues, this book does not use specific ethnic groups as the base from which to explore psychopathology. Although many of the case examples in the book come from ethnic/cultural groups in the Asia/Pacific region, reflecting the clinical experience of the authors, there has been no intention to focus on any particular group or groups, nor has there been any intention to describe or define the psychosocial characteristics of particular cultural groups. Instead, we choose specific areas of psychopathology, and then explore the various ways culture may influence or interact with these disorders.

The most common forms of psychopathology are covered, including depression, anxiety, personality disorders, and psychosis. Other chapters explore symptoms or conditions which have particularly notable cultural influence, including somatization, pain, dissociation, and posttraumatic stress. Suicidal and violent behavior are covered in two chapters about these important clinical problems. The chapters on adolescent and geriatric psychopathology take a developmental approach by focusing on these particular life stages. An overview and a summing up of the cultural issues in clinical assessment are presented in the introductory and concluding chapters. It is beyond the scope of this book to be totally comprehensive, and many important areas, such as substance abuse or eating disorders, have not been included. However, we believe that the book is sufficient in scope to provide guidance to the clinician for most types of mental health work.

Terminology is a difficult issue in any book about culture. For the sake of convenience in addressing cultural issues, ethnic or national terms are often used, such as "Japanese culture," or global terms, such as "Western culture," even though these terms do not necessarily represent a specific culture in an absolute manner.

The authors of this book are mostly faculty from the Department of Psychiatry, John A. Burns School of Medicine, University of Hawaii. Practicing and teaching in the multi-ethnic society of Hawaii, they naturally have great interest in culture. The idea for this book developed out of a series of symposia on cultural psychiatry. For more than a year, the authors met weekly to discuss cases and issues in transcultural assessment of psychopathology, and to debate clinical guidelines for such assessment. As a result, the chapters have a similar format and come together forming a coherent whole. We, as editors, would like to express our appreciation to them for working together enthusiastically on this project. Our thanks also extend to Carole Kleve for her assistance in preparing the manuscripts, to Kathy Reimers for her copy editing, and to Debbie Tanaka for editing and formatting the files to the publisher's specifications. Their invaluable assistance is very much appreciated.

This book is geared for clinical use. It aims to elaborate what is known and point out the limitations of our knowledge. It draws conclusions and recommendations concerning the conduct of culturally sensitive and relevant clinical assessments for patients with common types of psychopathology. The book is intended for psychiatrists, psychologists, social workers, and students interested in enhancing knowledge and skill in making culturally oriented assessments of psychopathology.

Wen-Shing Tseng, M.D.
Jon Streltzer, M.D.

CHAPTER ONE

Overview: Culture and Psychopathology

Wen-Shing Tseng, M.D.

PRELUDE: CASE VIGNETTES

Mental health clinicians frequently encounter cases with *unusual* clinical pictures that are different from textbook or standard classification categories and are puzzling to the clinicians in making their assessments. For instance, when an Asian patient complained of an "empty heart," the doctor needed to clarify whether the patient was suffering from the medical problem of a weak heart, with other cardiac-related somatic symptoms such as palpitations or shortness of breath, or from a low spirit, with feelings of emptiness and depression.

In a hospital setting, a Latino man shouted very loudly while dramatically and emotionally striking his own body with his fists when he learned of his spouse's death. The doctor was uncertain whether this was a *usual* acute grief reaction for a man of Latin background, or if the behavior was an excessively emotional and dramatic *hysterical* reaction that required psychiatric attention.

A Caucasian medical doctor was confused by a Polynesian woman patient, who, after being told by the doctor that she would not be discharged from the hospital, tied the cord to the light switch around her neck and refused to talk to the doctor. Suspecting that the patient might be suicidal, a psychiatric consultation was requested.

Most experienced clinicians are aware that the clinical picture of a patient is influenced by many factors, such as the patient's age, gender, and socioeconomic and educational backgrounds, as well as ethnic–cultural factors. Furthermore, the process of psychiatric evaluation itself is influenced by such factors in both the patient and the clinician, as is the interaction that takes place between them (Exhibit 1). The case vignettes described above illustrate that the clinical picture is colored by the cultural background of the patient, and the process of mental assessment is influenced by the cultural backgrounds of both the patient and the clinician to the extent that it may confuse or bias the clinician's assessment.

It is the intention of this book to explore how cultural factors may alter the presentation of mental symptoms, how cultural variables may influence the process of assessment, and how culturally relevant clinical evaluation is needed to make appropriate clinical assessments—an important task that is required of all psychiatrists and mental health professionals working in our increasingly polyethnic and multicultural society.

INTRODUCTION: UNDERSTANDING CULTURE

Anthropological Definition of Culture

In order to discuss cultural influences on psychopathology, let us first clarify the term *culture*. Scholars of behavioral science define culture in various ways. According to anthropologists Kroeber and Kluckhohn (1952, p. 181), "Culture consists of patterns, explicit and implicit, of and for behavior acquired and transmitted by symbols, constituting the distinctive achievement of human groups, including their embodiments in artifacts; the essential core of culture consists of traditional ideas and especially their attached values; culture systems may, on the one hand, be considered as products of action, on the other as conditioning elements of further action."

Exhibit 1

PROCESS OF CLINICAL ASSESSMENT OF A PATIENT

Presentation of Complaint/Problems	**Perception of Problems/Pathology**

Problem Presentation Style
Motivation/Expectation
Orientation to Care System
Concept of Problems

Sensitivity
Background Information
Familiarity of Problems
Definition of Pathology

Interaction

Presentation →

Assessment ←

Experience of Problems/Disorder	**Conceptualization of Problems/Disorder**

Coping Style
Perception of Stress

Theoretical Background
Classification System
Medical Culture

Encounter of Stress/Conflict	**Diagnostic Categorization**

PATIENT

Personality
Personal Background
Sociocultural Background

CLINICIAN

Professional Orientation
Personality
Sociocultural Background

Another anthropologist, Keesing (1976), emphasized that culture exists at two levels. The first is the realm of observable phenomena—the patterns of life within a community; and the second is the realm of ideas—the organized system of knowledge and beliefs that allows a group to structure its experiences and choose among alternatives.

The most current concept of culture includes the effects of "enculturation" on the mind–brain (Castillo, 1995). As a result of enculturation, every individual learns a language, a religion, or other meaning system specifying the operation of forces of nature in the world, as well as norms of behavior and patterns of experiencing the environment. All of these are structured in neural networks in the mind–brain. It has been found that the strengths of synaptic connections between individual neurons are determined by use patterns (Thompson et al., 1986). By the habitual act of thinking in a particular language, or believing in the forms of a particular religion, those forms of thought assume a type of physical reality in the organization of neural networks in the brain. In a very real sense, the social–cultural environment becomes physically structured in the brain of the individual. This process has frequently been referred to as "downward causation" (Sperry, 1987). That is, thinking as an activity pattern is *causal* in that it alters the brain at the level of dendritic branching, and the strengths of neurotransmitter properties in the individual synapse. This means the organization of culture has its psychobiological correlates in the organization of the mind–brain—in the microanatomy of the individual neuron and in the organizational formation of neural networks (Castillo, 1995).

As pointed out by Castillo (1995, p. 23), "For example, in order to speak Chinese one must have the neural networks for speaking Chinese structured in the brain—no Chinese neural networks, no speaking Chinese. The presence of Chinese neural networks, of course, results from enculturation. Someone who is genetically Chinese, but born and raised in the United States and fully assimilated into American culture, will have American neural networks—an American mind–brain." It is these culture-specific neural organizations that in turn influence most aspects of cognitive processing by individuals in the form of cognitive schemas (Sperry, 1987). These cognitive schemas structure experience of the world, and thus influence the development of psychopathology.

Two frequently used terms closely related to culture are race and ethnicity. The term *race* refers to a group of people that is characterized by certain physical features, such as color of skin, eyes, and hair, or physical size, that distinguish it from other groups. Modern anthropologists refer to race as *geographic race*. Geographic race is a human population that has inhabited a continental land mass or an island chain sufficiently long to have developed its own distinctive genetic composition, as compared with that of other geographic populations (Hoebel, 1972). African (Black), American (Native American), Asian (Yellow), Australian, European (White), Indian, and Polynesian are some of the major geographic races recognized around the world. Thus, race refers to a biological group that may or may not coincide with a culture system shared by the group. Although it may be possible to define races by biological or genetic factors, it must to be pointed out that races, by definition, are largely social. Essentially, when an ethnic group is assumed to have a biological basis, it is called a *race*.

The term *ethnicity* refers to social groups that distinguish themselves from other groups by a common historical path, behavior norms, and their own group identity. Thus, culture refers to behavior patterns and value systems, while ethnicity refers to a group of people that shares a common culture.

As culture is an abstract term, relatively difficult to identify and distinguish, reference is customarily made to ethnicity or country. For example, Japanese culture refers to the culture system that is shared by the people of Japan; and Jewish culture to the culture system shared by the Jewish ethnic group. However, caution is necessary in such use, as the unit of culture does not necessarily tie in with the unit of ethnicity or country. For instance, there have been a substantial number of Koreans living in Japan for nearly a century, but, after three or four generations, due to differences in the historical backgrounds of Japan and Korea, they still identify themselves as *Korean*, and are not accepted by other Japanese nationals as *Japanese*. Thus Japanese culture is not necessarily shared by "all" of the people of Japan; and Korean culture is shared by people not only living in Korea proper, but also by this group of people that is, in reality, Korean–Japanese.

Different Levels of Culture Addressed

In everyday life, culture may be perceived at different levels or in different dimensions. From the standpoint of behavior analysis, it is important to be aware of the different ways of grasping culture. They are:

Ideal Cultural Behavior

A desirable pattern of life prescribed by a certain group of people. This ideal does not necessarily match the actual behavior observed in the society. Ideal norms are generally selected and described by the members of a society in terms of group well-being; and they are often violated when individual self-interest induces another course of action (Hoebel, 1972).

Actual Cultural Behavior

A norm of behavior actually observed in life. The real culture is what the members of a society do and think in all their activities in fact (Hoebel, 1972). The gap between the ideal culture and the real culture may be great or small, depending on the societies in question.

Stereotyped Cultural Behavior

This refers to a certain behavior pattern that is described by an outsider to the group as if it represents the total behavior pattern of the group. The described behavior pattern is usually fragmented, exaggerated, or distorted. It may be merely a product of the outsider's own projection and not reflect the actual culture at all.

Deviated Cultural Behavior

The behavior pattern observed within a group is not necessarily homogeneous. Some of the members may manifest behavior patterns that are idiosyncratic and deviate from the pattern of the majority. Such deviated behavior may or may not be pathological.

Different Natures of Cultures Compared

When comparison is made between different cultural systems, it is necessary to understand the kind of cultural systems that are being compared. Otherwise, the comparison may be inappropriate and misleading.

Homogeneous versus *Heterogeneous*

The degree of variation within a cultural system may be minimal, and the culture homogeneous; or the differences may be so great that the nature of the culture is heterogeneous. If a culture is relatively homogeneous, any portion of the group will well represent the total of the society, and generalizations may be fairly inferred. In a heterogeneous culture, on the other hand, no one fragment of the society may be taken as a reflection of the totality. When a comparison is made between cultures, the degree of variation that exists within each culture is an important consideration.

Traditional versus *Contemporary*

Also deserving attention is the matter of cultural patterns that have existed in the past versus those that are observed at present within a society. Although, by definition, it is the nature of culture to maintain its characteristics, cultures also have a tendency to evolve over the course of time. What has been described as traditional may or may not be practiced anymore, or may continue to exist in a modified form. A time reference may be needed in referring to particular value systems or unique behavior patterns held by a society, to avoid confusing the present situation with the past.

Similar versus *Dissimilar*

It is important to examine the relative similarities and differences that may exist between the cultures being compared (the extent of cultural difference). For instance, a comparison made between a Caucasian American and an African American may not reveal obvious differences that can be attributed to culture. Because they are living in the same host society, the United States, any differences that may exist are minimized. However, a comparison of a Caucasian American and an African living in a traditional part of Africa may demonstrate great differences between them. The wider the culture gap, the easier it is to demonstrate the impact of cultural factors.

CULTURE AND PSYCHOPATHOLOGY

Type of Psychopathology

In order to discuss culture and psychopathology, it is first necessary to clarify the term *psychopathology*. In particular, it is helpful to distinguish different groups of psychopathology, which have varying cultural implications.

Major versus Minor Psychiatric Disorders

Mental disorders may be divided into major and minor disorders. Major psychiatric disorders are relatively severe, with gross impairment, including psychoses of various kinds, both functional and organic. Minor psychiatric disorders are usually less severe, allowing a person to maintain a reasonable connection to reality. Minor psychiatric illness includes adjustment disorders and a group of disorders formerly categorized as neuroses.

Major psychiatric disorders have prominant biological determinants and are less likely to be caused by psychological and sociocultural factors. The influence of cultural factors is secondary. Thus, culture may affect the phenomenology of, reaction to, and management and outcome of the disorder. On the other hand, the origin of minor psychiatric disorders is more intimately tied to psychological and contextual factors, and therefore sociocultural factors are more critical in their etiology.

Definitions of Normality and Pathology

To assess cultural influence on psychopathology, one must take into account the operating definitions of *normality* versus *pathology*. There are four ways to distinguish normality from pathology (Offer & Sabshin, 1974).

By Agreement of Experts

This first approach takes the view that normality or pathology can be distinguished clearly by the nature of the phenomenon itself, and can be judged by experts. In medicine, the occurrence of bleeding or a bone fracture, by the nature of the condition, is judged without doubt to be pathological and needing medical care. In psychiatry, if a person talks to nonexistent people, claims to be hearing the voice of a spaceman, or eats his or her own feces, he or she will be professionally considered to be suffering from a pathological mental condition. This approach maintains that certain conditions (manifested as signs or symptoms) are absolutely pathological in nature. A diagnosis can be made on such a condition that is applicable universally, beyond cultural boundaries.

By Deviation from the Mean

This second approach relies on mathematical measurement and uses a range of deviation from the mean to distinguish between normal and abnormal. For example, a diagnosis of hypertension, or underweight, is a medical condition that uses certain scales and measurements to define normality; a pathological condition is diagnosed when the measurement goes beyond the average range. In psychiatry, the measurement of IQ serves to distinguish normal or subnormal intelligence. The concept of mean is universal, yet the range of mean often needs adjustment for different populations. This is quite true when personality is to be assessed by using questionnaires cross-culturally.

By Assessment of Function

This third approach considers the effect of the thoughts, feelings, or behavior on function. Whether the condition provides (healthy) function or (unhealthy) dysfunction for the individual is the basis for judgment. Openly aggressive behavior that frequently disturbs the family, neighbors, or society is dysfunctional and therefore considered pathological. On the other hand, quiet, seclusive, and asocial behavior, if it does not cause any problems to other people, may not be considered dysfunctional, and thus, not labeled pathological. In sum, behavior is judged primarily by its impact on the individual, others, and the environment.

By Social Judgment

The fourth approach utilizes social judgment in deciding if behavior is normal or pathological. The decision is subject to the social knowledge and attitudes found among the members of the society. Thus, the conclusion is both subjective and collective. For instance, to walk naked in a public area may be seen as *normal* behavior in one society, *unusual* in another, and *obscene* in a third, depending on how each society defines the nature of such behavior, and its cultural tolerance of the action. The judgments made by a society may vary greatly, depending on its customs, beliefs, or values.

It is important for a clinician to be aware of which of the above approaches is being utilized in making a clinical judgment, to recognize the limitations of each approach, and to make whatever adjustments are necessary in putting together final assessment.

Different Levels of Cultural Impact on Psychopathology

Culture is a variable that influences psychopathology in a variety of ways. The following are a few of the levels of impact.

Phenomenology of Psychopathology (as a Symptom)

Cultural shaping of presenting symptoms is referred to as the pathoplastic effect of culture on pathology. For instance, the content of delusions or auditory hallucinations is subject to the environmental context in which the pathology is manifested. The content of an individual's grandiose delusion may be characterized by the belief that he is a Russian emperor, Jesus Christ, Buddha, or the president of the United States, depending on which figure is more popular or important. When a person becomes depressed, he may feel guilty for sins he has committed, or ashamed for socially noncompliant performance, or neither guilty nor ashamed. The relative emphasis on guilt or shame in the larger society shapes the nature of depressive delusions that may form in a susceptible member of that society.

Variations of Psychopathology (as a Syndrome)

The effect of cultural factors on pathology may be so prominent that it affects not only the level of symptom content, but also the syndrome as a whole. In this case, the concept of *subtype* or *variation* of a syndrome needs to be entertained.

For instance, Chinese in Hong Kong with anorexia nervosa are seldom concerned with being physically overweight. This is different from the anorexia nervosa recognized and described in Western society, and the syndrome is referred to as "non-fat concerned anorexia" (Lee et al., 1993). Similarly, the clinical picture of social phobia observed among Japanese is so different from that described in Western classifications that Japanese psychiatrists prefer to use the diagnostic nosology of *tanjinkuofusho* (anthrophobia, or interpersonal relation phobia) (Kimura, 1982) to distinguish it from common *social phobia* as described in the *Diagnostic and Statistical Manual of Mental Disorders—Fourth Edition* (DSM-IV) (American Psychiatric Association, 1994).

Unique Psychopathology (as a Specific Psychiatric Condition)

Finally, culture may contribute to the development of a unique psychopathology that is observed only in a certain cultural environment. This is referred to as a *culture-related specific psychiatric disorder* or a *culture-bound syndrome* (CBS). The occurrence of intense anxiety associated with the fear that the penis will shrink into the abdomen, resulting in death, is a unique psychopathology observed mainly in the South Asia region and is known as *koro* (impotence panic). It may occur as an epidemic (Tseng et al., 1988), involving several thousand victims within a short period of time. It is closely related to the local people's belief that the shrinking of the penis is a sign of the fatal exhausting of the *yang* element (Mo et al., 1995). *Koro*, as well as other kinds of unique psychopathology, such as *malgri* (territorial anxiety syndrome) (Cawte, 1976), or *amok* (non-discriminatory massive homocide) (Westermeyer, 1973) are classic examples of specific culture-related disorders observed only among certain peoples in their cultural settings.

Frequency of Psychopathology (as a Surveyed Psychiatric Condition)

It is obvious that culture affects psychopathology by the difference in frequency of pathology observed in various societies. If the variable of the sociocultural environment favors the development of a certain psychopathology, that pathology will be more prevalent; if not, it will be less prevalent.

It needs to be pointed out that there are many factors related to prevalence other than biology. The acceptance of the disorder by the environment, the availability of support, and the existing care system, all contribute to the prevalence of the disorder in the community. Schizophrenia, as a major psychiatric disorder, predominantly determined by biological factors, tends to have a narrow range of variation among different societies (Tsuang et al., 1995). In contrast to this, many psychiatric disorders, whose development is intimately tied to psychological factors and sociocultural variables, tend to have a wider range of variation of prevalence. The prevalence of suicidal behavior (Kok and Tseng, 1992), alcoholism (Day, 1995), and substance abuse (Anthony and Helzer, 1995) are examples of disorders whose frequency varies among different societies according to the sociocultural context, which contributes significantly to the occurrence of such disorders.

PROCESS OF CLINICAL EVALUATION

Psychiatric assessment results from a dynamic process that involves multiple levels of interaction between the patient (and sometimes the patient's family) and the clinician. This dynamic process involves a series of steps (Exhibit 1). It starts with the distress or problems experienced and perceived by the patient, and proceeds to the presentation of complaints made by the patient to the clinician. These complaints are perceived and understood as specific types of problems by the clinician. Finally, an assessment, which includes categorization and diagnosis, is made by the clinician of the disorder in question.

The Problems as Experienced by the Patient

This refers to the internal distress experienced by the patient. A person experiences *pain* when hit; feels *anxious* if worried about something; becomes *paranoid* if persecution by others is suspected; or has the feeling of going *downhill* if something of personal significance is lost. All these reactions to distress, which may be manifested as symptoms or signs, are subjective, experiential phenomena. These subjective reactions cannot be precisely measured from outside. It is thus impossible to know to what extent the actual *experience* of distress is influenced by cultural factors.

It is clear that the forerunner of the distress, namely the stress itself, can be impacted by sociocultural factors. Stress can be produced by culture in numerous ways. Stress can be produced by culturally demanding performance. For example, many cultures demand that a woman produce a male child; the society blames her, and the woman herself feels guilty, if she fails to bear a boy. Many societies expect children to achieve high academic performance. If a child fails to meet such parental expectations, he or she is shamed. Stress can be created by culturally maintained beliefs. For instance, if a person believes that it is very important to define the territory between sea and land, and he or she breaks a culturally held taboo and brings food across the land–sea territory, he or she may develop severe anxiety and associated somatic complaints, described as *malgri* reaction (Hippler and Cawte, 1978). A person may hold the cultural belief that it is fatal if his penis shrinks into his abdomen, and, in response to that belief, he may become fearful that his penis is "shrinking" and develop a panic attack, known as *koro* reaction (Mo et al., 1995). Stress can be generated by a culture's restriction of behavior, by culturally supported attitudes, or other culture-related factors, all of which may provoke distress in the individual.

The Problems as Identified by the Patient

Following the experience of distress and symptom manifestation, the next step is for the patient to perceive and interpret the distressful experience that he or she is having. How the patient perceives and interprets it is a psychological phenomenon that is subject to the influence of cultural factors in addition to other variables, such as the patient's personality, knowledge, and psychological needs.

Based on how the problem is understood and perceived, the patient will show a secondary process of various reactions to the distress experience. For instance, a person who interprets chest pain as nothing but chest pain will react to it lightly. However, if the pain is perceived and interpreted as a sign of an impending heart attack, the person may become very anxious, and even panic, further complicating the primary symptom of chest pain. Similarly, if a person believes that "shrinking of the penis into abdomen is fatal," he will react severely to any sign of penis shrinkage, even if the penis never shrinks into the abdomen. If a person does not adhere to such beliefs, he or she will be impervious to normal changes in his or her body. In other words, the perception and reaction to the primary symptoms will add secondary symptoms that compound the clinical picture. The forming of secondary symptoms is usually subject to cultural influences.

The Problems as Presented by the Patient

The next step deals with how the complaints or illness are presented by the patient to others—the process and art of *complaining*. Analysis of this process has shown that how the problem, symptom, or illness is presented or communicated to the clinician is based on the patient's (or the family's) orientation to illness, the meaning of the symptom, motivation for help-seeking, and culturally expected or sanctioned "problem-presenting style." It is a combination of the results of these factors that affects the process of complaining. Culture definitely plays a clear role in the complaining process.

For instance, when the patient presents a somatic complaint to the clinician at the initial session, there may be several alternative implications, namely: a physical condition is the patient's primary concern; somatic symptoms are being used as a socially recognized signal of illness; or complaints are a culturally sanctioned prelude to revealing psychological problems. Thus, the nature of the somatic complaint needs careful evaluation and understanding, rather than simply dealing with the somatic complaint itself (Tseng, 1975).

In the reverse situation, a patient may present many psychological problems to the therapist at the initial session, complaining that, as a small child, he or she was abused by an adult, never adequately loved by his or her parents, and is now confused about his or her own identity, unclear about the meaning of life, and so on. It is necessary for the clinician to determine how much of this psychologized complaint may merely reflect the patient's learned behavior from public communication about patienthood, and how much is really of primary concern. The performance of complaining or problem presentation is an art that does not directly reflect the distress or problem from which the patient is suffering. A dynamic interpretation and understanding is very necessary.

The Problems as Understood by the Clinician

A clinician, as a human being, as a cultural person, and as a professional person, will have different ways of perceiving and understanding the complaints that are presented by patients. Psychological sensitivity, cultural awareness, and professional experience, as well as medical competence, will all act together to influence the assessment of the problems a patient has presented. The cultural background of the clinician is a significant factor, and deserves special attention, particularly when the clinician is examining a patient with a diverse cultural background or a cultural background with which the clinician is unfamiliar.

> How the clinician's own cultural background affects the clinical assessment was shown in a study of the assessment of parent–child behavior by Japanese and American psychiatrists (Tseng et al., 1982). A series of videotaped family interaction patterns was shown to child psychiatrists in Tokyo and Honolulu. The clinicians of the two cultures reached remarkably different assessment conclusions. In one videotape a father did not interact with his daughter, leaving this role to his wife. Japanese child psychiatrists tended to view this as exhibiting "adequate" and "alright" parenting behavior,

while their American counterparts viewed such behavior as "not involved" and "inadequate" parenting behavior. The main reason for these different assessments derived from the clinicians' cultural expectations of a father's behavior. For Americans, it is culturally expected that the father, like the mother, should interact and be involved with all of their children, while the Japanese consider it the mother's job to interact and be involved with the children, and not the father's appropriate role. If a father interacts directly and too much with his daughter, it is considered "inappropriate behavior" for the father according to Japanese culture. This clearly demonstrates that a clinician's value system and cultural beliefs affect his way of making assessments.

It is well recognized that the clinician's style of interview, perception of and sensitivity toward pathology, and familiarity with the disorder under examination all influence the interactions between patient and clinician, which in turn influence the outcome of the clinician's understanding of the disorder (Tseng et al., 1992).

For example, an Asian patient's elaborate idiomatic complaints of suffering due to weakness of the kidney (psychosexual problem), elevated fire in the body or liver (anger or anxiety), loss of soul (depression or dissociation), disturbance from a deceased aunt's spirit, and so on, may not be fully comprehended with cultural empathy by an Occidental clinician; whereas the problems of polysubstance abuse or psychosexual problems presented by an Occidental patient may be unfamiliar to an Asian clinician, who may be at a loss as to how to relevantly explore and understand the problem.

A clinical study supports the fact that how familiar a clinician is with a patient's pathology will shape the result of clinical assessment. A group of case vignettes of social phobia was presented to clinicians in Tokyo and Honolulu, for their clinical diagnosis. More than 90% of the Japanese psychiatrists recognized the diagnosis of social phobia, compared to only a small percentage of the American psychiatrists. This illustrates that Japanese psychiatrists, who are familiar with social phobia, which is commonly seen in their clinical work, will give congruent diagnoses of social phobia when such cases are presented to them; whereas American psychiatrists, who are relatively unfamiliar with this condition, will not—they tend to give diagnoses of anxiety disorder, avoidant personality disorder, or others disorders (Tseng et al., 1992).

The Problems as Diagnosed by the Clinician

The final step in the process of evaluation is making a clinical diagnosis. Finding the appropriate clinical category for diagnosis is influenced by the professional orientation of the clinician, the classification system used, and the purpose of making the diagnosis (Cooper et al., 1972; Tseng et al., 1992). In many societies, a clinician needs to take into consideration the social impact of diagnostic labeling on the patient and his or her family when making a clinical diagnosis.

In order to understand why most of the psychotic inpatients in the United States were diagnosed as having schizophrenia while a much higher percentage of those in the United Kingdom were diagnosed as having affective disorders, a clinical investigation was conducted. A videotape record of a group of (psychotic) patients was presented to psychiatrists in both New York and London. Despite equivalent recognition of symptoms by both British and American psychiatrists, their diagnoses were different. British psychiatrists tended to diagnose affective psychoses in the same patients that American psychiatrists diagnosed schizophrenia. At the time of this investigation, American psychiatrists held broad concepts of schizophrenia, while British psychiatrists had a more restrictive view.

In sum, making a clinical diagnosis is a complex matter involving a *dynamic process* between the help-seeker and the help-provider. This diagnostic process is influenced in a variety of ways by the cultural background of the *patient* as well as that of the *clinician*. The clinician should be aware of how cultural factors will affect each step in the process involved in the interaction between the patient and the clinician.

CULTURE CONSIDERATIONS IN CLINICAL ASSESSMENT

Theoretical Considerations

Concepts of Disease and Illness

In medical anthropology, a distinction is made between the concepts of *disease* and *illness*. The term disease refers to the patho-

logical or malfunctioning condition that is diagnosed by the doctor or folk healer. It is the clinician's conceptualization of the
patient's problem, which derives from the paradigm of disease in
which the clinician was trained. For example, a biomedically oriented psychiatrist is trained to diagnose brain disease; a psychoanalyst is trained to diagnose psychodynamic problems; and a
folk healer might be trained to conceptualize and interpret such
things as spirit possession or sorcery. For a medically oriented
psychiatrist, a mental *disease* is used to describe a pathological
condition that can be grasped and comprehended from a medical
point of view—it provides an objective and professional perspective on how the sickness may occur, how it is manifested, how it
progresses, and how it ends.

In contrast to this, the term *illness* refers to the sickness that is
experienced and perceived by the patient. It is the patient's subjective perception, experience, and interpretation of his or her
suffering. Although these two terms, namely disease and illness,
are linguistically almost synonymous, they are purposely used
differently to refer to two separate conditions. It is intended to
illustrate that disease as perceived by the healer or doctor may or
may not be similar to illness as perceived and experienced by the
person suffering. This artificial distinction is useful from a cultural perspective, as it illustrates that there exists a potential gap
between the healer (or doctor) and the help-seeker (or patient) in
viewing the problems. Although the biomedically oriented physician tends to assume that disease is a universal and medical
entity, from a medical anthropological point of view, all clinicians' diagnoses as well as patients' illness experiences are cognitive constructions based on cultural schemas.

The potential gap between disease and illness is an area that
deserves the clinician's attention and management in making the
clinical assessment meaningful and useful, particularly in a
cross-cultural situation.

Range of Phenomenology of Psychopathology

Language reflects the concerns of the cultural group. For example, Eskimo people who are surrounded by snow year-round recognize and refer to many different kinds of snow, rather than having only one word for snow. Likewise, Micronesian people living
on small islands in the middle of the ocean distinguish many
types of clouds, rather than simply referring to clouds in general.
This helps them to predict weather conditions for survival in sail-

ing. Asian people use many different terms to express their concern with the delicate hierarchy of relations among family members. For instance, the Chinese use two terms, *gege* and *didi*, to address elder brother and younger brother, respectively, rather than simply referring to them both as *brothers;* three terms, *bobo, shushu,* and *jiujiu,* refer to paternal elder uncle, paternal younger uncle, and maternal uncle, respectively, rather than addressing them all by the single term *uncle,* as in English. In contrast, the Chinese are familiar with only one or two kinds of wine (mostly rice wine), whereas Westerners are familiar with endless varieties. In the Japanese language, there are many words that refer to the intimate dependency that exists in an interpersonal relationship, such as *amai, amaeru, amanzuru;* and *suneru, higamu, hinekureru,* and *uramu,* referring to various states of mind when the dependency needs are not satisfied. These linguistic phenomena reflect a characteristic of the Japanese people and their culture, in which dependence is valued, permitted, elaborated, and expected (Doi, 1973).

All the examples described above indicate that, beyond a universal base, there are variations in human thought or concern that are reflected in a people's use of language. In a similar way, it can be expected that human beings experience or manifest different spectrums, fields, or ranges of mental conditions, based on their life context or sociocultural background. Furthermore, it may be speculated that this phenomenon applies to pathological mental conditions. In addition to the basic, core, or universal pathology, people with different cultural backgrounds will experience and manifest different ranges of psychopathology. This is particularly true in the case of minor psychiatric disorders, which are more predominantly influenced by psychological and social factors.

This speculation can be illustrated by the study of folk terms used by people in different societies in describing their normal or pathological mental conditions. Beiser et al. (1976) investigated stress-related mental symptoms that were described by the people of Senegal in western Africa. Instead of using existing symptom questionnaires designed for Western populations, they constructed an indigenous questionnaire based on local ways of expressing disturbance. This was to avoid the danger of forcing data into categories or scales that exist in the mind of the investigator. The collected data were factor-analyzed into four clear-cut components, namely: Physiological Anxiety, Topical Depression, Health Preoccupation, and Episodic Anxiety. These four groups represented the spectrum of mental disturbance that was described and presented by the local people, which was different from the mental spectrum presented by other cultural groups.

In a similar way, a group of psychiatrists collaborated to conduct a multicultural study of minor psychiatric disorders in Asia (Tseng et al., 1990). The psychiatrists from China, Indonesia, Japan, and Thailand were asked to list the neurotic or emotional symptoms most commonly presented in their own clinical settings. Based on the compiled list, a Mental Symptom Questionnaire for Asian Population was constructed and given to the nonpsychotic psychiatric outpatient population at the sites of Bali (Indonesia), Chiang-Mai (Thailand), Kao-hsiung (Taiwan), Shanghai (Mainland China), and Tokyo (Japan). When the collected data were factor-analyzed, nine clusters emerged. Three of these clusters were related to the head, chest, and abdomen. Somatic symptoms for these Asian populations were not only prevalent but were elaborated. When the symptom profiles from the five sites were compared, it was found that the subjects from Kao-hsiung (Taiwan) and Shanghai (Mainland China) were almost identical, while those from Chiang-Mai (Thailand) were significantly different from the other sites. The findings supported the notion that people from different cultural backgrounds have different ranges or spectrums of commonly presented mental symptoms.

Netting Effect on Assessment

Closely related to the concept of variation of range of psychological expression is the concept of the "netting effect" on recognizing psychiatric symptoms. The concept of the netting effect is analogous to fishing with a net. The catch will vary depending on what *kind* of fishing net (e.g. the size or shape of the mesh) is used and also *where* the fishing net is cast, since different kinds of fish exist in different areas. Thus, the net determines the size and the kind of fish which may be caught.

In a similar manner, clinicians use different "fishing nets" to catch (or gather) pertinent history, symptoms, and signs from their patients. The fishing net used by the clinician is related to his or her professional knowledge, experience, laboratory instruments, and diagnostic classification systems, and influences the way he or she collects, organizes, and interprets information. In a cross-cultural setting, the clinical evaluation depends on how perceptive and sensitive the clinician is, and the method and criteria used to analyze and categorize the data—that is, the "netting effect."

Etic or Emic Approach

The terms *etic* and *emic* are originally derived from the linguistic terms *phonetic* (sound for universal language) and *phonemic* (sound for specific language). *Etic* is used to address things that are considered universal, while *emic* is culture-specific. In the field of research, the *etic* strategy holds the view that investigation can take place anywhere in the world, as the characteristics to be studied are universal; the *emic* approach takes the position that the characteristics are indigenous and distinctive, and only applicable to certain cultural groups (Draguns, 1989). At another level, the *etic* approach implies that research is conducted by an outsider; the *emic* approach, by an insider. Each approach has its own inherent advantages and shortcomings.

Applied to the clinical task of assessment, the cultural perspective defines an *etic* evaluation as one performed by a clinician who is outside of the cultural system. The etic evaluation may have the advantage of the outsider's fresh and objective perspective, but may be handicapped by the loss of meaning in interpreting the phenomena observed. In contrast, an emic evaluation is one carried out by a clinician of the same cultural group as the patient. The advantage of this approach is that meaningful interpretation may be obtained with cultural insight, the disadvantage is that it may be biased by subjectivity. In making a clinical assessment and interpretation, it is pertinent for the clinician to be aware of his or her position, either *etic* or *emic*, and to recognize its advantages as well as the shortcomings.

Practical Considerations

In actual practice, there are several challenges that need to be overcome by the clinician in order to conduct appropriate cross-cultural assessments with patients of different cultural back-grounds. Some of these challenges include the following.

Overcoming the Language Barrier

The first problem the clinician needs to solve is overcoming any language barrier that may exist with the patient. Clearly, a language problem will affect communication and limit the process and results of the clinician's evaluation. If there is no common language used between the clinician and the patient, an interpreter is needed. Body language is inadequate in making comprehensive mental health evaluations.

There is a skill involved in using an interpreter in a situation of psychiatric assessment (Kinzie, 1985). It is desirable to have an interpreter who has knowledge and experience in mental health work. The interpreter needs orientation, and perhaps training, for the work that is to be done. Word-for-word translation is needed for areas that are delicate and significant; summary translation for areas that require abstract interpretation; and meaning interpretation for areas that need elaboration and explanation in addition to translation. By coaching the interpreter in these different styles of interpretation, the process will be more efficient and useful.

Beyond the matter of how to interpret, it is necessary to consider the role of the interpreter, particularly his or her (social) relation to the patient, and how he or she feels and identifies with the patient and the patient's culture. For example, if a family member is used as an interpreter, this person may be functioning not only as a translator, but also attempting to convey needs of the patient and/or the family. These matters need proper attention and management, as they are all factors that will significantly affect the process and results of the interpretation.

A caution is needed when there is a common language between the clinician and the patient, making communication possible, but the common language is not the clinician's primary language. There may be a symbolic cultural meaning behind a word or a phrase that is beyond semantic understanding. Many subtle misunderstandings may occur without the clinician being aware of them (Hsu & Tseng, 1972).

Obtaining Cultural Background Information

Since a mental health worker is unlikely to be a trained anthropologist, it is unreasonable to expect him or her to have extensive knowledge about people of various cultural backgrounds. Yet, in clinical practice, it is very important to have a basic knowledge of the cultural background of a patient so that a meaningful understanding of the patient's behavior can be achieved. A clinician may read an anthropological book or consult with an anthropologist to gain the necessary information. Or, the clinician may consult with people from the same cultural background as the patient. One practical approach is to ask the patient or a member of his or her family to assist the clinician in understanding their cultural background. "How do your friends or the people in your community normally behave, think, and react in such a situation?" and "What is their interpretation of such behavior?" are the types of questions to be asked. The aim is to learn the common behavior that is collectively shared in the culture, rather than an individual, idiosyncratic response.

A caution is needed regarding reference to cultural matters. Sometimes, everything is attributed to ethnicity or culture, while at other times the existence of cultural impact is completely denied. The appropriate and objective utilization of cultural matters in interpreting the nature of behavior is in need of careful evaluation to avoid either overinterpretation or underinterpretation of the influence of culture.

Becoming Familiar with Cultural Variations of Psychopathology

There is no shortcut to learning about the types of psychopathology observed in various cultural groups. Contemporary psychiatry has not reached the point of providing comprehensive knowledge and information about this subject. There are many possible variations, particularly with psychopathology which is predominantly psychological and sociocultural in nature. It should also be noted that many publications overemphasize or exaggerate cultural impact on psychopathology. Numerous CBSs are named and reported, even though they are not necessarily or primarily related to culture in a strict sense (Tseng & McDermott, 1981). Learning objectively and accurately about the possible effects of culture on psychopathology is a major task for clinicians to undertake.

Becoming Culturally Sensitive

Although, practically, it is impossible to expect all clinicians to receive training as cultural psychiatrists or mental health workers, it should be the aim of every clinician or mental health worker to learn to be culturally sensitive. As long as clinicians are aware of the possible effect of culture on psychopathology and mental health practice, they will be more likely to search for and understand human behavior from a cultural dimension in addition to other dimensions that have an impact on behavior and psychopathology. This cultural sensitivity should be a basic expectation for every mental health worker.

EPILOGUE: DISCUSSION OF CASES

In the beginning of this chapter, three case vignettes were presented that deserve cultural elaboration before the chapter is closed. In the first case, a Chinese patient complained of an "empty heart." Clearly, he was using a traditional idiom to describe his distress. The idiomatic phrase originated in the Chinese medical concept of "vacant" or "empty" heart, referring to a low spirit, down heart, or low mood. Knowing the patient was using an idiom rooted in this traditional medical concept, the physician would not interpret the complaint literally as a problem of the heart organ, but would understand that the patient was reporting feelings of depression.

In the case of the Latino man, consultation with the patient's Latino friends revealed that the patient's behavior was considered *excessive* and *too theatrical*, and the label of *hysterical reaction* could be given to his dramatic reaction to the death of his wife. Consultation with people of the same cultural background is useful in this kind of situation to distinguish atypical from culturally normal behavior.

In the case of the woman who tied the rope around her neck, there was an interesting finding. This 66-year-old Samoan woman was admitted with congestive heart failure. In addition, she had significant multisystem disease, including chronic obstructive lung disease, diabetes mellitus, impaired renal function, and a history of myocardial infarction. She had reluctantly agreed to be hospitalized at the insistence of her family, although she preferred to stay at home and have the family take care of her. Two weeks into the hospitalization, the patient reported to the nurse that she was furious with her doctor and wished to be discharged. She believed that the doctor had promised her that she would not have to stay in the hospital very long and that he had lied to her. When the psychiatric consultant approached her, she looked away and mumbled, "I hate White people." Both her attending physician and the psychiatric consultant were White. The consultant ignored the comment and started "talking story" with her in a culturally appropriate way, asking about her family background. She indicated that her husband had died a few years before but she had 15 children. The consultant expressed great interest and appreciation of this fact, and asked about grandchildren. She stated proudly that she had 55. The consultant remarked that with her husband dead, she must now be the head of the family, and that obviously this was a very wonderful, large family and she must be an extremely important person. The patient became very pleased with the consultant and began to talk freely. At the end of the interview, she expressed great appreciation for the consultant's visit. She agreed to stay in the hospital and appreciated that the consultant would speak to her attending physician on her behalf. This case illustrates that, after successfully "culture-joining" with the patient, the doctor was able to learn the nature of her manifested behavior. Putting a rope around her neck was her way of showing her anger, and protesting to her doctor for not keeping his promise. It was not related to suicidal feelings at all!

These cases illustrate that, in order to grasp the nature of a patient's problems, culturally relevant inquiry and exploration is necessary, in addition to competent clinical knowledge and skill.

A clinician needs to know how cultural factors will shape the process and results of clinical evaluation. He or she also needs to learn how culture may have a different impact on various forms of psychopathology. The following chapters will examine and analyze the impact of culture on different kinds of pathology, including: anxiety, depression, pain, somatic complaints, dissociation, psychoses, post-traumatic stress disorders, suicidal behavior, violent behavior, and personality disorders. Assessment of psychopathology manifested in different stages of the life cycle, namely adolescence and old age, will also be explored. After reviewing different psychopathologies, an integrative summary and suggestions will be made in the concluding chapter of this book.

REFERENCES

Beiser, M., Benfari, R.C., Collomb, H., & Ravel, J. (1976). Measuring psychoneurotic behaviours in cross-cultural surveys. *Journal of Nervous and Mental Disease, 163*, 10–23.

Castillo, R.J. (1995). Culture, trance, and the mind–brain. *Anthropology of Consciousness, 6*, 17–34.

Cawte, J.E. (1976). Malgri: A culture-bound syndrome. In W.P. Lebra (Ed.), *Culture-bound syndromes, ethnopsychiatry, and alternate therapies* (pp. 22–31). Honolulu: University Press of Hawaii.

Cooper, J.E., Kendell, R.E., Gurland, B.J., Shaarpe, L., Copeland, J.R.M., & Simon, R. (1972). *Psychiatric diagnosis in New York and London* (p.125). London: Oxford University Press.

Day, N.L. (1995). Epidemiology of alcohol use, abuse, and dependence. In M.T. Tsuang, M. Tohen, G.E.P. Zahner (Eds.), *Textbook in psychiatric epidemiology*. New York: Wiley-Liss.

Doi, T. (1973). *The anatomy of dependence* (pp. 28–32). Tokyo: Kodansha International.

Draguns, J.G. (1989). Dilemmas and choices in cross-cultural counseling: The universal versus the culturally distinctive. In P.B. Pedersen, J.G. Draguns, W.J. Lonner, & J.E. Trimble (Eds.), *Counseling across cultures* (pp. 3–21). Honolulu: University of Hawaii Press.

Hippler, A. & Cawte, J. (1978). The Malgri territorial anxiety syndrome: Primitive pattern for agoraphobia. *Journal of Operational Psychiatry, 9*, 23–31.

Hoebel, E.A. (1972). *Anthropology: The study of man* (pp. 32–33, 232–233). New York: McGraw-Hill.

Hsu, J. & Tseng, W.S. (1972). Intercultural psychotherapy. *Archives of General Psychiatry, 26*, 700–705.

Jenkins, J.H. (1992). Too close for comfort: Schizophrenia and emotional over-involvement among Mexicano families. In A.D. Gaines (Ed.), *Ethnopsychiatry: The cultural construction of professional and folk psychiatries* (pp. 203–221). Albany: State University of New York Press.

Karno, M., Jenkins, J.H., de la Selva, A., et al. (1987). Expressed emotion and schizophrenic outcome among Mexican-American families. *Journal of Nervous and Mental Disease, 175*, 143–151.

Kasahara, Y. (1974). Fear of eye-to-eye confrontation among neurotic patients in Japan. In T.S. Lebra & W.P. Lebra (Eds.), *Japanese culture and behavior: Selected readings* (pp. 379–387). Honolulu: University Press of Hawaii.

Keesing, R.M. (1976). *Cultural anthropology: A contemporary perspective*. New York: Holt, Rinehart and Winston.

Kimura, S. (1982). *Nihonjin-no taijinkuofu (Japanese anthrophobia)*. Tokyo: Keiso Book Co.

Kinzie, D. (1985). Cultural aspects of psychiatric treatment with Indochinese refugees. *American Journal of Social Psychiatry, 5*, 47–53.

Kok, L.P. & Tseng, W.S. (1992). *Suicidal behavior in the Asia-Pacific region*. Singapore: Singapore University Press.

Kroeber, A.L. & Kluckhohn, C. (1952). Culture: A critical review of concepts and definitions. *Papers of the Peabody Museum of American Archaeology and Ethnology*, Vol 47 (p. 181).

Lee, S., Ho, T.P., & Hsu, L.K.G. (1993). Fat phobic and non-fat phobic anorexia nervosa: A comparative study of 70 Chinese patients in Hong Kong. *Psychological Medicine, 23*, 999–1017.

Leff, J. (1989). Family factors in schizophrenia. *Psychiatric Annals, 19*, 542–547.

Lopez, S. & Hernandez, R. (1987). When culture is considered in the evaluation and treatment of Hispanic patients. *Psychotherapy, 24*, 120–126.

Marcos, L.R. (1979). Effects of interpreters on the evaluation of psychopathology in non-English-speaking patients. *American Journal of Psychiatry, 136*, 171–174.

Marcos, L.R., Urcuyo, L., Kesselman, M., & Alpert, M. (1973). The language barrier in evaluating Spanish-American patients. *Archives of General Psychiatry, 29*, 655–659.

Margetts, E.L. (1958). The psychiatric examination of native African patients. *Medical Proceedings*, October, 679–683.

Mo, G.M., Chen, G.Q., Li, L., & Tseng, W.S. (1995). *Koro* epidemic in Southern China. In T.Y. Lin, W.S. Tseng, & E.K. Yeh (Eds.), *Chinese societies and mental health*. Hong Kong: Oxford University Press.

Offer, D. & Sabshin, M. (1974). *Normality: Theoretical and clinical concepts of mental health—second edition*. New York: Basic Books.

Sperry, R.W. (1987). Structure and significance of the consciousness revolution. *Journal of Mind and Behavior, 8*, 37–65.

Thompson, R.F., Donegan, N.H., & Lavond, D.G. (1986). The psychobiology of learning and memory. In R.C. Atkinson, R.J. Herrnstein, G. Lindzey, & R.D. Luce (Eds.), *Steven's Handbook of Experimental Psychology—Second Edition*. New York: John Wiley and Sons, Ltd.

Tseng, W.S. (1975). The nature of somatic complaints among psychiatric patients: The Chinese case. *Comprehensive Psychiatry, 16*, 237–245.

Tseng, W.S., Asai, M.H., Kitanish, K.J., McLaughlin, D., & Kyomen, H. (1992). Diagnostic pattern of social phobia: Comparison in Tokyo and Hawaii. *Journal of Nervous and Mental Disease, 180*, 380–385.

Tseng, W.S., Asai, M.H., Liu, J.Q., Wibulswasdi, P., Suryani, L.K., Wen, J.K., Brennan, J., & Heiby, E. (1990). Multi-cultural study of minor psychiatric disorders in Asia: Symptom manifestations. *International Journal of Social Psychiatry, 36*, 252–264.

Tseng, W.S. & McDermott, J.F. Jr. (1981). *Culture, mind and therapy: An introduction to cultural psychiatry* (pp. 203–221). New York: Brunner/Mazel.

Tseng, W.S., McDermott, J.F. Jr., Ogino, K., & Ebata, K. (1982). Cross-cultural differences in parent–child assessment: U.S.A. and Japan. *International Journal of Social Psychiatry, 28*, 305–317.

Tseng, W.S., Mo, K.M., Hsu, J., Li, L.S., Ou, L.W., Chen, G.Q., & Jiang, D.W. (1988). A sociocultural study of koro epidemics in Guangdong, China. *American Journal of Psychiatry, 145*, 1538–1543.

Tseng, W.S., Xu, D., Ebata, K., Hsu, J., & Cui, J. (1986). Diagnostic pattern for neuroses in China, Japan and America. *American Journal of Psychiatry, 143*, 1010–1014.

Tsuang, M.T., Tohen, M., & Zahner, G.E.P. (Eds.). (1995). *Textbook in psychiatric epidemiology*. New York: Wiley-Liss.

Vaughn, C., Doyle, M., McConaghy, N., et al. (1992). The relationship between relatives' expressed emotion and schizophrenic relapse: An Australian replication. *Social Psychiatry and Psychiatric Epidemiology, 27*, 10–15.

Westermeyer, J. (1972). On the epidemicity of amok violence. *Archives of General Psychiatry, 28,* 873–876.
Westermeyer, J. (1985). Psychiatric diagnosis across cultural boundaries. *American Journal of Psychiatry, 142,* 798–805.

CHAPTER TWO

Depression

Dykes M. Young, M.D.

CASE VIGNETTES

Case 1

Mrs. Etse, a 28-year-old Micronesian woman, began to complain of appetite loss and multiple aches and pains about two weeks prior to presentation. She had consulted the local folk medicine practitioner, and was treated with an unidentified herbal preparation, which did not relieve her symptoms. Her husband brought her to the medical dispensary in the capital city. At presentation the patient was disheveled, cachectic, dehydrated, and hypotensive. She expressed beliefs that her husband had been unfaithful and that she had been neglectful to her mother-in-law. When questioned, she acknowledged having thoughts of killing herself. She acknowledged feeling sad for some time, but did not associate her physical problems with her sadness. Instead she felt that her problems were due to possession by "sea ghosts."

Discussion

Though the patient was diagnosed with depression, her affective symptoms were not her primary concern. The patient's complaints were primarily of a somatic nature, and she attributed her illness to possession by sea ghosts. To the clinician not familiar with Micronesian culture, this belief may at first seem to be delusional. Cultures based on tradition, as opposed to those based on change, may understand depression to be caused by possession of some sort. Thus, it is essential that the clinician consider the patient's understanding of his or her illness and its cause in light of the patient's cultural background.

Case 2

Mrs. Mori, a 35-year-old Japanese-American, lost her 9-year-old son about three months prior to presentation. The boy died in an accident while on a camping trip. The loss was tragic for Mrs. Mori, but after a two-week leave, she returned to her office and resumed work as usual. Mrs. Mori mentioned to her Caucasian coworkers that she missed her dear son very much. Following her Buddhist beliefs, Mrs. Mori offered food to her deceased son's tablet at the family altar every morning. While offering the food, she would talk to her son about what had happened to the family the previous day. At night Mrs. Mori slept in her son's bed so that she "could dream about him at night." She claimed that once in a while her son's face appeared to her when she was awake. Every weekend for three months after her son's death, Mrs. Mori went to her son's grave, accompanied by her husband and her surviving son, and offered flowers at the grave site.

Upon learning of these practices, Mrs. Mori's colleagues felt that she was still severely depressed and had not yet recovered from the loss of her son. On the recommendation of her supervisor, Mrs. Mori consulted a psychiatric clinic, where she was seen by a psychiatrist of Asian background. Since Mrs. Mori did not have clinical signs of major depression, the psychiatrist concluded that Mrs. Mori was going through an *ordinary* mourning process, and that she was not pathologically depressed.

Discussion

Delineation of the boundary between normal and pathological bereavement is often problematic, even for the clinician evaluating the patient from his or her own culture. This process becomes even more confusing when the patient and therapist are of different cultural backgrounds. In order to distinguish between normal and pathological bereavement, the clinician must be familiar with the rituals and expectations surrounding the mourning process in the patient's culture. The duration of the mourning period, for example, may vary widely from one culture to another, as may the types of behaviors expected or permitted during mourning. Some cultures may consider it bizarre or even morbid for a mother to sleep in her deceased son's bed. Yet in another culture, such behavior may be an expected part of the mourning process.

Case 3

Mrs. Nguyen, a 50-year-old married Vietnamese woman, presented with multiple somatic complaints, poor sleep, decreased appetite, weight loss, constant fatigue, and suicidal ideation. Mrs. Nguyen revealed that much of her distress was due to an occurrence in Vietnam about which she carried much shame.

After the takeover of Saigon, Mrs. Nguyen's family was sent away for re-education. Mrs. Nguyen and her mother-in-law were permitted to remain in the family home in Saigon. As time passed and the fates of the relatives remained unknown, the mother-in-law became concerned that the family's home would pass to the government if she were to die without an heir. The mother-in-law urged Mrs. Nguyen to accept the title to the family home so that it would remain in the family. At first Mrs. Nguyen refused to accept the title, but eventually consented, with serious misgivings.

When Mrs. Nguyen's husband returned to Saigon, the mother-in-law had died and Mrs. Nguyen held the title to the house. Her husband and in-laws became furious with her. They accused Mrs. Nguyen of greed and of having coerced her mother-in-law into transferring the title. Mrs. Nguyen described "unresolvable shame," which she felt she would carry the rest of her life for having accepted the title.

Mrs. Nguyen described a sense of having lost self-esteem after emigrating from Vietnam. In the United States, Mrs. Nguyen felt ashamed of her acceptance of the title. She felt that her family respected her less and that because of her deed she was consigned to degrading tasks in the family business.

Discussion

While in Saigon, this patient was faced with a difficult decision. To the therapist, the choice was simple. For the patient, the choice was impossible: honor traditional mores regarding the passage of property, and lose the family home; or break tradition and accept the title. In the patient's culture only the most extreme mitigating circumstances might justify the breaking of traditional practices regarding the passage of property to the son. The American therapist had difficulty empathizing with the patient's dilemma. His culture allowed for passage of property according to less stringent guidelines. That which was stressful to the patient was a trivial matter in the eyes of the therapist.

Case 4

Mr. Dones, a 42-year-old Mexican-born American male, presented to a mental health clinic with severely depressed mood, insomnia, fatigue, poor concentration, hopelessness, decreased appetite, and psychomotor retardation of two months' duration. For several weeks, Mr. Dones had resisted his wife's encouragement to see a doctor. He claimed that although he was depressed, he did not need to see a doctor and that he could handle it on his own. He expressed concerns that his depression somehow made him less manly.

Discussion

Though Latina women may readily seek psychiatric treatment for depression, Latino men may not seek treatment until they suffer severe impairment of function, and then only with encouragement from their families. Once in treatment, the male Latino patient is at risk of dropping out. The Latino male may avoid treatment because depression may be perceived as a sign that he is less masculine. The likelihood of his continued treatment can be increased if the patient is praised for seeking help, and if he is reassured that his condition is severe enough to warrant it.

INTRODUCTION

Sharp pain seized Demeter's heart . . . She kept away from the gatherings of the Gods and high Olympus. She did not

by word or action acknowledge anyone; but without a
smile, not touching food or drink, she sat wasted with
longing . . . The earth would not send up a single sprout.
                                    —*Homeric Hymn to Demeter*,
                                    6th c. B.C.

Missing my dear mother, as a son,
    my liver and intestines are painfully broken!
Crying for my old mother, as a son
    my tears pour onto my chest!
Thinking about my old mother, as a son,
    to swallow food and tea is difficult!
Searching for my old mother, as a son,
    I cannot sleep day and night!
                                    —*Si-Lang Searching for Mother*,
                                    10th c. Beijing Opera

O that this too too solid flesh would melt,
Thaw and resolve itself into dew,
Or that the Everlasting had not fixed
His canon 'gainst self-slaughter. O God, God,
How weary, stale, flat, and unprofitable
seem to me all the uses of this world!

. . . I have of late, but
wherefore I know not, lost all my mirth, foregone all
custom of exercises; and indeed, it goes so heavily
with my disposition that this goodly frame, the
earth, seems to me a sterile promontory; this most
excellent canopy, the air, look you, this brave
o'erhanging firmament, this majestical roof fretted
with golden fire: why it appeareth nothing to me
but a foul and pestilent congregation of vapors.
                                    —Shakespeare, *Hamlet*, 1603

From its beginnings, the world's literature has been rich with
accounts of dysphoria, which many clinicians today would label
depression. The *Homeric Hymn to Demeter*, for example, describes
Demeter's sorrow following the abduction of her daughter Perse-
phone. Shakespeare's Hamlet recounts his symptoms of anhedonia,
hopelessness and suicidal ideation. Si-Lang of Chinese opera complains of somatic symptoms as part of his emotional angst.
    The European psychiatric tradition has focused on disturbances of
mood as the central feature of depression. The disease labeled depres-

sion, however, is a complex one involving alterations in many biological and psychosocial domains including those of mood and affect, immunological function (Wilson et al., 1990), interpersonal relationships, sleep architecture (Kupfer & Thase, 1983), perception, endocrinologic function (Thompson et al., 1992), and sensitivity to pain (Adler & Gattaz, 1993). Though the manifestations of the depressive syndrome are numerous, the etiology of depression is poorly understood. Thus, depression must be diagnosed, not by detecting the causative lesion, but rather by identifying the symptoms that are associated with the disorder. The distress caused by any particular symptom, and thus the emphasis placed on it, however, depend to a large extent upon the patient's value system. For example, if the patient values work productivity, then inability to work may be the depressed patient's most distressing symptom. However, if the patient values contentment and satisfaction, sad moods may cause the most distress. Similarly, if the patient embraces cultural prohibitions against suicide, then suicidal ideation may be the most distressing symptom.

Value systems are strongly influenced by culture. Thus, patients from different cultures, though all suffering from depression, may have markedly different presentations. Depression may manifest itself in three broad categories of symptoms: affective, behavioral, and somatic. If the clinician is not aware of the variability in the presentation of depression, he may fail to recognize depression in some cross-cultural patients. On the other hand, some cross-cultural patients may appear to be suffering from depression when they are not. These situations are more likely to arise when the clinician must assess the bereaved cross-cultural patient for depression.

Depressive disorders occur along a broad spectrum of severity, from mild dysthymia to severe major depressive disorder with psychotic features. In contrast to pathological depressive disorders, milder disturbances of mood may or may not be considered pathological. Differentiation of normal from pathological disturbances of mood should take into account the patient's occupational and social functioning in the context of the patient's culture.

REVIEW OF THE LITERATURE: CULTURE AND DEPRESSION

Historical Perspectives: East versus West

Hippocrates in the fourth century B.C.and Galen in the first century A.D. understood melancholia to be a physical illness caused by an overabundance of black bile. Kraeplin in the late nineteenth century, as well, understood depression to be a physical illness (Ackernecht, 1968). The symptoms of melancholia that both Hippocrates and Kraeplin described differ little from the symptoms ascribed to depression by Western clinicians today. Freud (1917), in *Mourning and Melancholia*, suggested that melancholia in some cases may be due to somatic causes, while in other cases it may be a psychogenic affection. Regardless of melancholia's etiology, Freud identified the following as its primary features: profoundly painful dejection, cessation of interest in the outside world, loss of the capacity to love, inhibition of all activity, and lowering of self-regarding feelings. Physical complaints were not identified by Freud as a feature of melancholia.

Since its beginnings, Western psychiatry has focused on the affective abnormalities seen in depression. Somatic complaints, when they are identified as part of the depressive syndrome by Western psychiatry, have been thought of as secondary to the disturbances of mood.

In order to understand the Eastern perspective toward depression, it is enlightening to consider the Buddhist view of suffering and how it contrasts with the Western perspective. According to Buddhist teachings, the Buddha was born a prince, but in adulthood converted to a life of spiritual teaching following his 49 days of rapture. Upon emerging from his meditation, the Buddha gave his first sermon, presenting the Four Noble Truths on which Buddhism is founded. It is noteworthy that the first of these truths is that life is *dukkha*, or suffering (Smith, 1991). This acceptance of suffering in Buddhist philosophy contrasts sharply with the Westerner's pursuit of happiness (Obeyesekere, 1985). Thus, the individual from a Buddhist culture who experiences depressed mood may be less likely than the individual from a Judeo–Christian culture to interpret this experience as an illness.

Epidemiology

Though Kraeplin, after visiting Java in 1904, identified the occurrence of manic depressive illness there, he suggested that unipolar depression was rare, and that when it did occur, it was "usually only mild and fleeting . . . ." This notion that depression is primarily an illness of Western cultures persisted into the 1960s (Nakane et al., 1991). As researchers began to look closely at other cultures, however, depression was found to occur in individuals from non-Western cultures as well (Singer, 1975; Jablensky et al., 1981; Lambo, 1960). Thus, the notion that depression is a disease that occurs exclusively in Western cultures has been all but dismissed.

Though depression has been identified in most, if not all, cultures examined, variation in the prevalence rates of the illness across cultures has been described. Blazer et al. (1994) determined the lifetime prevalence of depression in the United States to be 17.1%. In comparison to Whites and Hispanics, Blacks were reported to have a lower lifetime prevalence of depression at 11.9%. The reason for the lower prevalence rates among Blacks is not well defined. Prevalence rates for depression have also been reported to be lower in Asian countries compared to Western countries (Hirayasu, 1969; Nakane et al., 1988; Paykel, 1992). Hirayasu (1969) reported the lifetime prevalence of depression in Japan to be a surprisingly low 0.35%. Speculation as to the reason for the apparent lower prevalence rates for depression in Asian cultures abounds. Nakane et al. (1988) summarized this speculation by suggesting that prevalence rates for depression vary from culture to culture depending on which symptoms are recognized and emphasized by the patient and the clinician. Symptom recognition and emphasis is, in turn, influenced by the cultural values that shape psychiatry within that culture. More recently, however, Nakane et al. (1991) have suggested that prevalence rates for depression in Asian countries may be much higher than previously reported.

Comparisons of levels of anxiety and depression in Mexicans and Anglos show either no differences between cultures or that Mexicans have fewer symptoms than Anglos (Frerichs et al., 1981; Roberts, 1980). These findings, however, are inconsistent with the Mexican tendency toward belief in external locus of control and the correlation between belief in external locus of control and increased distress. Mirowsky and Ross (1984) theorized that distress resulting from belief in external locus of control is counterbalanced by support derived from stronger family and other social relationships, as they exist in Mexican culture.

Comparison of prevalence rates for depression derived from different studies poses a significant problem, in that investigators may use different criteria and instruments to make a diagnosis. Some epidemiologic studies may include only severe depression, while others may include cases of minor depression.

Despite variation in prevalence rates across cultures, Paykel (1992) reports that prevalence rates are consistently higher for women than for men across cultures for which data is available. Similarly, the World Health Organization (WHO) Collaborative

Study on the Assessment of Depressive Disorders (Thornicroft and Sartorius, 1992) shows little difference in outcome of depression across the cultures that have been studied.

INTERPRETATION AND PRESENTATION OF DEPRESSION: CULTURAL ASPECTS

Beliefs About the Cause of Depression

Ulrich (1993) described variations in the beliefs about the cause of depression in three women within a single family from an agrarian region of southern India. Each of these women had personally suffered from depression at some point in her life. The mother attributed her distress to ghost possession. The eldest daughter experienced her illness as a somatic problem, while the youngest daughter attributed her distress to depression. This remarkable family study succinctly describes the most common ways that the disease, which in the West is labeled depression, is understood. This study also illustrates a process described by Marsella (1979) in which, as traditional cultures become more Westernized, the manner in which depressed patients present begins to resemble that of the Western patient.

In traditional cultures, depression is often understood to be caused by spirit possession. The clinician treating a depressed patient from a traditional culture must exercise caution in differentiating a culturally sanctioned belief in spirit possession from psychotic features, lest the patient be unnecessarily treated with antipsychotic medication. On the other hand, the clinician must be careful not to assume that all unusual beliefs seen in the patient from an unfamiliar culture are culturally sanctioned, lest psychotic symptoms go undetected and untreated.

Though the presence of somatic complaints is not a *Diagnostic and Statistical Manual of Mental Disorders—Fourth Edition* (DSM-IV) (American Psychiatric Association, 1994) diagnostic criterion for major depression, it is generally accepted that such complaints are quite common in depressed patients across cultures (Jablensky et al., 1981; Silver, 1987; Nikelly, 1988; Chang, 1985). Furthermore, somatic complaints have been reported to be the predominant symptom of depressive conditions in some non-European cultures, for example neurasthenia and *hwa byung* (Lin et al., 1992). The depressed patient from a traditional culture may, for cultural reasons, attribute his or her complaints to a physical cause. The Western clinician, however, may regard the patient's belief in a physical cause for the distress as a form of denial seen in severe depression. Caution must be exercised when assessing the patient from a traditional culture who attributes his or her symptoms of depression to a physical illness. Such beliefs may indicate more about the patient's culture than the severity of his depression.

Examination of Asian cultural values suggests that the stigmatization of emotional or mental disorders results in an emphasis on the somatic nature of depression (Ots, 1990). In contrast, the European psychiatric tradition has legitimized the psychological basis of illness more than the Asian tradition, thus, the Western patient and clinician are more likely to attribute depression to psychological causes than are their Eastern counterparts.

Variations in Help-Seeking Behavior in Relation to Depression

Assumption of the "sick role" involves two steps that are of concern to the clinician working with a cross-cultural population. The first step involves the patient's acknowledgment that he or she is suffering from some form of distress. The second step involves the decision to seek help. Both of these steps are influenced by the patient's culture. Cultural values regarding what constitutes illness affect the first step. As mentioned previously, depressed mood in itself may not be regarded as a significant symptom by the individual who accepts suffering as a normal element of human existence. But, the clinician should be careful to distinguish the patient who readily accepts suffering from the severely depressed patient, who truly lacks insight into the presence of distress.

The second step in the process of seeking help involves making the decision to consult a clinician. This step is also strongly influenced by the patient's culture. The social stigma associated with emotional and mental illness often prevents depressed patients from seeking medical help for such problems. This stigma is by no means exclusive to any one culture, but Shanghai psychiatrist Xu (1987) has described an interesting phenomenon among Mainland Chinese which arises from attempts to avoid the stigma that mental illness carries. Mainland Chinese may refrain from seeking treatment for depression for fear of the detrimental effects that a label of mental illness may have on their prospects for marriage and employment. Instead, family or friends may be asked to discreetly consult with a psychiatrist who recommends medication which the patient then purchases and attempts to treat him or herself with. Despite the rigidly controlled drug industry in the United States, this phenomenon has been observed in a patient of Chinese descent in Hawaii.

The notion that depression is solely or partially due to a weakness of character may also prevent the depressed patient from seeking help. The case of Mr. Dones illustrates the greater reluctance of the Latino male in comparison to the Latina female to seek help for depression. The Latino male's reluctance to seek help is thought to be due to his attitude that he should be able to handle his problems on his own; or that his problems are not serious enough to warrant professional help.

Variations in Presentation of Depression

Lack of consistency in the presentation of depression across cultures tends to decrease the sensitivity of any method used to diagnose this disorder. For this reason, it is essential for the clinician working with a cross-cultural population to become familiar with these variations, in order to accurately assess the patient in whom depression is suspected. The clinician will also find it useful to have a framework for understanding the reasons that depression presents as it does across cultures.

Whereas the depressed European or American patient is likely to present with complaints of psychological problems, the depressed Asian patient is more likely to present with somatic complaints (Nikelly, 1988). In Asian cultures, the tendency to conceptualize depression as a physical problem is found not only in the patient but in the clinician as well (Nakane et al., 1988). The diagnosis of neurasthenia is frequently made by the Chinese clinician assessing patients who suffer from somatic pain, physical weakness, and dizziness. Neurasthenia is understood to be a physical illness, but in many cases patients diagnosed with neurasthenia may be suffering from depression (Ware & Kleinman, 1992). Neurasthenia may be the label for the same disease that Western clinicians label depression. Whether this is true or not remains to be seen, but this labeling difference may, in part, explain the lower prevalence of depression reported in Asian cultures.

A knowledge of why the cross-cultural differences in labeling exist is helpful to the clinician assessing the depressed patient. Though mental illness in Western culture is by no means free of social stigma, the depressed patient in Asian cultures suffers to a greater degree socially from being labeled mentally ill than the patient in Western culture. Therefore, in Asian societies, especially in China, clinicians prefer to give, and patients prefer to get, a diagnosis of a physical illness, such as neurasthenia. A diagnosis of neurasthenia suggests overwork; and the patient who suffers from the ill effects of overwork is likely to be revered rather than stigmatized in Chinese culture (Xu, 1987).

The Chinese patient is more likely to complain of somatic symptoms than the American patient (Nikelly, 1988). Further, both the Chinese clinician and patient are likely to minimize attention to affective complaints (Xu, 1987). Perhaps this is because the physician in China is seen as someone who treats physical symptoms, not mood problems, and because emotional disorders have never been regarded as the domain of traditional Chinese medicine (Zhang, 1989). When mood symptoms are acknowledged by the Asian patient and clinician, these symptoms are likely to be perceived as part of a medical illness. For example, in traditional Chinese medicine, melancholia is frequently understood to be a symptom of an abnormality of the spleen (Ots, 1990). The Chinese abide by different rules regarding the display of emotion (Wu, 1982; Chang, 1985). In general, the Chinese tend to be more guarded in the display of emotion. The Chinese frequently use metaphor in everyday language to express affective states (Chang, 1985; Nikelly, 1988). The clinician who is not aware of the affective significance of this form of expression may thereby fail to recognize the patient's somatic complaints as expressions of affective distress.

As alluded to earlier, the Buddhist tradition teaches that unhappiness or *dukkha* is a natural state. Thus, the patient from a Buddhist culture is less likely to consider dysphoria or existential angst to be a symptom of disease. It is, therefore, less likely that he or she would consult a physician for treatment of a depressed mood in the absence of other symptoms.

Studies of depression in Native Americans have shown differences in presentation across tribes. Depression in the Flathead has been described as often presenting with alcoholism and feelings of social loneliness (O'Nell, 1993). Studies of depressive syndromes among the Hopi reveal several native illness labels for depression. *Argumentativeness* is included as a symptom of several of these syndromes (Manson et al., 1985). That loneliness and argumentativeness have been identified as prominent features of depression in these Native American cultures is consistent with the high value that Native Americans, in general, place on functioning within a social context. Thus, the disruption of social interaction that may occur in depression is likely to be noticed both by the depressed individual and by those with whom the patient normally interacts.

Bereavement

Bereavement, the reaction to the loss of a loved person by death, is experienced internally in a uniform manner across cultures (Eisenbruch, 1984). Mourning, the social expression of bereavement, however, varies from culture to culture. Symptoms of depression are commonly observed during bereavement (Clayton, 1990). Differentiating depression from bereavement is sometimes problematic, even when therapist and patient are of similar cultural backgrounds. Add to this already challenging situation the fact that the practices and duration of mourning vary widely from culture to culture. This wide cultural variation is likely to confuse the clinician further when assessing the bereaved patient from another culture. The clinician must evaluate the bereaved patient according to the patient's cultural norms for expression of bereavement.

Uniformities in the Presentation of Depression

The bulk of the literature on cross-cultural assessment of depression, as well as the discussion herein, has focused on differences in the manner in which depression presents across cultures. Are there clinical features of depression that occur without regard to the patient's culture? And what is the clinical significance of these features in terms of diagnostic assessment?

Prior to this century, anhedonia, the failure to experience pleasure, was regarded as a critical feature in the diagnosis of melancholia. As the twentieth century progressed, however, anhedonia lost much of its significance as a central feature of depressive disorders (Snaith, 1993). In the 1970s interest in anhedonia as a feature of depression was resurrected by Klein (1974), when he proposed anhedonia as the best marker for predicting response to antidepressant medication.

Though Xu (1987) identified "loss of interest" as a symptom of *xin qi xu*, a depressive syndrome described in China, the prevalence of anhedonia occurring in the context of depression across cultures was not specifically addressed in the cross-cultural studies of depression reviewed here (Zhang, 1989; Ware & Kleinman, 1992;

Chang, 1985; Zung, 1969). Given the central role of anhedonia in depression proposed by Klein (1974), anhedonia is suggested here as a feature of depression that may occur without regard to culture. Though the importance of anhedonia as a consistent feature of depression across cultures is speculative at this point, the clinical utility of identifying anhedonia in the depressed patient lies in its putative power to predict response to antidepressant medication.

Kupfer and Thase (1983) have described disturbances of sleep observed in depressed subjects. Depressed individuals have more rapid eye movement (REM) sleep and a shortened latency to the first REM sleep period compared to control subjects. These abnormalities, though not pathognomonic for depression, have been found to occur consistently in depressed European, Latino, and Asian subjects (Mendelwicz & Kerkhofs, 1991). Though sleep studies are not currently employed in the diagnosis of depression, assessment of early morning awakening, an indicator of disturbed sleep often seen in depression, may have clinical utility in the diagnosis of depression across cultures.

SUGGESTED CLINICAL GUIDELINES

1. The Western clinician may find it difficult to diagnose depression in the patient who does not have prominent complaints of affective distress, such as sad mood. When depression is suspected in non-Western patients, the clinician should be alert to the patient's use of metaphor to express affective distress. Somatic complaints are often used as a metaphoric expression of affective distress by the non-Western patient.

2. The Western clinician may be tempted to minimize somatic complaints and aggressively seek conscious expression of affective distress when assessing the patient in whom depression is suspected. Somatic complaints should be attended to and not minimized. The clinician should bear in mind that somatic complaints may be offered by the patient in an effort to legitimize a visit to the doctor. However, the potential psychodynamic significance of somatic complaints should not be ignored. Be aware of the increased stigma associated with mental illness in other cultures. Allow the patient an opportunity to avoid the shame associ-

ated with mental illness. The chance to save face may determine whether the patient continues in treatment. Also, efforts to convince the patient from a "traditional culture" that his distress is due to psychological causes are not advisable (Zhang, 1989; Lambo, 1960), and will usually be unsuccessful at best. At worst, such efforts may result in a serious, possibly irreversible breach of empathy that could compromise the clinician's therapeutic capacity and the patient's willingness to remain in treatment.

3. An effort should be made to understand the patient's perception of the cause of his or her distress. According to the teachings of European and American psychiatry, the depressed patient who attributes his or her distress to a physical cause lacks insight and is more severely depressed than the patient who understands his or her distress to be due to depression. In the cross-cultural patient, attribution of illness to a physical cause does not necessarily indicate lack of insight; nor does it indicate a more severe case of depression.

4. The clinician should consider the occupational and social norms for the patient in light of the patient's culture when differentiating normal variation from pathological disturbances of mood. Occupational and social norms of the patient's culture should also be taken into account when grading severity of depression in the cross-cultural patient.

5. Thorough assessment of the depressed patient includes assessment of the stressors in the patient's life. Events seen as terribly stressful by the patient may seem trivial in the eyes of a therapist from another culture. Differences between the patient's and the clinician's value systems often make it difficult for the clinician to appreciate the importance of saving face, loyalty to family, and tradition in other cultures. Cultural consultation often helps the diagnostician to appreciate the significance of the patient's life events and the severity of the stressors in relation to depression.

6. The clinician should avoid the pitfall of overemphasizing culture in diagnosis. In order to accurately diagnose depression, the clinician must exercise care whenever signs

or symptoms that are potential indicators of psychopathology are interpreted as normal through ascription to culture. It may be tempting to attribute signs such as social withdrawal or blunted affect to "culture" rather than diagnosing depression. Before culture is utilized to explain possible psychopathology as normal, the clinician should be familiar with the patient's culture, either through personal experience or through cultural consultation.

REFERENCES

Ackernecht, E.H. (1968). *A short history of psychiatry*. New York: Hafner Publishing.

Adler, G. & Gattaz, W.F. (1993). Pain perception threshold in major depression. *Biological Psychiatry, 34*, 687–689.

American Psychiatric Association. (1994). *Diagnostic and statistical manual of mental disorders—fourth edition*. (DSM-IV). Washington, D.C.: American Psychiatric Association.

Bebbington, P. (1993). Transcultural aspects of affective disorders. *International Journal of Psychiatry, 5*, 145–146.

Blazer, D.G., Kessler, R.C., McGonagle, K.A., & Swartz, M.S. (1994). The prevalence of major depression in a national community sample: the national comorbidity survey. *American Journal of Psychiatry, 15*, 979–986.

Chang, W.C. (1985). A cross-cultural study of depressive symptomatology. *Culture, Medicine and Psychiatry, 9*, 295–317.

Clayton, P.J. (1990). Bereavement and depression. *Journal of Clinical Psychiatry, 51*, 34–38.

Eisenbruch, M. (1984). Cross-cultural aspects of bereavement, I. *Culture, Medicine and Psychiatry, 8*, 283–309.

Frerichs, R.R., Aneshensel, C.S., & Clark, V.A. (1981). Prevalence of depression in Los Angeles County. *American Journal of Epidemiology, 113*, 691–699.

Freud, S. (1917). Mourning and Melancholia. In J. Strachey & A. Freud (Eds.). *The standard edition of the complete psychological works of Sigmund Freud, Volume XIV* (pp. 237–258). London: Hogarth Press.

Hirayasu, T. (1969). An epidemiological and sociopsychiatric study on the mental and neurological disorders in an isolated island in Okinawa. *Psychiatria et Neurologia Japanica. 71*, 466–491.

Jablensky, A., Sartorius, N., Gulbinat, W., & Ernberg, G. (1981). Characteristics of depressive patients contacting psychiatric services in four cultures. *Acta Psychiatrica Scandinavica, 63*, 367–383.

Jacobsen, L. (1988). On the picture of depression and suicide in traditional societies. *Acta Psychiatrica Scandinavica, S344*, 55–63.

Klein, D.F. (1974). Endogenomorphic depression. *Archives of General Psychiatry, 31*, 447–454.

Kraeplin, E. (1974). Vergleicende psychiatre. In S.R. Hirsh, M. Shepherd (Eds.), *Themes and Variations in European Psychiatry* (pp. 3–6). Bristol: John Wright and Sons.

Kupfer, D.J. & Thase, M.E. (1983). The use of sleep laboratory in the diagnosis of affective disorder. *Psychiatric Clinics of North America, 6*, 3–25.

Lambo, T.A. (1960). Further neuropsychiatric observations in Nigeria. *British Medical Journal, 2*, 1969–1704.

Lin, K.M., Lau, J.K.C., Yamamoto, J., Zheng, Y.P., Kim, K.S., Cho, K.H., & Nakasaki, G. (1992). Hwa Byung. *Journal of Nervous and Mental Disease, 180*, 386–391.

Manson, S.P., Shore, J.H., & Bollm, J.D. (1985). The depressive experience in American Indian communities: A challenge for psychiatric theory and diagnosis. In A. Kleinman & B. Good (Eds.), *Culture and depression* (pp. 331–368). Berkeley: University of California Press.

Marsella, A.J. (1979). Depressive experience and disorder across cultures. In H. Triandis, J. Dragnus (Eds.), *Handbook of cross cultural psychology,* vol. 6 (pp. 237–289). Boston: Allyn and Bacon.

Mendelwicz, J. & Kerkhofs, M. (1991). Sleep electroencephalography in depressive illness. *British Journal of Psychiatry, 159*, 505–509.

Mirowsky, J. & Ross, C.E. (1984). Mexican culture and its emotional contradictions. *Journal of Health and Social Behavior, 25*, 2–13.

Nakane, Y., Ohta, Y., Radford, M., Yan, H., Wang, X., Lee, H.Y., Min, S.K., Michitsuji, S., & Ohtsuka, T. (1991). Comparative study of affective disorders in three Asian countries II. *Acta Psychiatrica Scandinavica, 84*, 313–319.

Nakane, Y., Ohta, Y., Uchino, J., Takada, K., Yan, H.Q., & Wang, Y.D. (1988). Comparative study of affective disorders in three Asian countries I. *Acta Psychiatrica Scandinavica, 78*, 698–705.

Nikelly, A.G. (1988). Does DSM-III-R diagnose depression in non-Western patients? *International Journal of Social Psychiatry, 34*, 316–320.

Obeyesekere, G.(1985). Depression, Buddhism and the work of culture in Sri Lanka. In A. Kleinman, B. Good (Eds.). *Culture and depression* (pp. 134–152). Berkeley: University of California Press.

O'Nell, T. (1993). Feeling worthless: an ethnographic investigation of depression and problem drinking at the Flathead Reservation. *Culture, Medicine and Psychiatry, 16*, 447–469.

Ots, T. (1990). The angry liver, the anxious heart and the melancholy spleen. *Culture, Medicine and Psychiatry, 14*, 21–58.

Paykel, E.S. (1992). Handbook of affective disorders—second edition. New York: Guilford Press.

Roberts, R.E. (1980). Prevalence of psychological distress among Mexican-Americans. *Journal of Health and Social Behavior, 21*, 134–145.

Shakespeare, W. (1963). *The tragedy of Hamlet* (I.ii. 129–137, II.ii. 303–311). E. Hubler (Ed.). New York: Penguin Books.

Silver, H. (1987). Physical complaints are part of the core depressive syndrome: Evidence from a cross cultural study in Israel. *Journal of Clinical Psychiatry, 48*, 140–142.

Singer, K. (1975). Depressive disorder from a transcultural perspective. *Social Science and Medicine, 9*, 289–301.

Smith, H. (1991). *The world's religions.* San Francisco: Harper.

Snaith, P. (1993). Anhedonia: a neglected symptom of psychopathology. *Psychological Medicine, 23*, 957–966.

Thompson, L.M., Rubin, R.T., McCracken, J.T. (1992). Neuroendocrine aspects of primary depression. *Psychoneuroimmunology, 17*, 507–515.

Thornicroft, G. & Sartorius, N. (1992). The course and outcome of depression in different cultures: 10–year follow-up of the WHO collaborative study on the assessment of depressive disorders. *Psychological Medicine, 23*, 1023–1032.

Ulrich, H. (1993). Cultural shaping of illness: A longitudinal perspective on apparent depression. *Journal of Nervous and Mental Disease, 181*, 647–649.

Ware, N.C. & Kleinman, A. (1992). Culture and somatic experience: The social course of illness in neurasthenia and chronic fatigue syndrome. *Psychosomatic Medicine, 54*, 546–560.

Wilson, S.N., Surman, O.S., Colvin, R., Ozonoff, D., Gelenberg, A.J., Jenike, M.A., Manschreck, T., & Pato, C. (1990). Unusual lymphocyte subset distribution in some depressed patients. *Journal of Clinical Psychiatry, 51*, 51–52.

Wu, D.Y.H. (1982). Psychotherapy and emotion in traditional Chinese medicine. In A.J. Marsella, G.M. White (Eds.) *Cultural conceptions of mental health and therapy* (pp. 285–301). Boston: D. Reidel Publishing Co.

Xu, J.M. (1987). Some issues in the diagnosis of depression in China. *Canadian Journal of Psychiatry, 32*, 368–370.

Zhang, M.Y. (1989). The diagnosis and phenomenology of neurasthenia, a Shanghai study. *Culture, Medicine and Psychiatry, 13*, 147–161.

Zung, W.W.K. (1969). A cross-cultural survey of symptoms in depression. *American Journal of Psychiatry, 126*, 116–121.

CHAPTER THREE

Anxiety Disorders

David M. Bernstein, M.D.

CASE VIGNETTES

Case 1

Mrs. C., a 23-year-old Caucasian female, was referred by her employer for psychiatric evaluation after experiencing difficulties functioning as an accounting assistant. After being on the job for approximately one month, Mrs. C. was called into the supervisor's office and informed that the other employees in the department had concerns about her mental health. Mrs. C's supervisor, citing her concerns about general employee morale and performance, recommended a psychiatric evaluation, adding, "I know it must be stressful taking a new job in a new city." Mrs. C., worried about losing her job, did not attempt to clarify her supervisor's concerns. Rather, she reluctantly agreed to an evaluation, and allowed her supervisor to share information about her job performance with the examining psychiatrist.

Mrs. C. underwent a standard psychiatric evaluation, which did not reveal evidence of obvious psychopathology. Mrs. C. was unable to elaborate on the reason for the referral, stating only that "my supervisor and the other people in my department think there's something wrong with me, but nobody will talk about it directly and I haven't asked. As far as I know, I think I am performing well." The examiner noted that Mrs. C. was a heavyset Caucasian woman, dressed very conservatively in a long-sleeved, closed-collared blouse and ankle-length skirt. She wore a scarf over her hair. A mental status examination was normal. A cursory developmental history indicated that Mrs. C. had grown up in New York, graduated from college with a degree in accounting, and recalled no difficulties in childhood or adolescence. She attended private schools throughout her education. She married at age 20, had a stable marital relationship, and was planning to have children. Her husband was recently promoted to a new position, which required the couple to move to their present city. Mrs. C. felt she was adjusting well to both the move and to her new job, and denied any psychiatric problems.

The psychiatrist contacted Mrs. C.'s supervisor for collateral history. Mrs. C.'s supervisor stated that Mrs. C. "never fit in with the other employees." She did not socialize, and became offended when the other women in the office suggested that she modify her wardrobe because "she dresses like an old lady." Mrs. C. refused to eat food offered to her by others, and brought her own food to work, which she would not store in the employee refrigerator. She would not use the supply of eating utensils in the employee lounge. Instead, she brought two different sets of personal eating utensils, cups, and plates, and kept them carefully separated from each other. Employees complained to the supervisor that she "acts as if we are all contaminated or something." They also noted that on occasion Mrs. C. seemed overly concerned with time. In fact, she anxiously rushed to complete her work on Fridays, and made a special arrangement with a coworker to cover for her so she could leave early, explaining only that she "had to be in her house before the sun went down." She absolutely refused to work on Saturdays, and declined to attend a department social event on a Saturday afternoon. Other employees complained of Mrs. C.'s "strange behavior," which her supervisor, on closer observation, noted for herself.

Based on this new collateral history, the psychiatrist arranged a second visit with Mrs. C. to explore more fully the possibility that her unusual preoccupation with cleanliness, including use of carefully delineated utensils, and wearing clothing that left little of her body, including her hair, exposed, was not an overlooked phobic disorder. He also noted that Mrs. C.'s seemingly ritualistic eating behavior and excessive concern with the exact time of sunset, may have reflected an underlying obsessive-compulsive disorder (OCD).

During the second visit, Mrs. C. admitted to the psychiatrist that the reports about her behavior were true. She explained, however, that she was an Orthodox Jew, and was therefore required to dress modestly, including covering her hair. Her observance of Jewish dietary laws (*Kashruth*) forbade mixing meat (*flaishedech*) and dairy (*milchedech*) products, and required separate eating utensils for each. She could not eat food offered by coworkers because it was "unkosher." Her observance of the Jewish Sabbath, which begins on sunset Friday night and ends on sunset Saturday night, prohibited her from work during this period. She attempted to complete her work on Fridays as soon as possible to allow for travel time home, where her role as female head of household required her to perform the Sabbath blessing ceremony, including the lighting of candles. Her observance of the Jewish Sabbath prevented her from work or social activities on Saturdays. When asked why Mrs. C. had not shared this information with her supervisor, fellow employees, or the psychiatrist, she replied that she wanted to be discreet about her religious requirements because she was the only Jew in the office. She also pointed out that Jewish tradition encourages one to practice one's religion discreetly when in a community of non-Jews. Psychiatric evaluation did not reveal any evidence of phobias, obsessions, compulsions, or excessive anxiety symptoms.

Case 2

Miss D., a 28-year-old single African-American female presented to an outpatient mental health clinic with complaints of anxiety and depression. She had been assigned to Hawaii to complete her final few months of active duty as a computer systems operator with the United States Army. Although she initially enjoyed her assignment, she noted that she "never really fit in because there are almost no Blacks in Hawaii except in the military." After her discharge from the Army, she decided to stay in Hawaii, and obtain a computer-related job in the civilian sector.

On presentation to the VA Mental Health Clinic, she had been out of the Army for two months and was still unemployed. She angrily descibed how prejudice against African Americans, which was magnified in the Asian-influenced culture of Hawaii, was responsible for her unemployment and anxiety in public. She reported that shortly after her discharge from the Army, while standing in line to purchase an item at a convenience store, she felt "like everybody was staring at me as if I was the first Black person they had ever seen." She became anxious and left the store without completing her purchase. Miss D. noted that while still on active duty she did her shopping at the PX, "where there were plenty of other Black people around and I never had a problem." Approximately two weeks later, while eating with a friend in a fast-food restaurant, she felt as though other patrons were staring at her, "like I didn't belong there. I've experienced prejudice before, and I recognize it when I see it." She expressed her discomfort to her friend, who was also African-American, but was annoyed when he told her that "it was all in my head. He felt perfectly comfortable." Despite feeling anxious, she finished her meal, and afterwards came to the conclusion that "compared to all these skinny little Japanese girls, I must look like some kind of giant Black freak. Back home nobody would care what I ate." Miss D. began to have frequent thoughts that when around Asians she had to carefully self-monitor her etiquette and food intake to avoid negative stereotyping of African-Americans as "uncivilized." She reported being extremely self-conscious in restaurants, and carried extra napkins with her to ensure that she could adequately wipe her face and hands. She stated that "all these Oriental people here are neat-freaks, and I am already discriminated against because I'm Black. I don't want to be sloppy, too."

Miss D. began to notice that she no longer felt comfortable eating on base or in other military settings, including parties at the homes of friends, even though her friends were almost exclusively African-Americans. She began to wonder "if I am going crazy. Why can't I just eat without thinking about it, like a normal person?" She began to experience feelings of depression, accompanied by crying spells. She rearranged her schedule so that she could eat meals alone, and avoided social events where she would be expected to eat in front of others. Her friends commented that she seemed depressed and withdrawn. One joked, "maybe you should see a psychiatrist." After much rumination, she presented to the VA Mental Health Clinic, complaining of anxiety and depression, which she attributed to "too much prejudice against Blacks in Hawaii."

A diagnosis of Social Phobia was made, and Miss D. was started on phenelzine. After approximately six weeks, she reported a significant decrease in phobic symptoms, and felt that she was "adjusting better to civilian life thanks to the medicine."

Case 3

Miss A., a 34-year-old Chinese-American female, was referred for psychiatric consultation by her internist for assessment of impaired social and occupational functioning. She had been in treatment for several years for chronic back pain resulting from a minor injury. Despite the absence of medical evidence of impairment, the patient insisted that she could not work, and refused referrals to occupational therapy and vocational rehabilitation. Other than attending medical appointments, during which only benign treatment was offered, Miss A. rarely left her home, complaining that she was easily tired and often in pain. She had no friends, and her social interactions were limited to accompanying her mother on shopping trips and errands. She had never had a date, and expressed no interest in romantic relationships, stating that her primary responsibility as an unmarried Chinese daughter was to care for her aging parents, and that it would be improper for her to express romantic interests. She resisted her physician's efforts to help her return to work, stating that she would find employment when she no longer had familial responsibilities, explaining to her non-Asian physician, "I don't expect you to understand this, but it is common in traditional Chinese families. I must put the welfare of my parents first." She gave a similar explanation for her lack of interest in pursuing friendships and romantic relationships, indicating that she would concern herself with these matters in the future. Her physician noted that Miss A. did not seem particularly troubled by her chronic physical symptoms, but insisted on regular medical appointments despite complaining of ineffective treatment.

Historical information revealed that Miss A. was the youngest of three siblings, and the only girl. Her parents, who were of Chinese ancestry, were born and raised in the United States, and were financially well-off, with no major health problems. Miss A. had few friends as a child, despite prodding by her parents to develop successful friendships, such as those of her brothers. After high school, on the urging of her parents, who were concerned by her lack of initiative and independent functioning, Miss A. joined the United States Army, where she worked in a clerical position for the minimal enlistment period, then returned home to live with her parents. Shortly after her return from the Army, Miss A. began to complain of aggravation of a back injury that she stated occurred in the military. Despite encouragement from her parents, she was unable to sustain employment for more than a few weeks, or complete a semester of college, which she attributed to easy fatigue and back pain. On focused psychiatric exam, Miss A. described separation anxiety since childhood, episodic panic attacks beginning in high school, and severe anxiety symptoms in public places unless accompanied by her family. A diagnosis of panic disorder with agoraphobia, and dependent personality disorder was made.

INTRODUCTION

The concept of anxiety as a pathologic component of mental illness is a central pillar of psychiatry. Anxiety, a universal experience that generally refers to a melding of somatic, cognitive, behavioral, and emotional features related to the fear response, challenges clinicians by its very ubiquitousness and complexity. In contrast to psychiatric symptoms such as hallucinations or thought disorganization, anxiety serves an adaptive function for humans and other animals. Manifestations of anxiety range from species-specific, biologically determined fight-or-flight responses in animals to complex sociocultural responses in humans. How then, does a clinician attempt to understand a phenomenon that involves such varied components as neurobiological arousal mechanisms, threat assessment, and a myriad of behavioral responses that range from individual actions to group behavior, all of which may be complicated by intrapsychic components such as cognitive schema and existential issues? To this confusion add the complex dimension of culture in both the etiology and elaboration of anxiety, and one quickly realizes why the psychiatric literature has approached the concept of anxiety from so many directions. Kirmayer et al. (1995), in a review of the cultural context of anxiety disorders, write, "The cultural determinants of anxiety symptoms and syndromes mean that anxiety must be understood not just in terms of cognitive or physiologic mechanisms, but also in terms of its social meanings and the roles, situations, and cultural practices that may engender anxiety and influence its intrapsychic and interpersonal management" (p. 504). This chapter will attempt to highlight, from a cultural psychiatric perspective, those aspects of anxiety and anxiety disorders that may be clinically useful for the mental health professional.

DEFINITION OF ANXIETY

Because of the tremendous overlap between anxiety disorders and other psychiatric disorders, such as mood, somatization, and psychotic disorders, a basic understanding of the meaning of the term *anxiety* is necessary. *The Oxford Psychiatric Dictionary—Fifth Edition* (Campbell, 1981) has no less than six pages elaborating the definitions and subtypes of anxiety, ranging from *signal anxiety* to *ego anxiety*. Anxiety has been defined in its simplest sense as the "feeling of apprehension caused by anticipation of danger, which may be internal or external" (p. 303) (Kaplan et al., 1994). Psychiatry has attempted to categorize anxiety based upon various nosologies, the two most important distinctions being presumed etiology and symptom clustering. Anxiety disorders categorized by etiology are dependent on the etiologic model used (e.g., the *castration anxiety* of the psychoanalytic model versus anxiety caused by a well-defined disease entity such as hyperthyroidism, pheochromocytoma, or substance-specific withdrawal, collectively grouped in the *Diagnostic and Statistical Manual of Mental Disorders—Fourth Edition* (DSM-IV) as "anxiety disorders due to a general medical condition"). Anxiety disorders characterized by clusters of core symptoms may range from the broad, multisymptom generalized anxiety disorder of the DSM-IV, or the neurasthenia of the *International Statistical Classification of Diseases and Related Health Problems— Tenth Revision* (ICD-10) (WHO, 1992), to commonly recognized specific phobic subtypes (e.g., simple phobia, social phobia, panic disorder, agoraphobia). If sufficiently rare or exotic, anxiety disorders can include both specific symptoms and presumed etiologies, such that they may even be designated as "folk illnesses" (Gaw, 1993) or culture bound syndromes (CBSs), which include such entities as *piblokto* (Arctic hysteria), and *koro* (genital retraction panic).

CROSS-CULTURAL PREVALENCE OF ANXIETY DISORDERS

Review of the literature on culture and anxiety indicates that the largest body of recent work attempts to address the epidemiology or cross-cultural prevalence of anxiety disorders. The National Comorbidity Survey (NCS), which was the first survey to use a structured psychiatric interview on a representative national sample in the United States ($n = 8098$), assessed lifetime and 12-month prevalence of DSM-III-R psychiatric disorders (Kessler et al., 1994). It indicated that the most common disorders were major depression (17%) and alcohol dependence (14%), followed by social phobia (13%) and simple phobias (11%), with approximately 25% of respondents reporting a lifetime prevalence of at least one anxiety disorder. The 12-month prevalence data indicated that, when viewed collectively, anxiety disorders were more prevalent (17%) than either substance use disorders (11%) or affective disorders (11%), which led the researchers to suggest that anxiety disorders are more chronic than either substance use or affective disorders. This study was an attempt to expand upon the Epidemiological Catchment Area (ECA) Study ($n > 20,000$), the major reference in psychiatric literature since the early 1980s (Robins et al., 1991), which indicated that, based on DSM-III (American Psychiatric Association, 1980) criteria, anxiety disorders have the highest six-month prevalence rate (8.9%) of all psychiatric disorders, subdivided as phobic disorders (7.7%), and OCD (1.5%).

PREVALENCE IN ETHNIC MINORITY POPULATIONS

The cultural psychiatry literature of the last 15 years has attempted to address the incidence and prevalence of various anxiety disorders in specific minority American populations, such as African Americans and Hispanics, and in population samples from other countries. For example, the epidemiology of OCD from community surveys in six countries (United States, Canada, Germany, Taiwan, Korea, New Zealand) and in Puerto Rico, indicated that with the exception of Taiwan, annual OCD prevalence rates are in the consistent range of 1.1–1.8 per 100 people, with variation exhibited in the predominance of obsessions or compulsions between countries (Weisman et al., 1994). Shrout et al. (1992), noted significant differences in the epidemiology of various anxiety disorders among Hispanic subgroups in the United States, such as a Los Angeles sample of Mexican-Americans and Mexican-American immigrants, compared to Puerto Rican islanders. Using the Diagnostic Interview Schedule (DIS), Shrout's group noted a lifetime prevalence of phobic disorder ranging from 17.7 % of Mexican-American natives, to 13.1% of Puerto Ricans, to 10% of Mexican-American immigrants. Explanations for the differences between the Mexican subgroups include the effects of acculturation and selection bias, such that only immigrants with less psychopathology complete a successful migration to the United States. Studies addressing the epidemiology of panic disorder in African Americans include the study of Horwath et al. (1993) of 4287 African Americans compared with 12,142 Whites distributed at five ECA study sites. The researchers concluded that panic disorder in the community is similar among African Americans and Whites with respect to lifetime prevalence, age at onset, years of disorder, symptom distribution, suicide attempts, and comorbidity with other psychiatric disorders. An update on the diagnosis of anxiety disorders in African Americans by Paradis et al. (1994) points to methodological problems in the ECA data, and references data based on the Anxiety Disorders Interview Scale-Revised (ADIS-R), indicating that anxiety disorders are significantly underdiagnosed in African Americans—nearly 25% of inner-city outpatients at a municipal hospital were diagnosed with Panic Disorder. International epidemiologic studies based on the DIS, such as Stefansson's (1993) study of lifetime prevalence of anxiety disorders in Iceland, using a sample of one half of the population born in 1931 (79.3% response rate), indicated that the overall prevalence of anxiety disorders was 44%, with generalized anxiety 22%, and the varied phobias affecting 18% of the study sample.

PROBLEMS OF CROSS-CULTURAL COMPARISON

The plethora of epidemiologic research on anxiety disorders in international samples, and in various minority samples in the United States, is plagued by concerns regarding methodology, most notably, the ability of survey instruments to operate across cultures. For example, Schwarz and Birn's (1995) comparison of dental anxiety (odontophobia) in Danish versus Chinese adults, using a standard survey instrument, indicated that dental anxiety was significantly higher in the Chinese as compared with the Danes. Interpretation of results, however, must account not only for possible translation errors or cultural differences in the emotional impact of descriptors, but must also take into account the important concepts of *behavioral norm* and *help-seeking behavior* within a culture. For example, in Hong Kong, most people visit dentists only after they have dental problems, which may predispose them to painful experiences, compared with the Danes, who, like many Westerners, incorporate the less traumatic practices of preventive dentistry, such as regular check-ups, into their health care behavioral norm.

Another problem with cross-cultural comparisons of anxiety disorders rests within the definition of the disorder itself, which may be highly variable across cultures. This problem is particularly relevant for assessment of anxiety disorders based upon the nosology of symptom clustering. For example, phenomena such as rarely leaving home, or the inability to leave home without being accompanied by a family member, a key component of agoraphobia, may not be pathological behavior for women, particularly young, unmarried women, in Islamic countries, where such behavior is culturally expected (El Aslam, 1994). Similarly, comorbidities associated with anxiety disorders, such as alcohol abuse, may not be relevant in cultures (e.g., Muslim societies) where alcohol use is restricted in the population in general, and especially so to subpopulations, such as women in Muslim, Asian, and Latin cultures, who statistically have higher prevalence rates of anxiety disorders than males in Western research samples. Fear of public speaking, a common diagnostic feature of social phobia, may not apply to subpopulations in cultures where public speaking is not an expected behavior. School refusal, an anxiety disorder recognized in childhood, may not be a relevant construct in undeveloped nations in which opportunities for formal education are lacking.

Tseng et al. (1986) outline a particularly useful paradigm to explain the variability of diagnosis of neurotic disorders across cultures. They posit three mechanisms by which reliance on characteristic symptom clusters may be problematic, including: (1) different diagnostic patterns among clinicians lead to different diagnoses for similar clinical phenomena; (2) cultural variation in symptom manifestation for the same disorder may lead to diagnostic variance; and (3) unique disorders may exist related to different sociocultural environments.

Attempts to address the problem of diagnostic variance resulting from poor inter-rater reliability across cultures has led to studies on the validity of rating scales among different groups, for example, retesting the validity of the Arabic version of the Hospital Anxiety and Depression (HAD) scale (El Rufaie and Absood, 1995). Attempts to address the problem of cultural variation in the symptom manifestation of anxiety disorders leads to the interesting concept of *idioms of distress*, which, in turn, is related to the meaning of anxiety within a particular culture. Attempts to address the problem of disorders having a unique etiology or manifestation in a particular sociocultural environment leads to the area of folk illnesses or CBSs as pathologic manifestations of anxiety.

VARIATIONS OF ANXIETY DISORDER MANIFESTATION

An *idiom of distress* is the manner in which symptoms present in a given sociocultural context. In a study of nonpsychotic mental illness in Zimbabwe, *spiritual distress* was identified as a subtype of mental illness (Patel, 1995). Among the Shona, six idioms of spiritual distress resembled the psychological construct of anxiety, among which were four cognitive idioms whose core features were worry and panic. Other examples of idioms of distress include phenomena such as somatic symptoms. Clinicians attempting to diagnose and treat anxiety disorders across cultures must become familiar with various idioms of distress that reflect anxiety symptoms in their patients.

A study of New York Puerto Ricans by Rogler et al. (1994) indicated that the prevailing idioms of distress in their sample were based upon two major themes, anger and injustice, and correlated widely with professionally developed measures of anxiety, depression, and somatization and with utilization of professional mental health care. In the Chinese medical model, where the heart is a metaphor for anxiety, patients may present with the complaint of *anxious heart (xin Ji)*, used to describe anxiety accompanied by palpitations (Ots, 1990). The Japanese literature describes a syndrome known as *taijinkyofusho* (TKS) or *anthrophobia*, which relates to a constellation of phobic symptoms manifested by complaints that one is offensive to others by virtue of body odor or physical appearance, accompanied by behavioral symptoms such as inappropriate avoidance of eye contact (Russell, 1989). Kasahara (1970) described the manifestations of phobia as varying depending upon cultural context, describing some phobias as *egoistic* or guilt-based, and others as *altruistic* or shame-based. Thus, in contrast to the fear of public embarrassment that is characteristic of social phobia in the West, fear of embarrassing or offending others is a major source of anxiety in Japanese society, and may lead to unique symptom manifestation, such as avoiding eye contact or covering one's nose.

Similarly, cultural values may provide the substrate for anxiety disorders in some societies but not in others. For example, the value placed on marriage and fertility in Middle Eastern, Asian, and Indian cultures is often unappreciated by Western clinicians. In a fascinating article, Inhorn (1994) describes the magnitude of the fear of reproductive infertility among Egyptian women, for whom individual and societal status is determined by the ability to bear children. She notes that the syndrome of *Kabsa*, female infertility attributed to symbolic pollution, is viewed by the urban and rural poor of Egypt as the major cause of female infertility, and as such is greatly feared by Egyptian women as a threat to their future fertility, their marital relationship, and, on a larger scale, to pronatalist, religious Egyptian society. So great is their fear that Egyptian

women employ a variety of rituals to either prevent or cure this condition. Many of the rituals are abhorrent by Western standards,
involving such practices as insertion of grilled cat placenta in the
vagina and bathing with a body part (e.g., the brain) of a still-born
infant. Indian literature notes fear of remaining unmarried as a
major factor contributing to *obsessional neurosis* (Akhtar, 1978).
Anxiety symptoms related to perceived semen loss *(dhat* syndrome
in India, and *shen-k'uei* in China) may reflect male versions of fer-
tility-related anxiety disorders (Simons & Hughes, 1993). The value
placed on body image among American women, which often leads
to such practices as surgical breast augmentation, or the obsessive
calorie-counting, compulsive exercise and binge-purge behavior of
bulimia and anorexia nervosa, may appear puzzling to non-Western
societies, in which these disorders may not be recognized. American literature increasingly describes a syndrome known as *homo-
phobia* or *erotophobia* as an anxiety syndrome manifested by fear of
homosexuals (Ficarrotto, 1990). This "syndrome" is likely related to
the sociopolitical climate of American society, where discrimination
based on sexual preference is widely recognized.

Culture may also affect the manner in which anxiety symptoms
are manifested or recognized as pathological. In an excellent study
of the phenomenology of OCD in Egypt, Okasha et al. (1994) note
that both obsessions and compulsions are influenced by the Egyptian Moslem culture. Compared to British samples, where obsessions were predominantly related to orderliness and aggression, the
obsessions of the Egyptian sample were concerned mostly with religious matters, and matters related to cleanliness and contamination. They point out that Islamic religion, which places a high
emphasis on cleanliness and ritual purity, may explain this variance. Moslems are required to pray five times per day, with each
prayer preceded by a ritualistic cleansing process or ablution. Strict
fundamentalist Moslems may be required to perform a complex ritualistic ablution for even touching a woman; Okasha et al. (1994)
write, "The female gender is surrounded by so many religious and
sexual taboos that the issue becomes a rich pool for worries, rumi-
nations, and cleansing compulsions in women susceptible to developing OCD" (p. 195).

The grouping of anxiety disorders by a combination of symptom
cluster and perceived etiology is best illustrated in the area of CBSs.
Although CBSs will not be covered in detail here, several CBSs may
be grouped under the heading of anxiety disorders, including *koro*
(genital retraction panic) among Chinese, *ataque de nervios* (an
acute onset panic-like response) among Hispanics, *dhat* or *jiryan*

(anxiety due to semen loss) among Asian Indians, *kayak angst* (fear of capsizing and drowning) among Inuit Eskimos, frigophobia or *pa leng* (constitutional weakness caused by exposure to cold, or deficiency of the *yang* force), and *taijinkyofusho* (anthrophobia) among Japanese. Literature on refugee mental health currently recognizes an entity called Sudden Unexpected Nocturnal Death Syndrome (SUNDS) among the Hmong, characterized by overwhelming fear and paralysis associated with the belief that an evil spirit is preventing a sleeping person from breathing, and which may result in death (Adler, 1995). The important construct for the clinician to grasp is that these anxiety disorders reflect varying clusters of symptoms, including somatic, dissociative, and psychotic symptoms, that are rooted in the unique cultural context and medical belief system of the afflicted patient.

CASE DISCUSSIONS

Case 1

This case illustrates the importance of assessing a patient's religious practices during the psychiatric examination. For many people, religion dictates behavioral practices and prohibitions, social interactions, and expected role functioning. The inability to comply with the requirements of one's religion is a common source of anxiety. Indeed, preventing people from practicing their religion, or forcing them into practices that conflict with their religious beliefs (e.g., forcing a Muslim to eat pork) can generate a level of anxiety so extreme that it is often used as a method of torture in countries where state-sponsored torture is practiced. Many religious rituals, particularly those involving ritual cleanliness, such as dietary practices, or restrictions that affect social relations as related to menstruation, may be mistaken for compulsions or phobic symptoms by the clinician who is unfamiliar with these practices. Religious prohibitions on various aspects of social behavior, such as physical contact and verbal communication, may also appear as anxiety-related symptoms, and can lead to a misdiagnosis of simple or social phobia. For example, Buddhist monks take great precautions to avoid even the slightest physical contact with women, as do male orthodox practitioners of Islam. In Orthodox Judaism, males and females are not allowed to pray together, and are physically separated in synagogues. In this case, Mrs. C.'s seemingly excessive concern with the time of sunset, adherence to dietary rituals, and limits on both social and occupational functioning due to requirements of the Jewish Sabbath, may appear within the spectrum of anxiety disorders to the uninformed clinician.

Case 2

The central feature of social phobia is the irrational fear of public embarrassment. Common symptoms include fear of being under scrutiny when performing common activities, such as writing in public, using public restrooms, or speaking in public. Individuals with social phobia experience anxiety symptoms when in situations in which they feel they are being scrutinized by others. This may lead to depression and phobic avoidance behavior. Although age of onset is generally prior to age twenty-five, like other anxiety disorders, it may be subclinical for many years and intensify after a significant psychosocial stressor. The ECA study showed rates of social phobia were highest among women and persons who were younger, less educated, single, and of lower socioeconomic class.

Miss D. exhibits typical features of social phobia, including fear of public scrutiny, anxiety and self-consciousness when performing a common activity (eating) in public, and phobic avoidance. Although the onset of her illness is unknown, it intensified to the point of clinical presentation following a major psychosocial stressor, the abrupt transition from military to civilian life in an environment lacking familial social support. This diagnosis could easily be missed because, as presented by Miss D., it could be attributed to the commonly recognized experience of prejudice felt by African Americans in mainstream American culture, and more so in Hawaii, where their minority status is exaggerated due to demographic factors. By attributing Miss D.'s self-consciousness as a compensatory response to her minority status, the clinician may overlook her psychiatric symptoms, which, in fact, reflect an irrational fear of public embarrassment. Some diagnostic clues include presence of her symptoms in situations where her minority status is not a factor (e.g., at social gatherings of other African Americans). Collateral data shared by the patient that her feeling of being scrutinized in the fast-food restaurant based on her ethnicity was not shared by her African-American companion, who noted that it was inappropriate, is also a tip-off. The specific preoccupations of Miss D. (neatness and proper social behavior, such as table manners) are not related to her ethnic minority status. This case illustrates how the core features of an anxiety

disorder may be misattributed as normal by both patient and clinician if they appear to fit within an accepted cultural construct, such
as racial discrimination against minorities.

Case 3

This case illustrates the importance of assessing the degree of cultural influence on a patient's symptom presentation in order to
accurately determine psychopathology. Miss A. rationalized her
social and occupational impairment as "normal behavior" in the
context of traditional Chinese family values. She portrayed herself
as a traditional, unmarried Chinese daughter, whose social and
occupational impairment by "Western" standards might in fact,
reflect normal role expectations in the context of traditional Chinese culture. Thus, her lack of romantic relationships was consistent with the expectation of modesty, and her refusal to separate
from her parents and function independently was evidence of filial
piety, which emphasizes subjugating one's own personal needs and
autonomy for the higher Confucian ideal of honoring one's parents.
    Examination of Miss. A.'s history indicates that her family of origin,
although ethnically Chinese, functioned more in line with mainstream
American culture than with traditional Chinese culture. Her parents
were American-born and raised, and valued independent functioning
in their daughter, to the extent that they persuaded her to enlist in the
military in the hope that it would provide her with self-confidence and
independent living skills. While parental encouragement of a military
experience for character development, and as a foundation for
autonomous functioning is not uncommon in mainstream American
culture, it would be a highly aberrant strategy for raising a daughter in
the context of traditional Chinese cultural values. When presenting to
her non-Asian physician, Miss. A. used the facade of being a caricature
of a "traditional Chinese daughter" to mask the dysfunction caused by
a chronic, untreated anxiety disorder. Her on-going, albeit unsuccessful treatment for vague somatic symptoms (easy fatigue and chronic
back pain) legitimized Miss A.'s dysfunction to her parents as the
product of a genuine medical disability.

SUGGESTED CLINICAL GUIDELINES

  1. Recognize that "anxiety" is a complex concept that incor-
     porates emotional, cognitive, and behavioral components,

all of which may be shaped by culture. A patient may present with primary emphasis on any of these subcomponents, or on a combination of several. For example, the DSM-IV diagnosis of panic disorder requires the presence of a "panic attack" followed by either a *cognitive* change (persistent worry about having another attack, or worry about the implications/consequences of the attack) or a *behavioral* change (significant change in behavior related to the attacks). The definition of the phenomenon labeled a panic attack requires the presence of a combination of affective, somatic, and cognitive components, with a minimum of 4 out of a choice of 13 being necessary to establish the diagnosis. Note that for the symptoms listed in the DSM-IV definition of a panic attack, 10 of 13 involve *somatic* symptoms (e.g., palpitations, nausea, dizziness, etc.), while the remaining 3 involve *cognitions* (e.g., fear of losing control, fear of dying, and depersonalization), of which 2 also involve *affect* or emotion (fear). In making the diagnosis of an anxiety disorder, such as panic disorder, from a cultural psychiatric standpoint, one must ask the following questions:

a. What, if any, role does culture play in the presentation of *cognitive* symptoms in anxiety disorders? For example, is "fear of going crazy," a core symptom in panic disorder, an easily recognized symptom in cultures whose definition of sanity may be different from our own? Is the cognitive experience of depersonalization (defined in DSM-IV as "being detached from oneself"), a pathological construct in those cultures, such as the Buddhist culture of Thailand, where meditation to attain this state is a culturally sanctioned, even idealized, practice? Are "recurrent and persistent thoughts" concerning cleanliness, a common pathologic symptom of OCD, "pathological" in cultures, such as the Islamic culture of Egypt, or orthodox Judaic cultures, where constant concern about "contamination" and "purity" is required in order to practice religious rites appropriately? Is the cognitive component of "fear" in itself culturally determined? For example "fear of blood" is a common simple phobia in industrialized countries, where exposure to blood is not common in everyday life, and, when it does occur, is often associated with trauma. In non-industrialized countries, where animals are purchased live at the market and slaughtered prior to cooking, exposure to fresh blood may not only be commonplace, but may also be desirable (proving to the purchaser of this expensive commodity that the animal is fresh or healthy). Thus, the same experience (blood exposure), may have different cognitive meanings depending on the culture.

b. What, if any, role does culture play in the presentation of *behavioral* symptoms of anxiety disorders? Normal and abnormal behavior is highly culturally dependent, and within a given culture may be influenced by factors such as gender and social status. The "compulsions" or pathologic behaviors that define OCD, such as ritualistic hand-washing, may be accepted and required behaviors in certain cultural contexts, such as orthodox Islamic societies. If one is required to pray five times per day, and praying must be accompanied by ritualized hand-washing, one automatically meets the "C" criteria in the DSM-IV definition of OCD, which states that the "compulsive" behaviors: "are time-consuming" (take more than an hour a day); or "significantly interfere with the person's normal routine, occupational functioning, or usual social relationships" (American Psychiatric Association, 1994). As described in Case 1, the Orthodox Jewish woman's religious requirements necessitated a combination of ritualistic behavior and avoidant behavior that was time-consuming, and impacted on her social and occupational functioning.

c. What, if any, role does culture play in the *affective* symptoms of anxiety disorders? Anxiety, as an affective state, while universally common, may present differently across cultures. Some cultures may not have a unique name for the affect state of anxiety. For example, Malasi et al. (1991) point out that in Arabic, the word for anxiety or "tension" (*deega*) also describes the affect state of depression. In some cultures the affect state of anxiety is viewed primarily in terms of somatic symptoms, which may vary depending upon the culture's view of the relationship between *soma* and *psyche*. While the affect state of anxiety is closely linked with the fear response, and as such has a species-specific component (e.g., startle response), the internal experience of fear, and its external expression, whether by words or behavior, is in itself shaped by many cultural variables.

2. Anxiety may present as an "idiom of distress." Clinicians attempting to assess anxiety disorders must be familiar with the major idioms of distress that represent anxiety within the culture of their patient. Idioms of distress may include somatic symptoms, particular behaviors, or cognitive schema. The CBSs, such as "ataque de nervios" among Hispanics, "neurasthenia" among Chinese, and "dhat" among Asian Indians, may be idioms of distress reflecting an anxiety state, expressed as seemingly unique syndromes.

3. Cultural values may provide the substrate for the genesis of anxiety disorders. The experience of anxiety, including its cognitive, affective, and behavioral components, may reflect an individual's feeling of being in conflict with cultural values or norms. Thus, in cultures placing a high emphasis on fertility, infertility or the perceived threat of infertility may produce an anxiety response in vulnerable persons. Cultures that place a high value on a particular physical appearance may engender an anxiety response in those individuals who are unable to fit the desired physical stereotype of beauty (e.g., the anxiety component of anorexia nervosa and bulimia). Cultures that place a high value on marriage, religious observance, or financial success may play a causal role in anxiety syndromes among their members who are seen as deviant by their inability to fulfill expected norms. The clinician must therefore ask, "What does the culture expect of this individual, and is this individual's inability to provide it the source of his or her anxiety?"

4. Anxiety symptoms are commonly mislabeled, or misattributed by both patient and therapist, depending on perceived causation. The etiologic model of anxiety, which varies across cultures, can lead to variability in symptom presentation and diagnosis. While an American psychoanalyst may have no problem diagnosing "castration anxiety" as the cause of psychopathology in his patient, clinicians from cultures with other theoretical constructs may be unable to make use of this concept. Similarly, Chinese clinicians may have no problem attributing a patient's palpitations and anxiety to *xin ji* (anxious heart), which postulates a dysregulation or imbalance in *yin yang* forces central to the Chinese medical model.

5. Anxiety presenting as a CBS depends upon the clinician's cultural point of view. *Kayak angst* among the Inuit Eskimos, which causes social impairment associated with anxiety, and phobic avoidance, may appear as an exotic syndrome in cultures where individual fishing in often treacherous open oceans is not a central part of life. One could posit that the intense fear of public speaking or urinating in the presence of others (seen in social phobia), or the intense fear of exposure to blood (a common simple phobia), may be viewed as CBSs to clinicians from non-Western cultures in which these situations may have very different frequencies of occurrence and social implications.

In conclusion, when approaching anxiety from a diagnostic perspective, the clinician should be cognizant of the complexities inherent in the very concept of anxiety. These complexities are compounded by the influence of culture in symptom labeling, etiology, cognitive, behavioral, and affective manifestations of anxiety, whether as a unique symptom, or as a symptom cluster that forms part of a larger syndrome. In other words, the term "anxiety disorder" poses diagnostic problems associated with both the "anxiety" and the "disorder" component of the diagnosis, which cannot be separated from cultural context.

REFERENCES

Adler, S. (1995). Refugee stress and folk belief: Among sudden deaths. *Social Science and Medicine*, *40*, 1623–1629.

Akhtar, S. (1978). Obsessional neurosis, marriage, sex and fertility: Some transcultural comparisons. *International Journal of Social Psychiatry*, *Fall 24*, 164–166.

Campbell, R.J. (1981). *Psychiatric dictionary, Fifth edition*. New York: Oxford University Press.

El Aslam, M.F. (1994). Cultural aspects of morbid fears in Qatari women. *Social Psychiatry and Psychiatric Epidemiology*, *29*, 137.

El Rufaie, O.E., & Absood, G.H. (1995). Retesting the validity of the Arabic version of the Hospital and Anxiety and Depression (HAD) scale in primary health care. *Society of Psychiatric Epidemiology*, *1*, 26–31.

Ficarrotto, T.J. (1990). Racism, sexism, and erotophobia: Attitudes of heterosexuals towards homosexuals. *Journal of Homosexuality*, *19*, 111–116.

Gaw, A.C. (1993). *Culture, Ethnicity, and Mental Illness*. Washington: American Psychiatric Press.

Horwath, M., Johnson, J., & Horning, C. (1993). Epidemiology of panic disorder in African-Americans. *American Journal of Psychiatry, 150,* 465–469.

Kaplan, H.I., Sadock, B.J., & Grebb, J.A. (1994). *Synopsis of Psychiatry—seventh edition.* Williams and Wilkins: Baltimore.

Kasahara, Y. (1970). Fear of eye-to-eye confrontation among neurotic patients in Japan. In T.S. Lebra & W. Lebra (Eds.), *Japanese culture and behavior: Selected readings (1974).* (pp. 396–406). Honolulu: University Press of Hawaii.

Kessler, R., McGonagle, K., Zhao, S., Nelson, C., Hughes, M., Eshleman, S., Wittchen, H., & Kendler, K. (1994). Lifetime and 12-month prevalence of DSM-III-R psychiatric disorders in the United States. *Archives of General Psychiatry, 51,* 8–19.

Kirmayer, L., Young, A., & Hayton, B. (1995). The cultural context of anxiety disorders. *Psychiatric Clinics of North America, 18,* 503–536.

Malasi, T.H., Mirza, I. A., & el-Islam, M.F. (1991). Validation of the Hospital Anxiety and Depression Scale in Arab patients. *Acta Psychiatrica Scandinavica, 84,* 323–326.

Okasha, A., Saad, A., Khalil, A., El-Dawla, A., & Yehia, N. (1994). Phenomenology of obsessive-compulsive disorder: a transcultural study. *Comprehensive Psychiatry, 35,* 191–197.

Ots, T., (1990). The angry liver, the anxious heart and the melancholy spleen: the phenomenology of perceptions in Chinese culture. *Culture, Medicine and Psychiatry, 14,* 21–58.

Paradis, C., Hatch, M., & Friedman, S. (1994). Anxiety disorders in African-Americans: an update. *Journal of the National Medical Association, 86,* 609–612.

Patel, V. (1995). Spiritual distress: an indigenous model of nonpsychotic mental illness in primary care in Harare, Zimbabwe. *Acta Psychiatrica Scandinavica, 92,* 103–107.

Robins, L.N., Locke, B.Z., & Regier, D. A. (1991). *Psychiatric disorders in America: the epidemiological catchment area study.* New York, N.Y.: Free Press.

Rogler, L., Cortes, D., & Malgady, R. (1994). The mental health relevance of idioms of distress: anger and perceptions of injustice among New York Puerto Ricans. *Journal of Nervous and Mental Disease, 182,* 327–330.

Russell, J. (1989). Anxiety disorders in Japan: a review of the Japanese literature on shinkeishitsu and taijinkyofusho. *Culture, Medicine, and Psychiatry, 14,* 21–58.

Schneier, F., Johnson, J., Hornig, C., Liebowitz, M., & Weissman, M. (1992). Social phobia: comorbidity and morbidity in an epidemiologic sample. *Archives of General Psychiatry, 49,* 282–288.

Schwarz, E. & Birn, H. (1995). Dental anxiety in Danish and Chinese adults—a cross-cultural perspective. *Social Science and Medicine, 41,* 123–130.

Shrout, P., Canino, G., Bird, H., & Rubio-Stipec, M. (1992). Mental health status among Puerto Ricans, Mexican Americans, and non-Hispanic Whites. *American Journal of Community Psychology, 20,* 729–753.

Simons, R.C., & Hughes, C.C., (1993). Culture-bound syndromes. In A.C. Gaw (Ed.), *Culture, ethnicity, and mental illness.* (pp. 75–93). Washington D.C.: American Psychiatric Press.

Stefannson, J.G. (1993). The lifetime prevalence of anxiety disorders in Iceland as estimated by the United States National Institute of Mental

Health Diagnostic Interview Schedule. *Acta Psychiatrica Scandinavica,* *88*, 29–34.

Tseng, W.S., Xu, D., Ebata, K., Hsu, J., & Cui, J. (1986). Diagnostic pattern for neurosis in China, Japan and the United States. *American Journal of Psychiatry, 143*, 1000–1014.

Weisman, M.M., Bland, R., Canino, G., Greenwald, S., Hirn, H., Lee, C., Newman, J., Oakley-Brown, M., Robin-Stipes, M., Wickramaratne, P. et al. (1994). The cross-national epidemiology of obsessive-compulsive disorder. *Journal of Clinical Psychiatry, 53*, 3 (supplement), 5–10.

WHO. (1992). *International statistical classification of diseases and related health problems*, Tenth revision (ICD-10). Geneva: World Health Organization.

CHAPTER FOUR

Somatization

Steven L. Chaplin, M.D.

CASE VIGNETTES

Case 1

Mrs. Chang, a 56-year-old married woman from Mainland China, was brought to see a psychiatrist by her daughter. Mrs. Chang was visiting the daughter, who had studied in an American university, completed a graduate degree, and now lived in the United States. In the past, Mrs. Chang had traveled to the United States and other Western countries for business reasons. This trip was strictly a social visit. The daughter had noted some strange behavior in her mother during the visit. She had given some precious items to her daughter with a solemnity that seemed uncharacteristic. She had also made numerous statements to the effect that she would not be seeing her daughter again. As the time for her mother's return to China approached, the daughter became increasingly concerned and persuaded her to see a doctor.

During the interview, Mrs. Chang told the doctor that she suffered from "weakness within the heart" and had "difficulty sleeping at night." Initially, she was reluctant to talk, but she became more animated when discussing her problems with sleep. She described intermittent, restless sleep that often prevented her from sleeping well for several days. She stated that it was because she had "too much fire in the liver," and pointed to a sore on her lip as proof of that assessment.

Upon further questioning, she related that her sleep problems had begun a year before, soon after she retired from work. She had attained a rather important position as a chief architect and supervised a staff of over 100 people. She had even been able to travel outside China on business during the latter part of her career. However, she had been forced to retire in accordance with government regulations.

After retiring, she had complained that she had nothing to do, and that her life was without purpose. Her husband, also a professional, was still employed. She described him as a quiet person by nature who offered her little comfort. Later, she volunteered the information that he had had an extramarital affair several years prior, and that their relationship had been strained since then.

At the conclusion of the session, the psychiatrist explained that he believed her problems were mostly related to her postretirement adjustment. He recommended that she attempt to reopen dialogue with her husband, and encouraged her to seek activities and friends outside of her home. He finally offered to prescribe medication for her "depression." She agreed to talk more with her husband and to try to cultivate outside activities. However, she claimed that she did not understand the term "depression," and reminded the doctor that she suffered "weakness within the heart," "too much fire in the liver," and "difficulty sleeping."

Case 2

Ms. Gonzales is a 48-year-old Hispanic female who was born and raised in southern California. She is divorced, unemployed, and lives with her 20-year-old daughter who is single and employed. Ms. Gonzales was referred to a mental health clinic because she was complaining of poor sleep and low energy as well as loss of sexual desire. Four years previously, she had a bout of shingles that forced her to quit working. Shortly thereafter she was diagnosed with fibromyalgia. She stated that "my body hasn't been the same since."

She began having multiple aches and pains following the shingles episode and underwent ankle and back surgery. The back surgery did not improve her back pain. Now she is quite upset that she consented to the surgery. However, she maintains that she can deal with the pain she suffers. It is the poor sleep and tiredness that concerns her most.

After screening for occult medical illness, she was started on an antidepressant drug. Some improvement in sleep was experienced, but she continued to mention her dissatisfaction with her sexual drive. She had undergone a total hysterectomy two years ago, and had stopped menstruating one year prior to the operation. She had not been sexually active since her divorce six years earlier.

During the first several therapy sessions, new somatic symptoms appeared. The muscle aches and pains worsened to the point of keeping her bedridden at times. She also complained of headaches, dyspepsia, and nervousness. As therapy progressed she managed to taper off an antianxiety medication that she had taken for approximately three years. She was also able to reduce the potency of the pain medication for the muscle aches. Furthermore, she was able to talk about her sense of loss as her daughter became more independent and about her residual anger toward her former husband. She would mention muscle pains only during periods of increased stress.

Case 3

Mr. Sione is a 50-year-old minister from Western Samoa. He is quite famous there as a biblical scholar and leader in the religious community. Over a period of several months he began experiencing weakness in his legs to the point where he was unable to walk. He was excused from some of his duties at the high school where he teaches. He continued to give lectures but did not have to mete out corporal punishment to students, which is a common form of punishment in Samoa. He previously had been given the task of paddling students because the principal knew that he would be fair and not as harsh as some other teachers. An initial workup in Samoa found no obvious cause for his leg weakness. He came to Hawaii for further medical evaluation because his inability to walk did not remit.

In Hawaii, he underwent some neurologic tests without any pathological findings. His neurologist told him he could walk and attempted to lead him about the room. At this point, Mr. Sione collapsed on the floor, unable to support his own weight. A psychiatrist was called to consult. Further history revealed two prior episodes of leg weakness. Once as a teenager he had fallen out of a tree and spent several weeks in bed. He recalled this time fondly, saying that he had never received so much attention from his family, since he was from a large family and often felt ignored. Another episode occurred during school when he worked at a construction job and had to climb out on a ledge high above the ground. He felt weak in the legs and was not required to work at such heights again.

While in Hawaii for the medical evaluation, he seemed to be having a great time. His wife, with whom he had a good relationship, had come with him. When not undergoing tests, she would help him get around the hospital. The psychiatrist noted that he avidly watched violent television shows. As they discussed this topic over a couple of sessions, it became clear that he was fascinated by violence but at the same time he found it quite repugnant. He began to talk about the conflict he experienced in Samoa over being the teacher who was supposed to physically punish students. He felt this was against his religious training, even though it was culturally accepted. He also worried that he might secretly enjoy the punishment that he inflicted and felt aghast at this possibility. As his stay in Hawaii neared an end, the psychiatrist said he was allowed to return to work, in a wheelchair if necessary, but under no circumstances would he be permitted to mete out corporal punishment to students. He accepted this prohibition. He was able to walk onto the departing airplane that week and was able to return to teaching.

INTRODUCTION

Somatization is inextricably entwined with culture. When somatic symptoms are difficult to classify, they expose the cultural construction of disease and the culture's influence on help-seeking behavior. It is the goal of this chapter to tease out the cultural components of somatic complaints that do not appear to have a medical basis.

Definitions

Somatization is not a codified diagnosis in the *Diagnostic and Statistical Manual of Mental Disorders—Fourth Edition* (DSM-IV)

(American Psychiatric Association, 1994) or the *International Statistical Classification of Diseases and Related Health Problems— Tenth Revision* (ICD-10) (World Health Organization, 1992). Rather, it is a trait or behavior that may appear in a number of disorders, including: somatoform, mood, anxiety, psychotic, dissociative, and personality disorders. Nevertheless, it is most closely associated with the somatoform disorders whose unifying concept is that psychological distress is expressed in somatic complaints. It is distinguished from psychosomatic diseases, which present as verifiable physiologic disturbances, although psychological factors are thought to play a causative role. In the DSM-IV, the somatoform disorders include somatization disorder, undifferentiated somatoform disorder, conversion disorder, pain disorder, hypochondriasis, body dysmorphic disorder, and a not otherwise specified category. The ICD-10 includes two additional categories: somatoform autonomic dysfunction and neurasthenia.

Somatization disorder is the successor to Briquet's syndrome, or hysteria. The stringent diagnostic criteria, 13 out of 35 symptoms for DSM-III-R (American Psychiatric Association, 1987) or eight symptoms from four body systems for DSM-IV, has made this specific disorder rare. The Epidemiologic Catchment Area (ECA) study found only a 0.1% lifetime prevalence based on earlier criteria (Robbins et al., 1984). More recent surveys using the new, broader criteria still find only 0.2% to 2% prevalence rates (American Psychiatric Association, 1994). These low rates contrast starkly with the experience of primary care physicians, who claim that 25% to 72% of patient visits are due to psychosocial distress presenting as somatic complaints (Purcell, 1991). Escobar (1987) has argued for operationalizing the definition of these somatic complaints into a somatization trait construct, but most commentators continue to place these somatic presentations in the undifferentiated somatoform disorder category.

This definition of somatization, which emphasizes symptoms, is not without controversy. The main alternate view emphasizes the role of somatization as an idiom of distress (Katon et al., 1982). This definition expresses the function the symptoms may serve in contradistinction to the atheoretical stance of the DSM-IV. This chapter will use somatization in the sense conveyed by undifferentiated somatoform disorder but will also explore the cultural meaning of somatic symptom presentation. In addition, some of the other somatoform disorders will be briefly reviewed from a cross-cultural perspective.

SOMATIZATION IN DIFFERENT CULTURES

A classic study by Zola (1966) demonstrated the influence of cultural background on the symptomatic presentation of patients. He reported that Italian-American patients complained of more somatic symptoms involving more body locations than Irish-American patients. The stage was set for a multitude of cross-cultural comparisons. Kirmayer (1984), in an excellent overview, provides examples, from every corner of the world, of somatic presentations in the absence of significant physical findings. From this plethora of studies, three groups have garnered the most commentary: Asians, Hispanics, and refugees.

The Asian Cases

The most extensive literature on the cross-cultural nature of somatization concerns the purported tendency of Asians, in particular the Chinese, to somatize. Kleinman (1977) reported increased somatization among patients in Taiwan that he diagnosed as depressed. Thereafter, an extensive literature on Chinese somatization followed. A recent study in Britain found that in a primary care setting, Asian patients (from India, Pakistan, and Bangladesh) reported significantly more somatic and depressive symptoms than Caucasian patients (Farooq et al., 1995). Although fewer studies have been reported, Japanese patients are described as prone to somatize as well (Yamamoto, 1982). An excellent review of the Chinese literature is provided by F.M. Cheung (1995). Kleinman and Mechanic's (1980) influential observations on normal and abnormal behavior in Chinese culture and Tseng's (1975) cogent hypotheses to explain increased somatization led to an abundance of facts interlaced with myths in Cheung's view.

Because roughly one-fourth of the world's population is Asian, understanding increased somatization in this cultural group would advance cultural psychiatry's relevance. Explanations for this trait among the Chinese have included Tseng's (1975) hypotheses that the Chinese (1) are exposed to Chinese traditional medicine's emphasis on the symbolic correspondence between human emotions and body organs, (2) find physical complaints more socially acceptable, (3) are reluctant to openly express sexual or aggressive feelings, and (4) have hypochondriacal worries conditioned by the Chinese media.

While each of these explanations is plausible, each has been used to challenge the legitimacy of increased somatization in the Chinese. Tung (1994) states that the Chinese use body-related verbal expressions in an all-encompassing fashion that says more about their values, beliefs, and world views than any somatizing characteristic. He gives many examples of Chinese words such as *xin jin*, which means "mood," but whose individual Chinese characters mean "heart" and "area" or "territory." The implication is that psychological constructs are naturally expressed in the metaphors of the body. He finds traditional Chinese medicine's relating each emotion to specific organs in the body not as evidence of a somatizing trait but as eliminating the mind–body dualism of Western culture.

The stereotype of the inscrutable Chinese or the deferent Japanese may lead therapists to presume that they do not express emotion overtly or discuss personal matters openly. Questions not asked or nuances not pursued remain mysteries. It is all too easy to take the patient's somatic complaints at face value. In a study of depressed Chinese patients in a general medical clinic, patients initially expressed somatic complaints but admitted affective symptoms when asked about them directly (Cheung et al., 1980-1981). Recently, Cheng (1995) extended this finding to a community sample. He reported that his questionnaire survey of neuroses in a community population revealed that although many of the subjects (83.7% of cases) reported somatic symptoms, all of them manifested certain kinds of emotional symptoms with varying degrees of severity, as well. Furthermore, the weighted prevalence rates of somatic symptoms were very similar to those found in a British community survey (Jenkins, 1985) using the same operational definition. Cheng emphasized that the cultural differences were revealed by the manner in which the patients reported their symptoms, more than by what they actually manifested (or suffered from). This finding supports the difference between the concepts of disease and illness, and, hence, further emphasizes the need to understand the cultural pattern of presenting problems.

The Hispanic Cases

Escobar (1987) has commented on the unique tendency of Hispanic populations to present with somatic complaints. Mezzich and Raab (1980) compared depressed Peruvian outpatients with a group of inpatients in the United States and found the Peruvian patients reported a higher proportion of somatic symptoms. Escobar et al.

(1983) then compared depressed Hispanic patients in a Colombian hospital and predominantly non-Hispanic patients in two hospitals in the United States, and concluded that depressed Colombians somatized more than depressed Americans.

The large Epidemiologic Catchment Area (ECA) study data from Los Angeles (Burnam et al., 1987) compared the prevalence of disorders diagnosed using the DSM-III (American Psychiatric Association, 1980) between Mexican Americans and White non-Hispanics. There were no differences found for most DSM-III diagnoses, including somatization disorder. However, the paucity of somatization cases precluded logistic regression analysis. Escobar et al. (1987) looked explicitly at the somatization symptoms reported and found that Mexican-American females reported a higher mean number of symptoms than White non-Hispanic females. This correlation was highest for women over the age of 40 and for those whose level of acculturation was the lowest, that is, those who identified most with the Mexican culture. Among the male respondents, no significant differences were found. The authors commented that culturally related factors such as migration, acculturation, and social role norms affect levels of somatization for Mexican-American women, but perhaps older Mexican-American men minimize symptoms due to "machismo" and stoicism. In his most recent review of the transcultural aspects of somatization, Escobar (1995) cites his earlier findings, which showed Puerto Rican respondents to have the highest levels of somatization among several ethnic groups studied in the United States: a 0.7% prevalence of DSM-III Somatization Disorder and a 20% prevalence using his more lenient criteria. He ascribes the higher rates to the following: stigmatization of mental illness, men's fear of appearing weak, less psychological-mindedness, and societally sanctioned entry into the health care system. While these specific factors of Puerto Rican culture may influence the higher rates in this study, it should be noted that the same factors express themselves in many other cultural groups.

The Refugee Cases

The 1980s might be described as the decade of the refugee. Displaced persons from war, civil strife, drought, and natural disasters reached truly epic proportions. Health workers began to notice the frequent somatization of refugees, and several studies were reported. The most common reasons for referring Southeast Asian refugees to a psychiatric clinic in Canada were bodily complaints thought to be somatic manifestations of anxiety and depression (Nguyen, 1982). Lin et al. (1985) found a very high rate of somatization among Asian refugees and immigrants at a primary care center in the United States. Somatization accounted for 27% of the immigrants' clinic visits and 42% of the refugee visits. This study found somatization associated with decreased resources such as large households with low income, female-headed households, and limited English proficiency. Ethnicity was found to be independently associated with somatization; the Mien refugees had the highest rate, the Filipino immigrants the lowest.

Westermeyer et al. (1989) also found high rates of somatization in Hmong refugees in the United States. They found a correlation between higher somatization and lesser acculturation as measured by use of the American mass media, friendship with native-born Americans, and degree of participation in various cultural activities. They concluded that social isolation and cultural alienation from the majority culture may foster somatization.

It seems likely that the increased somatization among refugees and immigrants is partly explained by the stresses of their status. Many decades ago, Tyhurst (1951) studied displaced persons in Canada after World War II and found the changing social factors of these patients (as opposed to individual factors) to be the primary determinant of the consistency in their symptom patterns, which included a high degree of somatization. The increase may also be due, in part, to the simple fact of the cultural gap between the displaced person and the health provider.

SOMATOFORM DISORDERS AND SOMATIZATION

Hypochondriasis

Hypochondriasis and somatization have been closely associated, and have even frequently been seen as overlapping concepts. The DSM-III-R classified hypochondriasis as a somatoform disorder. This nosology has been challenged, however. Several authorities have questioned the distinction between the two disorders as defined in the DSM-III-R (Schmidt, 1994) and, presumably, DSM-IV, since it only adds an insight specifier to the criteria. Nevertheless, Schmidt concludes that the literature allows one to distinguish the two concepts on the basis of the presence or absence of a hypochondriacal attitude: an unjustified health anxiety or disease conviction, and preoccupation with signs from one's own body. somatization disorder lacks the disease conviction, and has the physical complaint itself as the focus of the patient's concerns.

There are few studies that specifically examine hypochondriasis with respect to cultural features. The DSM-IV admonishes clinicians to cautiously diagnose hypochondriasis "if the individual's ideas about disease have been reinforced by traditional healers who may disagree with the reassurances provided by medical evaluations" (American Psychiatric Association, 1994, p. 464). Little is said in the research literature about the variance of hypochondriasis among cultures, although this is a ripe area for stereotypes. An early review of hypochondriacal states (Kenyon, 1976) noted how, historically, hypochondriasis was seen as peculiarly British and named "the English malady." Being British, the author included Continental nationalities by relating that the French tend to be preoccupied with their livers and the Germans with their bowels.

A review concurrent with the DSM-III nosology made observations about cultures differing in their belief systems about disease, their attitudes toward different parts of the body, and the varying stigmata of psychiatric illness (Barsky & Klerman, 1983). These observations would apply equally to somatization disorder and do not elucidate any unique cultural components of hypochondriasis. While one's culture might influence which diseases would be a focus of preoccupation, the very diseases that are endemic in an area will influence the hypochondriacal focus. One study of the cross-national prevalence of neurotic symptoms actually found no difference in the presentation of hypochondriasis (Saz et al., 1995). Thus, hypochondriasis, if influenced by cultural factors, is likely subject to the same factors germane to somatization.

Conversion Disorder

Conversion disorder is defined as the sudden onset of symptoms that suggest a neurological or general medical condition for which there is no pathophysiologic explanation (American Psychiatric Association, 1994). The symptoms tend to follow the patient's model of illness rather than neuroanatomical pathways (Kirmayer et al., 1994). Culture influences models of illness and would be expected to affect the presentation of conversion disorder.

The generally held view, as expressed in the DSM-IV, is that the disorder is more prevalent in developing regions of the world, where rural populations are larger and the socioeconomic status is lower

(American Psychiatric Association, 1994). The greater prevalence reported in less developed regions may be a reflection of the population's better understanding of illness. In populations where Western medical paradigms are widely accepted, somatic symptoms are more "realistic" and, hence, not called conversion symptoms.

As Kirmayer and Weiss (1993) have suggested, all conversion symptoms could be construed as culturally sanctioned in that they are meaningful ways of expressing distress in a particular culture. As a means to express distress, the symptoms of conversion disorder may reflect more the local cultural ideas about what is acceptable for entry into the sick role or for solving an underlying psychological conflict than any underlying pathophysiology.

Among the somatoform disorders, conversion disorder is the only one in which the diagnosis is specifically excluded if the symptoms represent culturally sanctioned behavior or experience (American Psychiatric Association, 1994). Such culturally sanctioned syndromes as *ataques de nervios* and *falling out* involve dramatic symptoms such as fainting episodes and temporary blindness that seem to meet the criteria of conversion disorder, yet they are accorded special status. The spectrum of culturally influenced presentations from somatization through conversion disorder to culture-bound syndromes (CBSs) merely highlights the tension between the universal and the local with which psychiatric nosologies struggle. Culture plays a permissive role in determining which symptoms will be recognized. This role is very broad in somatization, becomes much narrower in conversion disorder, and is defining in CBSs.

It must be acknowledged that few studies have closely examined the cross-cultural prevalence of conversion disorder, and more data are needed before making definitive conclusions on the role of culture. Freud, who coined the term, lived in one of the most sophisticated urban centers of Europe and drew his case studies from the culturally elite. Furthermore, conversion disorders are still being reported in developed countries (Viederman, 1995). Clearly, cultural influences are complex.

Neurasthenia

Neurasthenia is a diagnosis that enjoyed considerable popularity in the United States and western Europe in the early part of the twentieth century. It was a term revived by the American neurologist George Beard to describe an array of somatic and psychological symptoms, including: fatigue, weakness, diffuse aches and pains, gastrointestinal problems, sleep difficulties, and autonomic nervous system involvement. The concept was first taken up from the United States by physicians in Europe and then in Asia (Ware & Kleinman, 1992). While the number of cases diagnosed in the Western world tapered off, the diagnosis burgeoned in China. By the 1980s it was the most common neurotic diagnosis in China (Cheung, 1991). Since the Chinese Classification of Mental Disorders tightened the criteria for neurasthenia, it is now much less frequently diagnosed. In its place is the increased diagnosis of depressive neurosis (Lee, 1994), which tends to confirm Kleinman's (1982) original thesis that most neurasthenia cases would be diagnosed as major depression according to the DSM-III.

Yet, even in the Western world there are many patients who present with neurasthenic symptoms but do not receive a diagnosis of depression. Analogous to China's diagnostic reconceptualization of neurasthenia, the DSM first endorsed, then limited or excluded its diagnosis. A diagnostic entity with a similar symptom profile then took root in the United States. Chronic fatigue syndrome was associated in the United States with credible reports of a link between chronic Epstein–Barr virus infection and symptoms of fatigue. However, careful follow-up studies revealed little evidence for this hypothesized link (Wessely, 1990). Nevertheless, chronic fatigue syndrome emerged as the neurasthenia of the 1980s.

Abbey and Garfinkel (1991) explain the striking parallels between neurasthenia and chronic fatigue syndrome in sociocultural terms. They note that both disorders arose during times of preoccupation with commerce and the changing role of women. They also view the disorders using the scientific paradigms extant at the time. Their conclusion is that these represent illness behaviors shaped by the culture.

A tragic incident occurred in Japan in 1982 when a pilot for Japan Airlines, who had been experiencing auditory hallucinations and delusions, caused the crash-landing of a large airliner. His symptoms had developed over a five-year period, but he had only received a diagnosis of psychosomatic disorder, a depressive state, or a malfunction of the autonomic nervous system. Munakata (1989) views this case as one of the tragic examples of using diagnoses like neurasthenia to disguise a diagnosis of schizophrenia. He ascribes this pattern to the widespread stigma of mental illness in Japan. Neurasthenia is used as a disguise diagnosis, he relates, for a host of psychiatric disorders, because it is seen as a legitimate physical illness. Thus, physicians collude with patients to avoid the social prejudice against mental illness, sometimes with disastrous consequences. Extensive social prejudice toward mental illness still exists in Europe and the United

States. Munakata (1989) believes, however, that the burden on Japanese doctors to reduce the psychological suffering of patients when a diagnosis of mental illness is made makes the disguising of diagnoses especially prevalent in Japan.

CASE DISCUSSION

Case 1

The case of the woman from Mainland China illustrates that patients can use various somatic idioms, such as "weakness within the heart" or "too much fire in the liver," to communicate to a doctor the suffering they experience. According to traditional Chinese medical concepts, the different emotions of anger, sorrow, sadness, and courage are associated with specific visceral organs. Being familiar with such concepts, ordinary Chinese will generally understand the idiomatic meaning of "weakness within the heart" as implying that one's mood is down, and "too much fire in the liver" as being anxious or irritated. When a person develops a herpes rash around the lips it is usually interpreted as a sign of tension—a condition associated with "too much fire in the liver." The prescribed remedy is taking the foods or drinks that are considered cold elements to reduce the excessive heat in the body. These idiomatic ways to describe one's state of mind may not be understood and appreciated by non-Chinese physicians who are unfamiliar with the terms.

The most important lesson to learn from this patient is that although she kept using somatic idioms, she is not necessarily somatizing her psychological problems. She understood clearly that her problems were related to her sudden retirement coupled with her marital problems—a psychological way of interpreting her reaction to the stress. She agreed that she needed to change her attitude and adapt to a new pattern of life if she were to enjoy her remaining years. Nonetheless, she remained unfamiliar with the English (psychiatric) term of depression, and continued to refer to her problems under the rubric of insomnia and organ system derangements.

Case 2

The Hispanic woman referred to therapy with a diagnosis of fibromyalgia soon revealed a pattern of increased somatic symptoms when stressors increased in her life. Far from being laconic or unable to express her emotions, she was often quite histrionic. Whether physicians overlooked the possible presence of depression because of physician–patient cultural differences, or whether the work-related onset clouded the presentation, it was not until the patient was encouraged to speak about interpersonal problems that a depressive component to her complaints became clear. The symptoms of sleep disturbance and loss of energy characterized as vegetative symptoms have been shown in cross-cultural studies to be core symptoms of depression (Katon et al., 1982). Somatization in the presence of depression is not culture specific, but in cultures where somatization has been alleged to be more prevalent, clinicians should be even more assiduous at probing for depressive symptoms. This patient certainly did not have a complete remission of the fibromyalgia symptoms; nevertheless, antidepressant therapy coupled with interpersonal psychotherapy lessened her suffering.

Case 3

The case vignette of the Samoan minister illustrates the typical conversion symptoms of a pseudoneurological disorder, which greatly affected his functioning and allowed him to avoid onerous duties. He even seemed to be relatively unconcerned—the classic *la belle indifference*.

Samoan society, especially Western Samoa, where the patient lived, has a medical system that includes traditional healers and concurrent use of herbal medicines. Coming from this tradition, the patient did not have an exclusively Western-influenced repertoire of symptoms to draw on. This hypothesis fits the generalization that populations in less developed regions are more likely to exhibit conversion symptoms. Beyond that generalization, however, is the further cultural impact the patient experienced. He lived in a society that condones fairly harsh corporal punishment, but his religious beliefs apparently frowned on such punishment and it was personally repugnant to him. This conflict alone could have driven the production of the paralysis. Or, the conflict may have been deeper, involving his choice of vocation, and the repression of aggressive impulses. In either case, the conversion symptom afforded him the opportunity to solve a difficult psychological dilemma. When the consulting psychiatrist was able to offer an alternative solution, the need for the disabling symptoms was resolved.

CONCLUSIONS

As noted throughout this chapter, widely held precepts regarding somatization and culture have not always withstood scrutiny. What can be said is that the somatic expression of psychological distress is widespread across cultures. Furthermore, somatization is a widespread occurrence in Western society. In a summary of several studies, Swartz et al. (1989) state that 60% to 80% of the normal population experiences at least one such symptom in any given week, and that 20% to 84% of patients presenting to physicians have somatic complaints without a discernible physical basis. Any study positing higher somatization rates in non-Western cultures must contend with these high rates of somatization in the United States.

There are many credible studies that indicate higher somatization in certain groups—lower socioeconomic status, rural residence, and ethnic groups that discourage the expression of emotion (Barsky & Klerman, 1983). There have also been several reasonable hypotheses to explain somatization, for example, the social stigma of mental illness (Goldberg & Blackwell, 1970), the social requirement of obtaining a sick role (Mechanic, 1978), and the need for idioms of distress (Kleinman, 1980), to name some prominent ones. Because intracultural diversity is so great, it will help to focus on cultural factors framed in these ways rather than as cultural stereotypes.

While stigmatization of mental illness exists in all societies, it does seem more harsh or, at least, leads to more serious consequences in some. In Japan, for example, there is a family registry called *kosekitohon* that can be consulted if mental illness in a family pedigree is of concern. The legitimacy of an illness and entry into the sick role is culturally influenced. Medical practitioners control entry into the medical system in overt and subtle ways, and much of patients' presentations can be explained by the patient seeking to conform to the practitioner's belief system. Patient and practitioner often share belief systems, and somatization becomes a cultural trait only observed from the outside. When practitioner and patient start with different belief systems, the divergence is more apparent within that particular culture. One author has even explained conversion reaction as the inability of either the patient or the doctor to accept the terms of the transaction between them with dignity (Rabkin, 1964).

Although his work has been criticized for misreading the psychological impact of China's social problems (Young & Xiao, 1993),

Kleinman's view that the great majority of the world's people experience human suffering in non-dualistic metaphors that do not separate the mind and body, as Western medical culture often does, continues to offer the best overall understanding of culture's influence on somatization.

SUGGESTED CLINICAL GUIDELINES

1. Have an awareness of the ubiquity of somatization. Somatization has been found wherever it has been sought. The prevalence of a disorder should always influence how intensely it should be looked for in a population. As the prevalence studies cited above have indicated, somatization is present across cultures.

2. Thorough interviewing is essential. Although elementary, this dictum cannot be overemphasized. As the study by Cheung et al. (1980–1981) illustrates, persistence in asking about underlying psychosocial problems often reveals their importance despite an initial presentation that is limited to somatic complaints. Of course, the more familiar the interviewer is with the idioms of distress in a particular culture, the more cognizant of the meaning of somatic symptoms that practitioner will be. It is when patient and practitioner come from different cultural backgrounds that the practitioner must be especially attuned to the presence of somatization.

3. Demonstrate, if possible, a familiarity with the psychosocial constructs that the patient understands. Not only does a cultural difference between patient and practitioner make interpretation of symptoms more problematic, but this very relationship influences the presentation of symptoms. The patient may present in a manner that he believes the practitioner's culture expects. By demonstrating familiarity with psychosomatic constructs that the patient understands, the practitioner may gain the patient's trust to elaborate on the psychological component of symptoms. For example, extrapolating from Lin's (1983) observations, one could use the CBS of *Hwa-Byung*, which most Koreans

have heard of, to help Korean patients accept that anger and stress can result in physical illness.

4. Gather collateral information. Collateral information can be especially useful for somatizing patients. When there is a question of whether or not the somatic symptoms represent masked depression, for example, finding out from family or friends what behaviors the patient manifests can help resolve this question. The somatizing patient whose family reports that he thoroughly enjoys his usual activities is not likely to be depressed. How the patient's symptoms affect the patient's role in the family can also help clarify the cultural perspective. The family is a microcosm of the culture, and allows close observation of what effects the patients' symptoms produce. This observation can elucidate cultural factors that might not be readily apparent.

5. Avoid cultural stereotypes that obscure more salient factors in the presentation of somatic symptoms. Personality factors and demographics may explain a particular patient's somatization better than ethnicity. Concentrating on cultural differences in patients may lead to missing other important diagnostic signs. Cultural sensitivity is not a fixation on culture.

What these various recommendations all have in common is a heightened awareness of cultural differences and increased sensitivity to those differences. Jablensky et al. (1994) emphasize that culture should not be a synonym for unexplained variance. By talking more with patients and trying to understand their conceptions of the meaning of symptoms, practitioners can ultimately better serve their needs.

REFERENCES

Abbey, S.E. & Garfinkel, P.E. (1991). Neurasthenia and chronic fatigue syndrome: The role of culture in the making of a diagnosis. *American Journal of Psychiatry*, *148*, 1638–1646.

American Psychiatric Association. (1980). *Diagnostic and statistical manual of mental disorders—third edition*. (DSM-III). Washington, D.C.: American Psychiatric Association.

84 *Somatization*

American Psychiatric Association. (1987). *Diagnostic and statistical manual of mental disorders—third edition, revised.* (DSM-III-R). Washington, D.C.: American Psychiatric Association.

American Psychiatric Association. (1994). *Diagnostic and statistical manual of mental disorders—fourth edition.* (DSM-IV). Washington, D.C.: American Psychiatric Association.

Barsky, A.J. & Klerman, G.L. (1983). Overview: Hypochondriasis, bodily complaints, and somatic styles. *American Journal of Psychiatry, 140,* 273–283.

Burnam, M.A., Hough, R.L., Escobar, J.I., Karno, M., Timbers, D.M., Telles, C.A., & Locke, B.Z., (1987). Six-month prevalence of specific psychiatric disorders among Mexican Americans and Non-Hispanic Whites in Los Angeles. *Archives of General Psychiatry, 44,* 687–694.

Cheng, T.A. (1995). Neurosis in Taiwan: Findings from a community survey. In T.Y Lin, W.S. Tseng, and E.K. Yeh (Eds.), *Chinese Societies and Mental Health* (pp. 167–175). Hong Kong: Oxford University Press.

Cheung, F.M. (1995). Facts and myths about somatization among the Chinese. In T.Y. Lin, W.S. Tseng, & E.K. Yeh (Eds.), *Chinese Societies and Mental Health* (pp.156–166). Hong Kong: Oxford University Press.

Cheung, F.M., Lau, B.W.K., & Waldmann, E. (1980–81). Somatization among Chinese depressives in general practice. *International Journal of Psychiatry in Medicine, 10,* 361–74.

Cheung, P. (1991). Adult psychiatric epidemiology in China in the 80s. *Culture, Medicine and Psychiatry, 15,* 479–496.

Escobar, J.I. (1987). Cross-cultural aspects of the somatization trait. *Hospital and Community Psychiatry, 38*(2), 174–180.

Escobar, J.I. (1995). Transcultural aspects of dissociative and somatoform disorders. *Psychiatric Clinics of North America, 18,* 555–569.

Escobar, J.I., Burnham, M.A., Karno, M., Forsythe, A., & Golding, J.M. (1987). Somatization in the community. *Archives General Psychiatry, 44,* 713–718.

Escobar, J.I., Gomez, J., & Tuason, V.B. (1983). Depressive phenomenology in North and South American patients. *American Journal of Psychiatry, 140,* 47–51.

Farooq, S., Gahir, M.S., Okyere, E., Sheikh, A.J., & Oyebode, F. (1995). Somatization: A transcultural study. *Journal of Psychosomatic Research, 39,* 883–888.

Goldberg, D.P. & Blackwell, B. (1970). Psychiatric illness in general practice. A detailed study using a new method of case identification. *British Medical Journal, 2,* 439–443.

Jablensky, A., Sartorius, N., Cooper, J.E., Anker, M., Korten, A., & Bertelsen, A. (1994). Culture and schizophrenia: Criticisms of WHO studies are answered (editorial). *British Journal of Psychiatry, 165,* 434–436.

Jenkins, R. (1985). *Sex Difference in Minor Psychiatric Morbidity.* Psychological Medicine Monograph Supplement 7. Cambridge: Cambridge University Press.

Katon, W., Kleinman, A., & Rosen, G. (1982). Depression and somatization: A review, part I. *American Journal of Medicine, 72,* 127–135.

Kenyon, F.E. (1976). Hypochondriacal states. *British Journal of Psychiatry, 129,* 1–14.

Kirmayer, L.J. (1984). Culture, affect and somatization, part I. *Transcultural Psychiatric Research Review, 21,* 159–188.

Kirmayer, L.J., Robbins, J.M., & Paris, J. (1994). Somatoform disorders: Personality and the social matrix of somatic distress. *Journal of Abnormal Psychology, 103*, 125–136.

Kirmayer, L.J. & Weiss, M. (1993). Somatoform disorders. In J.E. Mezzich (Chair, National Institute of Mental Health (NIMH) Group on Culture and Diagnosis), *Revised Cultural Proposals for DSM-IV* (pp. 61–82). NIMH-Sponsored Group on Culture and Diagnosis.

Kleinman, A. (1977). Depression, somatization and the 'new cross-cultural psychiatry.' *Social Science and Medicine, 11*, 3–10.

Kleinman, A. (1980). *Patients and Healers in the Context of Culture: An Exploration of the Borderland Between Anthropology, Medicine and Psychiatry.* Berkeley, California: University of California Press.

Kleinman, A. (1982). Neurasthenia and depression: A study of somatization and culture in China. *Culture, Medicine and Psychiatry, 6*, 117–190.

Kleinman, A. & Mechanic, D. (1980). Mental illness and psychosocial aspects of medical problems in China. In A. Kleinman and T.Y. Lin (Eds.), *Normal and Abnormal Behavior in Chinese Culture* (pp. 331–356). Dordrecht, Holland: D. Reidel.

Lee, S. (1994). Neurasthenia and Chinese psychiatry in the 1990s. *Journal of Psychosomatic Research, 38*, 487–491.

Lin, E.H.B., Carter, W.B., & Kleinman, A.M. (1985). An exploration of somatization among Asian refugees and immigrants in primary care. *American Journal of Public Health, 75*, 1080–1084.

Lin, K.M. (1983). *Hwa Byung*: A Korean culture-bound syndrome? *American Journal of Psychiatry, 140*, 105–107.

Mechanic, D. (1978). *Medical Sociology—second edition.* New York: Free Press.

Mezzich, J.E. & Raab, E.S. (1980). Depressive symptomatology across the Americas. *Archives of General Psychiatry, 37*, 818–823.

Munakata, T. (1989). The sociocultural significance of the diagnostic label "neurasthenia" in Japan's mental health care system. *Culture, Medicine and Psychiatry, 13*, 203–213.

Nguyen, S.D. (1982). Psychiatric and psychosomatic problems among Southeast Asian refugees. *Psychiatric Journal of the University of Ottawa, 7*, 163–172.

Purcell, T.B. (1991). The somatic patient. *Emergency Medicine Clinics of North America, 9*, 137–159.

Rabkin, R. (1964). Conversion hysteria as social maladaptation. *Psychiatry, 27*, 349–363.

Robbins, L.N., Helzer, J.E., Weissman, M.M., Orvaschel, H., Gruenberg, E., Burke, J.D., & Regier, D.A. (1984). Lifetime prevalence of specific psychiatric disorders in three sites. *Archives of General Psychiatry, 41*, 949–958.

Saz, P., Copeland, J.R.M., de la Camara, C., Lobo, A., & Dewey, M.E. (1995). Cross-national comparison of prevalence of symptoms of neurotic disorders in older people in two community samples. *Acta Psychiatrica Scandinavica, 91*, 18–22.

Schmidt, A.J.M. (1994). Bottlenecks in the diagnosis of hypochondriasis. *Comprehensive Psychiatry, 35*, 306–315.

Swartz, M., Landerman, R., Blazer, D., & George, L. (1989). Somatization symptoms in the community: A rural/urban comparison. *Psychosomatics, 30*, 44–53.

86   *Somatization*

Tseng, W.S. (1975). The nature of somatic complaints among psychiatric patients: The Chinese case. *Comprehensive Psychiatry, 16,* 237–245.

Tung, M.P.M. (1994). Symbolic meanings of the body in Chinese culture and "somatization". *Culture, Medicine and Psychiatry, 18,* 483–492.

Tyhurst, L. (1951). Displacement and migration: A study in social psychiatry. *American Journal of Psychiatry, 107,* 561–568.

Viederman, M. (1995). Metaphor and meaning in conversion disorder: A brief active therapy. *Psychosomatic Medicine, 57,* 403–409.

Ware, N.C. & Kleinman, A. (1992). Culture and somatic experience: The social course of illness in neurasthenia and chronic fatigue syndrome. *Psychosomatic Medicine, 54,* 546–560.

Wessely, S. (1990). Old wine in new bottles: neurasthenia and 'ME'. *Psychological Medicine, 20,* 35–53.

Westermeyer, J., Bouafuely, M., Neider, J., & Callies, A. (1989). Somatization among refugees: An epidemiologic study. *Psychosomatics, 30,* 34–43.

World Health Organization. (1992). *International statistical classification of diseases and related health problems—tenth revision.* Geneva: WHO.

Yamamoto, J. (1982). Japanese Americans. In A. Gaw (Ed.), *Cross-Cultural Psychiatry* (pp. 31–54). Littleton, Mass.: J. Wright.

Young, D. & Xiao, S. (1993). Several theoretical topics in neurosis research. *Integrative Psychiatry, 9,* 5–9.

Zola, I.K. (1966). Culture and symptoms: An analysis of patients' presenting complaints. *American Sociological Review, 31,* 615–630.

CHAPTER FIVE

Pain

Jon Streltzer, M.D.

CASE VIGNETTES

Case 1

A 34-year-old Italian-American construction worker received emergency surgery for acute appendicitis from a Chinese-American surgeon. Postoperative pain medication consisted of 75 mg of meperidine every four hours as needed for pain. Three hours after each injection, the patient demanded more medication, screaming for the nurses when they delayed responding because it was too soon for more medication. The surgeon berated the patient for his behavior and reduced the meperidine dose to 50 mg. This infuriated the patient, who continued to complain loudly that he was in pain. A psychiatric consultant recommended increasing the dose and frequency of pain medication, and the surgeon was told that the patient was emotional and fearful of pain because of his cultural background. The surgeon accepted this, and the rest of the hospital course was uneventful.

Case 2

A 79-year-old white Anglo-Saxon man was dying of lung cancer which had widely metastasized to bones and other parts of his body. He lay in bed quite emaciated, but denied any significant pain and was taking no pain medication. He stated that he had had a good life and was prepared to die. He enjoyed having visitors and was pleased to talk about his past, his philosophies, and other topics. He did not spontaneously discuss his illness, but it did not disturb him to do so.

Case 3

A 49-year-old first generation Filipino woman had been employed for several years as a laundry aide. One day she bumped her head as she was pulling clothes out of a large laundry machine. Despite the fact that she did not even sustain a bruise, she complained of head, neck, shoulder, arm, back, and leg pain for the next several years and was unable to return to work. Repeated neurological exams were negative. She was not reassured by physicians' statements that she was healthy and had no serious injury.

Case 4

A 28-year-old Japanese-American hemodialysis patient had severe bone pain from renal osteodystrophy. The patient complained of pain, but talked little about his life or about his feelings regarding his disease. It was thought that his inability to express his feelings was cultural and that perhaps he was depressed but unable to report it. When his mother visited him in the hospital, however, she noted that her son had always been quiet and unrevealing about himself in contrast to all his siblings who tended to be quite expressive and outgoing.

Case 5

A 42-year-old Jewish man complained of chronic back pain following a minor injury. Over the years the pain spread to include the neck, both legs, and headaches. Objective findings were minimal, while subjective complaints were unimproved by a variety of treatments. The man's Jewish physician was puzzled by his condition, but found him to be quite likable, and reluctantly kept prescribing the narcotic analgesics he insisted on getting.

INTRODUCTION

Relief of pain has been a critical part of the practice of medicine throughout history. Our ability to assess pain, however, remains at a fairly primitive level compared to our diagnostic abilities in other areas of medicine. There are no laboratory tests or imaging techniques that can give accurate information about the experience of pain. Furthermore, recent technological advances have been disappointing in their attempts to find the causes of pain. For example, with regard to chronic back pain, a condition which has historically perplexed physicians, there were great expectations that computerized tomography and MRI scans would be able to pinpoint pathology in the lower back and thus clearly explain not only why patients had pain but also where it originated. Despite initial hopes and the subsequent integration of these tests into clinical practice, controlled studies have now revealed a lack of correlation between anatomical abnormalities found in these imaging studies and clinical symptoms (Weisel et al., 1984; Jensen et al., 1994). The abnormalities sought to explain chronic low back pain appear quite commonly in the normal asymptomatic population.

Thus, to understand the patient's experience of pain, clinicians must continue to rely primarily on the patient's verbal expression of pain supplemented by an interpretation of behaviors that are perceived as being related to pain. All doctors are familiar with the wide variation of descriptions of pain and behaviors associated with pain. It is reassuring when pain complaints and behaviors correlate closely with objective pathological findings, but all too often, this is not the case.

Individual factors are thought to commonly influence the perception of pain. Furthermore, a patient's personality is a critical influence on the way pain is reported. In trying to understand the experience of pain, therefore, we need to understand the individual. In this regard, the individual's culture is often felt to profoundly affect pain behavior.

Possibly the most famous study relating culture to pain was published by Zborowski in 1952. He studied veterans with chronic pain and divided them into ethnic groups. He concluded that behavioral responses to painful illness were specific to the patient's ethnic group. He defined one group as "old Americans." These patients were White Anglo-Saxon Protestants whose families had lived in the United States for several generations. These patients were characterized as stoic in response to their pain. This stoicism was in marked contrast to two other ethnic groups, Jews and Italians. These groups did not hesitate to complain about their pain. They were quite expressive and emotional.

The Jews and Italians differed from each other, however, in other respects. The Italians were eager for pain relief, whereas the Jews were fearful of medication that would take away their pain. They wanted to be able to monitor their pain, which they perceived as a sign of how their illness was doing. Zborowski considered them to be future-oriented. In contrast, the Italians were present-oriented, and wanted to have their immediate suffering relieved.

Cases 1 and 2 above are consistent with Zborowski's observations. In Case 1, an Italian-American man complains vociferously of pain and wants immediate relief. The surgeon, from a different cultural background, is concerned and possibly even offended by the patient's behavior, and is not so concerned about the patient's experience of pain. In Case 2, the Anglo-Saxon man appears quite stoic and denies discomfort even though he lies in bed in a curled-up position. He makes no demands on his physician and seeks no sympathy.

Zborowski's study has been repeatedly cited as demonstrating cultural differences in response to pain, and has stimulated many further studies in this area. This literature on culture and pain may be divided into four categories: experimental pain, chronic pain, cancer pain, and acute pain.

EXPERIMENTAL PAIN

The following are some of the more significant studies of experimental pain. In 1944, Chapman and Jones focused radiant heat on the foreheads of subjects and concluded that southern Blacks tolerated this less than North Americans of northern European descent. Mediterranean subjects and Jews also exhibited less tolerance. Little can be concluded from this study which provided no statistical analysis and did not even include basic demographic data such as gender of the subjects. One can imagine, however, that the relationship between the experimenters and the subjects could have strongly influenced the results.

In a much more sophisticated design in the mid-1960s, Stern-bach and Turskey used transcutaneous electrical stimulation to induce pain (Sternbach & Turskey, 1965; Turskey & Sternbach, 1967). Studying groups similar to those of Zborowski (1952) and Chapman and Jones (1944), they found that North American Protestants tolerated pain better than ethnic Italians. Ethnic Jews also tolerated pain better than ethnic Italians. The differences were statistically significant at $p > .01$. The results only partially confirmed the conclusions of the earlier investigators.

A remarkable study, because of the number of subjects involved, was performed by Woodrow et al. (1972). Over 40,000 patients who were obtaining routine health screening as part of a Kaiser Foundation Health Plan in California were tested by applying pressure to the achilles tendon with a vise-like apparatus. The apparatus was tightened until the subject could not tolerate the pain. Because of the large number of subjects, all differences were highly significant. Caucasians (83% of subjects) tolerated more pain than Blacks, who in turn tolerated more pain than Asians (4% of subjects). There were prominent differences by gender and age. This study tried to control for socioeconomic effects by looking at educational level but analyses of variance were not done.

Knox et al. (1977) also demonstrated more pain tolerance in Caucasians than in Asians. Pain was induced by immersing an arm in a bucket of ice water and then recording the number of seconds that the subject could tolerate the freezing cold before pulling the arm out of the water. An interesting twist was added to this study. It was hypothesized that the Chinese subjects from Asia might respond to pretreatment with acupuncture better than the North American subjects. In fact, acupuncture had no effect on either group of subjects, although the Chinese liked it better.

Of particular interest are the studies by Lambert et al. (1960) and Poser (1963). In these studies, pain was inflicted on Jews and Christians. Manipulating the design by changing the ethnicity of the experimenter influenced the results. Furthermore, when either group was told that the other group had performed better, repeating the experiment resulted in markedly increased pain tolerance for that group.

Overall, there are no clear-cut cultural differences to be found in response to experimental pain. The various studies that have been done tend to use different types of pain under different circumstances. The experimenters have been quite ingenious in devising techniques to induce pain, but the results have been somewhat conflicting and there are numerous confounding variables. What does appear to have clearly emerged from this literature, however, is that the conditions of the experimental situation and variables associated with the experimenter can be critical in determining the results. This has implications for clinical pain. For one thing, one must be extremely careful in translating the results of data gained in experimental pain studies to clinical situations. For another, one might not expect the responses in any given clinical setting to necessarily be the same in a different clinical context.

CHRONIC PAIN

Relatively few studies have looked at culture in regard to chronic pain. Let us return to Zborowski's study (1952) to analyze it further. His findings actually mimic those of Chapman and Jones from 1944 in that White Americans of northern European ancestry tolerate pain better than other ethnic groups. Zborowski, however, presented us with no data. He did not mention the responses to pain of two of the groups in his study (Irish and "others"). He told nothing about the pain medications being used, the duration of the pain, concomitant psychiatric conditions such as war trauma, and so forth. Zborowski did note that an undetermined number of patients did not fall into the expected pattern. He suggested those patients had less identification with their cultural group. Although the stereotypes deployed by Zborowski have become a prominent part of pain literature, the actual evidence for them is slim to nonexistent beyond anecdote.

In 1992, a more sophisticated study of chronic pain patients was published by Bates and Edwards. This study resembled that of Zborowski but with greatly improved methodology. Structured questionnaires were utilized to study patients attending a chronic pain clinic. Patient groups included old Americans, Irish, Italians, French Canadians, Poles, and Hispanics. The Hispanics showed the clearest differences among the groups. They complained of more pain than the other groups, and were also less likely to be working, were more expressive of their pain, sought more advice about their pain, felt more unhealthy in general, and believed more strongly that the presence of pain meant that an unhappy life was inevitable.

The Hispanics differed from the other groups, however, in being substantially less educated. Their average educational level was eighth grade, compared to high school for the other groups. The data indicated that Hispanics were somewhat more likely to be on workers' compensation and they had a higher percentage of back pain as opposed to other more well-defined conditions. This study tried to control for pain medications. The level of medication use was not defined well, however, and it was impossible to tell the degree of regular narcotic use and potential dependency issues. Narcotic dependency can be a significant issue in a high percentage of chronic pain patients (Streltzer, 1994). This would be expected to influence pain complaints greatly and should be taken into account.

An example of the increasingly sophisticated approach to culture in the work of Bates and Edwards (1992) is the objectification of the concept of *heritage consistency*, defined as the degree to which a member of an ethnic group identifies with and practices customs common to his or her ethnic background. Patients with high heritage consistency had less pain. Generation effects were also noted.

Overall, the data did not refute the thesis that old Americans and also Poles tended to be more stoic. The results were not statistically significant, however, and were somewhat inconsistent.

A recent study from the multiethnic society of Hawaii (Streltzer et al., 1995) compared somatoform pain patients (having chronic pain grossly disproportionate to objective medical findings) with an injured control group that did not develop a somatoform pain disorder. There was no clear difference in ethnic distribution between the chronic pain patients and the general population or the control group, except for a suggestion that chronic somatoform pain was more common in the first generation Filipino group. There was no reason to suspect that Filipino culture was predisposed to chronic pain, but immigration status may well have been related. Immigrant Filipino workers typically had low-paying jobs requiring physically hard work. A liberal workers' compensation system provided replacement wages and lump-sum settlements for injured workers. Compensation issues were rated as highly significant in 49% of cases. Thus, chronic disability may have provided appreciable secondary gains for these unskilled, immigrant workers.

Another significant finding in this study was that one-half of the somatoform pain patients were dependent on daily narcotic pain medications. This suggests great difficulty in proper assessment of these patients. It is likely that cultural issues contributed to this difficulty.

CANCER PAIN

At the 7th World Congress on Pain in Paris, France in 1993, reports were presented from various countries describing the state of cancer pain and its treatment. Four countries, all European, reported similar results. In Denmark, Norway, France, and Germany, cancer pain was considered to be very frequent and undertreated. In China, however, cancer pain was considered to be much less of a problem. Only 30% of patients were considered to have significant pain in the terminal stages versus estimates of about 70% in the West. Only 4% of Chinese cancer patients were treated with narcotic analgesics. The Chinese physicians who presented their results concluded that narcotics were rarely needed. This is in marked contrast to the European physicians, who concluded that there was a great need for narcotic analgesics and that these medications were greatly underutilized.

These reports are intriguing. Do the Chinese actually experience less pain? Does their attitude about life and death insulate them from severe pain, or do Chinese patients not communicate their pain to their physicians? Perhaps the pain is the same, but physicians do not recognize it as readily. It is also possible that the culture of the physician is the critical variable. Perhaps Chinese physicians expect their patients to be stoic and not to demonstrate significant pain. In contrast, European cultures may be more encouraging of pain behavior and provide more support as a result. Or perhaps the key is the interaction between the patient and the physician. Perhaps Chinese patients attempt to please their physicians more and believe that pain reports will be more disturbing to their physicians.

A recent investigation by Cleeland et al. (1994) studied 871 outpatients with cancer in the eastern United States. They found that the cancer patients reported much more pain than their oncologists believed they had. Using a formula that matched the type of analgesic drug to the severity of reported pain, they found that patients were generally undertreated. This was most strikingly the case with groups that they termed "minorities." Although this term was not defined, the paper implies that most of the minorities were Blacks and Hispanics. The ethnic groups of the treating physicians were not described.

ACUTE PAIN

Observations of women during the process of childbirth provide a fascinating perspective into the cultural variations of the response to acute pain. While the physiological basis for labor pain is presumably similar in all cultures, the behavioral response may range from screaming and writhing in agony to a quiet, stoic acceptance, and this response seems to correlate with cultural expectations about whether childbirth should be painful and whether it is shameful or acceptable for women to express pain (Newton & Newton, 1972).

Studies of acute pain have generally utilized a specific clinical situation, such as obstetrical pain or dental pain, and subjective measurements of pain recorded for patients of varying ethnic groups. As with experimental pain situations, results have been mixed. For example, Flannery et al. (1981) found no differences in episiotomy pain among Blacks and several White ethnic groups. Weisenberg et al. (1975) also found no differences in reported acute dental pain in Black, White, and Puerto Rican patients. On the other hand, Faucett et al. (1994) found Whites to report less dental pain than Blacks or Latins, particularly among women. Complicating the conclusions of the study, however, was the fact that the group of Whites represented at least 21 different ethnicities, and the Latin group at least eleven.

A cross-cultural study of acute clinical pain was done by Streltzer and Wade (1981). Two hundred and seventy-five consecutive surgery patients receiving elective gall bladder removal were included in the study. No measures of subjective pain were used. Neither were physicians or nurses asked to rate the patients' pain. Instead, the treatment of pain was used as the only dependent variable. Overall, significant undertreatment of pain was found. This was consistent with other studies of the time. The typical postoperative pain medication was 50 to 75 mg of meperidine every three to four hours as needed for pain. This dosage was found to be inadequate for much acute pain. It is also a much lower dose than was typically prescribed in the 1960s and before. It is a much lower dose than is commonly prescribed today, when intravenous morphine is often used through a technique called patient-controlled analgesia.

In this milieu of undertreatment of pain, there were differences among ethnic groups. Caucasians received the most pain medication. Filipinos, Japanese, and Chinese received the least. Hawaiians were intermediate. A number of factors were controlled, including age, sex, anesthesiologist ratings of preoperative physical condition, surgical complications, time under anesthesia, number of postoperative hospital days, surgeons, and specific hospital wards. There was a significant age effect, with older patients receiving less pain medication. Multiple regression analyses revealed that all the factors studied accounted for only 15% of the variance in amount of pain medications received. Thus, it is presumed that individual factors accounted for the bulk of the variance. Of the factors studied, however, ethnic group accounted for the largest proportion, about 6% of the variance. Statistically, this percentage was highly significant. Thus, there appeared to be a very real difference in the way patients were treated according to their ethnic group, although this explained only a small part of the total amount of pain treatment.

In trying to explain this result, the ethnicities of the surgeons were identified. Surgeons' orders were almost identical irrespective of ethnic group. The difference in treatment appeared to be at the nurse's discretion. Because of multiple shifts and changing assignments, it was impossible to identify nursing ethnic groups in relation to the patients' treatment.

The following cases illustrate the tendency toward undertreatment in all ethnic groups in this study. A 41-year-old Chinese female had an order for 50 to 75 mg of meperidine every three hours as needed for pain. On one day the patient was treated with 75 mg, with good relief being reported after each dose. On all the other postoperative days, the patient was treated with 50 mg of meperidine and the patient was noted to request more pain medication. On the fourth postoperative day, the order for intramuscular meperidine was discontinued and 50 mg orally was ordered for complaints of pain. This is a very small dose. The patient reported little relief with this medication and received it only infrequently. On the sixth postoperative day, the physician's note included the following: "Subjective: Patient complains of pain. Objective: Patient has dependent personality. Assessment: Psychological factors." A 28-year-old Filipino housewife received only 200 mg total of meperidine and none after the first postoperative day. At one point she complained of being unable to walk straight due to the pain. The nurse's response was recorded as: "Encourage to walk straight," and no pain medications were given. A 54-year-old Caucasian female registered nurse complained of abdominal pain. The treatment response, according to the nurse's notes, was "needs encouragement to cough and deep breathe." A 74-year-old Caucasian female complained of pain postoperatively. She was given 50 mg of meperidine by injection, and one-half hour later the nurse noted "no relief." The patient received her next pain injection eight hours later. She had on order medication every three hours as needed for pain. A 52-year-old Hawaiian male received pain injections for two days postoperatively. Then he refused pain medications, but appeared to be in much pain. No explanation for his refusal was documented in the chart. In contrast, for a 43-year-old

Caucasian wife of a physician, the nurse's notes included the comment "give Demerol to relieve pain well."

In summary, all ethnic groups studied were undertreated for pain but the Asian groups more so. The differences appeared to be at the level of nurse–patient interaction. In a milieu of undertreatment of pain, perhaps cultural factors associated with Asians allowed them to be more undertreated. Perhaps they were less vocal or more stoic. The nurses may have felt that giving less narcotics meant better nursing care. Perhaps the Asian groups were more eager to please their nurses.

CONCLUSIONS

There are remarkably few studies of cultural issues in clinical pain. It has been difficult to progress beyond stereotypes. In general, however, some conclusions can be reached. Zborowski (1952) identified cultural factors as important in understanding clinical pain. Studies have consistently indicated that this is indeed the case. Zborowski's original interpretations seem to be simplistic and inadequate, however. Stereotypes do not hold up well under the scrutiny of more sophisticated studies.

There appear to be interactive effects between culture and gender, educational level, and socioeconomic status used in determining pain perceptions and behavioral response.

There is increasing evidence that cultural issues are important at the level of interaction between the patient and the doctor or nurse. The expression of pain is not only influenced by the patient's perception of pain, but also by the patient's perception of the way the doctor will respond to his behavioral response to pain. A given patient may respond differently according to the doctor's personality or cultural group. Likewise, the doctor may respond differently to patients of the same or differing cultural groups.

In the assessment of pain, contextual issues must be taken into account. There are major differences between acute and chronic pain. Different cultures may respond differently to these types of pain. The source of pain is an important issue, for it carries different meanings. For example, cancer pain may be viewed much differently than benign pain. With regard to chronic pain, dependency on narcotic pain medications is commonly an issue. Compensation and disability status are important and interact with socioeconomic status.

All of these factors influence an individual's perception of pain independently, as well as in combination with the individual's cultural group. These factors also have meaning for the doctor, and thus affect the doctor–patient interaction from both sides.

SUGGESTED CLINICAL GUIDELINES

While the literature does not provide definitive answers to the role of culture in clinical conditions involving pain, it does provide a basis for understanding the issues. The following guidelines are derived from research literature in conjunction with clinical experience working in a multicultural environment with pain patients.

1. Pain is possibly the most difficult somatic complaint to assess, due to its entirely subjective nature. There is wide individual variation in response to painful stimuli. The physician should express interest in the patient's cultural background so that the patient will feel understood. The physician may search for and gain insight into the meaning of pain to the patient.

2. Cultural stereotypes often do not hold up in practice (see Case 4). The clinician must guard against assessing the pain experience of the patient too quickly based on the patient's presumed cultural background.

3. In the management of pain, particularly cancer and chronic pain, it is often helpful to assess the degree of *suffering* associated with the pain. Chronic pain patients, for example, may complain greatly but show little objective evidence of suffering. In cancer pain, the opposite may be true (see Case 2). This seemingly paradoxical situation may become clear when the pain is understood in the context of the patient's values, beliefs, and life experiences—his or her culture.

4. The physician's own background may influence his or her assessment of the patient's pain. For example, physicians who expect stoicism may devalue a patient's pain complaints and treat the pain minimally (see Case 1). In acute pain and cancer pain, the physician must guard against

underestimating the extent of pain if he or she is unfamiliar with the patient's cultural background, or undertreatment can result. Alternatively, the physician who identifies with the patient, or is overly eager to be liked, may be excessively responsive to the patient's subjective complaints of chronic pain and ignore inconsistent objective findings. The physician who most comfortably identifies with the patient's background may be most subject to manipulation by the patient for narcotic analgesics (see Case 5).

5. The patient may respond to the physician according to the patient's assessment and cultural expectations of the physician. If the patient does not expect the physician to be understanding and sympathetic, the patient may withhold complaints of pain. On the other hand, some patients may feel the physician will only respond to them if they exaggerate and dramatize their pain complaints.

6. In addition to direct influences on pain complaints, culture may influence the development of *secondary gain*, in which illness is reinforced by outside factors. This is particularly problematic with chronic pain patients. Cultural values related to dependency may influence how readily the sick role is assumed and also determine whether family response will tend to reinforce the sick role. Cultures may vary in tolerance for disability. Secondary gain may be more critical in determining disability in immigrant and unacculturated groups.

REFERENCES

Bates, M.S. & Edwards, W.T. (1992). Ethnic variations in the chronic pain experience. *Ethnicity and Disease*, *2*, 63–83.

Chapman, W.P. & Jones, C.M. (1944). Variations in cutaneous and visceral pain sensitivity in normal subjects. *Journal of Clinical Investigation*, *23*, 81–91.

Cleeland, C.S., Gonin, R., Hatfield, A.K., Edmonson, J.H., Blum, R.H., Stewart, J.A., & Pandya, K.J. (1994). Pain and its treatment in outpatients with metastatic cancer. *New England Journal of Medicine*, *330*, 592–601.

Faucett, J., Gordon, N., & Levine, J. (1994). *Journal of Pain and Symptom Management*, *9*, 383–389.

Flannery, R.B., Sos, J., & McGovern, P. (1981). Ethnicity as a factor in the expression of pain. *Psychosomatics*, *22*, 39–50.

Jensen, M.C., Brandt-Zawadzki, M.N., Obuchowski, N., Modic, M.T., Malkasian, D., & Ross, J.S. (1994). Magnetic resonance imaging of the lumbar spine in people without back pain. *New England Journal of Medicine, 331,* 69–73.

Knox, V.J., Shum, K., & McLaughlin, D.M. (1977). Response to cold pressor pain and to acupuncture analgesia in Oriental and Occidental subjects. *Pain, 4,* 49–57.

Lambert, W.E., Libman, E., & Poser, E.G. (1960). The effect of increased salience of a membership group on pain tolerance. *Journal of Personality, 38,* 350–357.

Newton, N. & Newton, M. (1972). Childbirth in crosscultural perspective. In: J.G. Howells (Ed.), *Modern perspectives in psycho-obstetrics* (pp. 150–172). New York: Brunner/Mazel.

Poser, E.G. (1963). Some psychosocial determinants of pain tolerance. Read at XVI International Congress of Psychology, Washington, D.C.

Sternbach, R. & Turskey, B. (1965). Ethnic differences among housewives in psychophysical and skin potential responses to electrical shock. *Psychophysiology, 1,* 241–246.

Streltzer, J. (1994). Chronic pain and addiction. In H. Leigh (Ed.), *Consultation–liaison psychiatry: 1990 and beyond* (pp. 43–51). New York: Plenum Press.

Streltzer, J., Eliashof, B.A., & Kline, A.E. (1995). Associated features of somatoform pain disorder. *Psychosomatic Medicine, 57,* 92.

Streltzer, J. & Wade, T.C. (1981). The influence of cultural group on the undertreatment of postoperative pain. *Psychosomatic Medicine, 43,* 397–403.

Turskey, B. & Sternbach, R. (1967). Further physiological correlates of ethnic differences in response to shock. *Psychophysiology, 4,* 67– 74.

Weisel, S.W., Tsourmas, N., Feffer, H.L., Citrin, C.M. & Patronas, N. (1984). A study of computer-assisted tomography. 1. The incidence of positive CAT scans in an asymptomatic group of patients. *Spine, 9,* 549–551.

Weisenberg, M., Kreindler, M.L., Schachat, R., & Werboff, J. (1975). Pain: Anxiety and attitudes in Black, White and Puerto Rican patients. *Psychosomatic Medicine, 37,* 123–135.

Woodrow, K.M., Freidman, G.D., Siegelaub, A.B., & Collen, M.F. (1972). Pain tolerance: Differences according to age, sex and race. *Psychosomatic Medicine, 34,* 548–556.

Zborowski, M. (1952). Cultural components in responses to pain. *Journal of Social Issues, 8,* 16–30.

CHAPTER SIX

Dissociation

Richard J. Castillo, Ph.D.

CASE VIGNETTES

Case 1

Mrs. Lee, a 35-year-old Taiwanese housewife and the mother of three children, was brought by her family to see a psychiatrist. She had been a successful spirit medium, practicing for two years since the delivery of her second child. However, one month before, following the delivery of her third child, she began to lose her self-control. She would speak in tongues and go into possession trances, even when she was not being consulted by a client. She became hyperaroused, talked all day, and was unable to sleep at night. Because of her overtalkativeness and excitement, and her inability to extract herself from her possession trance, her family decided to bring her to the hospital for treatment.

Mrs. Lee's history revealed that she was born to a very poor family. As a young girl she deeply regretted her family's poverty and fervently wished to someday become rich and successful. When she grew up she entered into an arranged marriage, but was disappointed with her husband, who was unsuccessful and unambitious. Shortly after the birth of her first baby she had a mental breakdown. She became excited and talked a great deal, saying that she was going to start an international business, and singing songs all day. Her mental condition returned to normal within a couple of weeks. However, two years later, shortly after the birth of her second child, she experienced a second mental breakdown. This time she experienced drowsiness, feelings of personal strangeness, and auditory hallucinations in the form of a god's voice speaking to her. Against her own will she began to speak with a masculine voice. At this point, she realized that she was possessed by the "thief-god" she had worshipped since she was a little girl. According to local belief, there once was a thief who stole from the rich and gave to the poor. After his death, this thief was worshipped as a god by the local people. It was this thief-god who possessed her.

As a result of her experience, she realized that the thief-god wanted her to become a spirit medium, allowing him to serve the poor people through her. Without further training she began to practice as a spirit medium at home. Soon she was known in her neighborhood as a spirit medium who could help poor people become rich. During her consultations, she would go into trances in which she became "possessed," speaking and behaving as the thief-god. In her practice she often saw five to ten clients in an evening, which did not interfere with her daytime duties as a housewife and mother. She practiced in this way for almost two years, until the birth of her third child.

Discussion

This case illustrates that dissociation can be either normal or pathological, even in the same individual, depending on the cultural context and type of symptoms. In this case, dissociation was occurring in response to environmental stress (childbirth), which is typical. However, the individual learned to control her dissociative experiences and use them as a tool in her occupation as a spirit medium. In the non-Western cultural context, dissociative experiences of this type can be considered normal behavior, and the individual should not be considered to be suffering from a mental disorder. Trance-related hallucinations in themselves are not enough to consider someone from a non-Western society mentally ill.

However, when Mrs. Lee lost control of her possession trance experiences and was unable to come out of the trance state, she could be considered to be suffering from a mental disorder. Her life was clearly disrupted by her symptoms, and she was experiencing social and occupational impairment. In the local culture and by her family she is now considered to be ill. Thus, for dissociation to be considered pathological, there should be significant impairment present, and the symptoms should be considered an illness in the indigenous culture.

Case 2

Mr. Williams is a 26-year-old Caucasian-American man who had begun the practice of yoga meditation seven years prior to being seen by a psychiatrist for treatment of panic attacks. For seven years he had been very regular in his meditation practice, meditating 20 to 30 minutes twice daily, and had become very familiar with the practice and subjective experience of meditative trance. After seven years, he began attending month-long intensive meditation "residence courses," during which he meditated several hours a day.

His first panic attack occurred the day after he had returned from a two-week residence course. He woke up in the middle of the night feeling removed from himself. He felt as if he was some "thing" other than himself. His perception of the environment also took on a flattened two-dimensional quality and looked somehow unreal. He thought he was going crazy. It was at this point that he began to feel panic. He was visiting his parents' house at the time of the episode. They took him to the emergency room, where he was treated with antianxiety medication and released.

Mr. Williams had no further episodes until about six weeks later, when he returned to the meditation academy for another one-month residence course. The very first night there he awoke in the middle of the night with the same feelings of depersonalization and derealization. He immediately became highly anxious, again thinking that he was going insane. The next morning he spoke to one of the meditation instructors and explained his experiences. The meditation instructor informed him that the experiences were nothing to be alarmed about, and that he was not going crazy. She interpreted the experiences according to the Hindu yogic model of consciousness and reality, which views a division in consciousness between an observing self and a participating self to be a goal of meditation practice. She explained that these experiences were signs he was progressing on the path to "enlightenment." Her explanation of the situation made sense to him, and he began to feel better immediately.

During that month-long residence course and on many subsequent occasions he had similar experiences. At first he was slightly frightened by them, but gradually, as he became more knowledgeable about how to interpret them according to the yogic model, the experiences became a normal part of his life. Even though the dissociative experiences continued to occur, he was no longer bothered by them, had no further anxiety reactions, and was not impaired in his occupational or social functioning.

Discussion

This case illustrates that depersonalization and derealization can be the basis of panic attacks if an individual holds catastrophic interpretations of these experiences, such as, "I am going crazy." This case also illustrates that depersonalization, even if it is recurrent and severe, need not impair functioning. The case also demonstrates the trance-related nature of depersonalization and derealization. These experiences were created by intensive practice of meditative trance. This is important, because many non-Western cultures have institutionalized forms of religious and healing trance practices. These practices are likely to produce dissociative symptoms. In the case of a Westerner engaging in Eastern trance practices, it is quite possible that this individual will not have the proper cultural background and training to interpret the resultant dissociative experiences in a way that is non-threatening, thus they result in anxiety or other pathological reactions.

Case 3

Swami Turiyananda is a 73-year-old Hindu monastic living in northern India. When he was 7 years old his mother died of an agonizing infection on her face that was left untreated. The young boy watched his mother die, and her death was such a shock that he turned inward to fill the void left by her loss. He remembers having his first religious visions around this time in his life. Since early childhood, he has had religious visions in which he saw Hindu deities and heard their voices.

At the age of six he was initiated into the practice of yoga meditation by the family priest. He was taught how to repeat the mantra

Jai Hanuman (a typical mantra given to young boys) over and over. After his mother's death, he spent hours every day in meditation. His grandmother told him religious stories, and as a result he became very religious. He observed and memorized the *pujas* (rituals of worship) that were performed in the local temple and then did them himself in private. This gave him great pleasure. His family members nicknamed him "Pujari" (performer of *pujas*) as a child because of his religious inclinations. He recalls having visions of Hanuman and other Hindu deities starting at this young age.

He never had any interest in getting married. His father and stepmother tried to arrange marriages for him three times, but each time he met only with the parents, never the girls. Once a pre-marriage ceremony was arranged with a prospective bride, but he refused to attend and ran away for the day. He had no interest in women or sex and to this day has remained celibate.

In 1952, he ran for office in the provincial assembly as a Socialist Party candidate and was narrowly defeated. He continued to work full-time for the Socialist Party until 1954, but was demoralized after his election defeat. It was at this point that he decided to renounce the world, and go to the Himalayas to live the spiritual life of a Hindu monastic.

Swami Turiyananda has no contact whatever with his own family. When his stepmother recently died he even refused to attend the funeral in order to avoid contact with his family members. When asked about this he said that his siblings would want to treat him as their brother instead of as a saint. This was unacceptable to him because he views himself as a saint.

Swami Turiyananda has permanent dissociation characterized by a division in consciousness between an "observing self" and a "participating self," as well as frequent religious visions characterized by visual and auditory hallucinations of Hindu deities. None of this causes him any emotional distress or impairment. His mood is generally one of mild euphoria, and his religious visions validate his position as a holy man in the eyes of the local population.

Discussion

This case illustrates that dissociation can become severe, involving a permanently divided consciousness, as well as auditory and visual hallucinations, and yet be nonpathological. Swami Turiyananda and others like him dissociate through the use of meditative trance, thus creating a divided consciousness and gaining the ability to directly experience the deities of their religion.

The observing self produced by the division of consciousness is constructed through culture-based cognitive categories as a religious *sacred self*. Swami Turiyananda refers to this as self-*realization*. Because this special state of consciousness is so highly valued in Hindu culture (self-realization being the goal of the religion), the actual lived-experience is one of mild euphoria, and does not involve social or occupational impairment. This case illustrates that yogic self-realization is constituted in a dialectical relationship between culture and individual consciousness. Trance experience is used to create a permanently altered state of consciousness that is valued in the culture and given a special meaning. The case also illustrates that hallucinations do not need to be considered symptoms of psychosis, and can be considered nonpathological in non-Western cultural contexts.

THE DISSOCIATIVE DISORDERS

Dissociation is characterized by a loss of the integration of faculties or functions that are normally integrated in consciousness. This lack of integration can affect memory, sensory modalities, motor functions, cognitive functions, and personal identity or sense of self. Cultural meaning systems affect the subjective experience and expression of dissociation. There are particularly noticeable differences between societies that are *modern* in their cultural meaning systems (possessing a modern, scientific worldview), and those that are *premodern* (possessing a traditional, nonscientific worldview).

Dissociative disorders cover a wide variety of symptoms with much cultural variation. The dissociative disorders in the *Diagnostic and Statistical Manual of Mental Disorders—Fourth Edition* (DSM-IV) are dissociative amnesia, dissociative fugue, dissociative identity disorder (formerly multiple personality disorder), depersonalization disorder, and dissociative disorder not otherwise specified, with a subtype most relevant to non-Western cultures of dissociative trance disorder (American Psychiatric Association, 1994).

Dissociative Amnesia

Dissociative amnesia is characterized by an inability to recall important information that is too extensive to be explained by ordinary forgetfulness. This information is usually of a traumatic or stressful nature. This is because dissociative amnesia is typically an adaptive response to some sort of emotional trauma or extreme stress (American Psychiatric Association, 1994).

Cross-culturally, dissociative amnesia is quite common. However, it is usually indigenously seen as a symptom of some larger culture-bound syndrome (CBS) such as *amok* in Malaysia or spirit possession in South Asia. It is not usually perceived as a separate disorder in itself, as it is in DSM-IV. This is probably because the symptom of amnesia will always be seen in the context of a local explanatory model, such as sorcery or attack by spirits. Thus, although the symptom of psychogenic amnesia is very common cross-culturally, dissociative amnesia as a separate disorder is mostly found in Western or modern societies.

Dissociative Fugue

Dissociative fugue is characterized by sudden, unexpected travel away from home or one's customary place of work. It is accompanied by an inability to recall one's past, and also a confusion about personal identity. In some cases, a person moves away from home and assumes a new identity with no memory of his or her former self. Fugues can last from a few hours to several months. Once the individual returns to the prefugue state, it is typical that he or she has no memory for the events that occurred during the fugue. During the fugue, a separate stream of consciousness takes over control of the body and personal identity. Thus, an individual acts as if he or she is a different person, or is unsure of his or her identity. In the typical case seen in modern societies, a person in a fugue condition does not act in an overtly unusual fashion indicating psychopathology. Thus, they do not attract attention, and appear to be normal unless questioned carefully about their personal identity or personal history (American Psychiatric Association, 1994).

Cross-culturally, taking on a new identity for brief periods of time and leaving one's home is a common type of dissociative behavior. However, in premodern societies, this type of behavior is usually structured in some type of CBS that differs from the usual modern case. For example, *pibloktoq* among the native Arctic peoples, and *grisi siknis* among the Miskito Indians of Central America are characterized by trance, amnesia, and leaving home. However, in these syndromes the individuals act wildly, running aimlessly, and sometimes assaulting others or harming themselves (Dennis, 1985; Gussow, 1985). Moreover, these syndromes are indigenously seen as spirit attack (*grisi siknis*), or no illness at all (*pibloktoq*). They have their own typical subjective experience, idioms of distress, indigenous diagnosis, treatments, and outcomes. Thus, it is probably inappropriate to classify these "running" syndromes as dissociative fugue. In general, dissociative-type syndromes resembling dissociative fugue are common in many cultures, but they have their own culture-based presentations. Thus, dissociative fugue as defined in DSM-IV is primarily a syndrome observed in modern societies.

Dissociative Identity Disorder

Dissociative identity disorder (DID) is characterized by the presence of two or more distinct identities or personality states that recurrently take control of an individual's behavior. This is accompanied by amnesia (American Psychiatric Association, 1994). Dissociative identity disorder is an illness caused by spontaneous trance reactions to traumatic stress, usually occurring in childhood, and has shown a particularly strong overlap of symptoms with schizophrenia (Fink & Golinkoff, 1990; Kluft, 1987; Ross & Anderson, 1988; Ross & Gahan, 1988; Ross et al., 1989; Steinberg et al., 1994). In one study which the authors describe as "potentially paradigm-threatening," DID patients were found to have more of Kurt Schneider's *first-rank* symptoms of schizophrenia than schizophrenics (Ross et al., 1989). In another study, DID patients did not differ statistically in the number of first-rank symptoms from patients diagnosed with schizophrenia (Fink & Golinkoff, 1990). Schneider's first-rank symptoms form a major portion of the diagnostic criteria for schizophrenia in the DSM-IV.

Mental patients with dissociative pathology have frequently been misdiagnosed with schizophrenia. This error is hardly surprising, since they report such a high number of first-rank symptoms. The misdiagnosis of DID as schizophrenia usually occurs on the basis of first-rank symptoms, including *auditory hallucinations* (primarily voices), *made feelings* (feelings which appear to have been imposed by some external entity), *made impulses* (impulses to carry out an action imposed by an outside entity), and *made volitional acts* (actions experienced as being under the control of an external agency). In the DID patient, these are the voices and influences of the alternate personalities, usually arguing or commenting on the patient's activities, or interfering with the patient's primary personality.

The studies of first-rank symptoms in dissociative patients have yet to make a significant impact on official psychiatric nosology. The DSM-IV still largely ignores the presence of first-rank symptoms in DID. This is because schizophrenia is considered a psychotic disorder, and DID is classified as a dissociative disorder. Psychosis and dissociation are presumed to be two separate processes in the biomedical paradigm, one biological and the other psychological. Thus, any similarities in symptomatology have been largely ignored.

In general, DID appears to be primarily a modern syndrome because of differing cultural meaning systems. In premodern societies, individuals tend to dissociate into gods, ghosts, demons, and other supernatural entities. This is in contrast to the mostly human personalities of DID observed in modern societies. This creates important differences in subjective experience, idioms of distress, indigenous diagnoses, treatments, and outcomes (Castillo, 1994a,b).

Depersonalization Disorder

Depersonalization disorder is characterized by a persistent or recurrent feeling of being detached from one's mental processes or body. Typically, the patient feels separate from his or her body, thinking processes, or emotions. He or she may feel a lack of control over his or her actions, speech, or thoughts, as if someone or something else were in control. There is usually the experience of passively observing one's actions or thoughts, as if someone else were performing them. Reality testing remains intact (American Psychiatric Association, 1994).

Depersonalization is a common experience worldwide, both in psychiatric and normal populations. Depersonalization in itself is not an indication of psychopathology. However, depersonalization is a symptom common to many types of mental disorders, including all of the dissociative disorders, schizophrenia and other psychoses, posttraumatic stress disorder, panic disorder, and various phobias. Thus, depersonalization is probably an adaptive trance response to extreme stress or anxiety.

Cross-culturally, depersonalization is a very common experience. However, depersonalization disorder is found primarily in modern societies. In premodern societies, depersonalization is typically experienced and diagnosed in various CBSs related to spirit attack, or spirit possession. Alternatively, depersonalization forms the basis of many religious experiences deliberately induced through trance practices, for example, yogic meditation (see Case 2; Castillo, 1990, 1991).

Dissociative Disorder Not Otherwise Specified

Dissociative disorder NOS is used for cases that do not fit the diagnostic criteria of the major categories of dissociative disorders. Most relevant to this discussion is a subtype that has been designated dissociative trance disorder (DTD), which was included in the DSM-IV (American Psychiatric Association, 1994) specifically for premodern cases. The diagnostic criteria for DTD highlight the distinction between *trance* and *possession trance* made by Bourguignon (1973). This new diagnostic category has a dual structure subsuming pathological dissociation of two overall types, trance syndromes and possession trance syndromes.

Trance, defined in the DSM-IV as a temporary marked alteration of consciousness based on a narrowing of awareness, can manifest in a wide variety of symptoms and syndromes across cultures. Many of these CBSs would qualify for a diagnosis of DTD.

For example, *ataques de nervios*, a Latin American trance syndrome, is characterized by trembling, heart palpitations, heat in the chest rising to the head, faintness and seizure-like episodes, and sometimes hallucinations. It is indigenously attributed to acute anxiety-provoking experiences, particularly related to family conflict, fear, and grief (Lewis-Fernandez, 1992; Spitzer et al., 1994).

Latah (which is usually thought of as a Malay–Indonesian syndrome, although similar syndromes are found elsewhere), is typically a trance syndrome characterized by an extreme response to startling stimuli. Attention becomes highly focused and the person exhibits anxiety and trance-related behavior, such as violent body movements, assumption of defensive postures, striking out, throwing or dropping held objects, the mimicking of observed movements, and sometimes extreme suggestibility or obedience (Simons, 1985).

Pibloktoq (also sometimes called arctic hysteria), is a Polar Eskimo trance syndrome. It is characterized by short-lived episodes (five minutes to one hour) of extreme anxiety responses in which the person will tear off his or her clothes and run into the snow or across the ice, screaming incoherently. There is amnesia for the episodes, which are indigenously attributed to sudden fright, intense fear, and imagined or actual personal abuse (Foulks, 1985; Gussow, 1985).

And *amok*, a Southeast Asian syndrome usually associated with trance, is characterized by a short-lived (a few minutes to several hours) sudden outburst of unrestrained violence, usually of a homicidal nature, preceded by a period of anxious brooding, and ending with exhaustion. There is amnesia for these episodes, which are indigenously attributed to interpersonal conflict, intolerably embarrassing or shameful situations, loss of honor, and personal abuse (Carr, 1985).

Trance syndromes can be distinguished from possession trance syndromes, which are characterized by the replacement of the primary personality by a new identity, usually a ghost, demon, or deity. The behavior of persons with possession trance syndromes is usually more complex, with a more complete alternate personality whose behavior follows pre-established cultural patterns. Thus, persons behave as a particular spirit or demon from the indigenous cultural repertoire, in most cases speaking and performing actions as the spirit or demon, sometimes over lengthy periods of time.

However, there is no clear boundary between these two variations and some syndromes fall in between. For example, spirit possession among female factory workers in Malaysia is characterized by extreme anxiety episodes in which the victims are screaming, crying, and flailing about uncontrollably, with apparently great strength. This is attributed to spirit possession, but the behavior exhibited is relatively simple compared to the elaborated behavioral characteristics of spirits that possess persons in India (Castillo, 1994b; Lewis-Fernandez, 1994).

Thus, given the wide variety of possible symptoms, diagnosticians should not consider DTD to be a single disorder, but a variety of disorders based on a common dissociative process with various types of cultural structuring. The symptoms of trance and possession trance syndromes that would be appropriately diagnosed as DTD can vary widely in different cultures. For example, North American Charismatic Christians can be possessed by satanic demons, while Taiwanese are possessed by local gods and ghosts. In the multiethnic population of India symptoms vary by religion, region, and caste.

What is clear is that populations form cultural repertoires of dissociative experience. A cultural repertoire of possessing agents may include stable characteristics of gender, personality, behavior, and social (supernatural or natural) status. Therefore, the cultural complexity of pathological trance syndromes should be noted in diagnosis and treatment of premodern forms of dissociative disorders.

SATANIC RITUAL ABUSE AND FALSE MEMORY SYNDROME

Contrary to the thinking of Freud and his followers, all evidence indicates that incest, other sexual abuse, and physical abuse of children are surprisingly common (Briere & Runtz, 1988; Craine et al., 1988; Kaplan, 1995). Also, there is now considerable evidence linking dissociative disorders with spontaneous trance reactions to childhood physical and sexual abuse (Chu & Dill, 1990; Coons, 1994; Dell & Eisenhower, 1990; Hornstein & Putnam, 1992; Waldinger et al., 1994).

However, the relation between dissociation and childhood abuse remains somewhat problematic. That is because it is well-known that memory is unreliable. Having a memory of childhood abuse does not necessarily mean it actually occurred. Many clinicians today doubt the occurrence of childhood abuse in some such adult psychiatric patients, claiming that memories of childhood abuse may be implanted in patients through hypnotic suggestion by therapists (Merskey, 1994), or manufactured by the patients themselves because of cultural influences in the media (North et al., 1993).

It is possible that persons experiencing dissociative or other types of psychiatric symptoms may be influenced by numerous accounts in the media of childhood abuse causing adult mental distress. A distressed person influenced by the cultural concept of the "wounded inner child" may focus on ideas of childhood abuse in his imagination, and subjectively experience those events as actually having happened. The ability to focus attention on imagination can create lifelike realism in subjective experience and thus create "memories" of abuse. Therefore, the power of the mind to create subjective reality needs to be recognized in the creation of illness experience and in explanatory models for illness. The current epidemic of psychiatric patients who have experienced childhood abuse in the United States may be a manifestation of an American CBS related to the extensive publicity regarding child abuse in recent years.

Moreover, beginning in the mid-1980s, literally hundreds of people in North America began to report dissociated memories of childhood abuse during satanic rituals that occurred years earlier

(Greaves, 1992). Some clinicians practicing in the area of dissociative disorders accepted these accounts of satanic abuse at face value, thus validating their clients' abuse experiences. In many cases, this validation led clients to accuse family members of satanic and other abuse. This prompted the creation of the False Memory Syndrome Foundation, an organization of persons and families accused of child abuse, usually by their adult children. Their position is that incompetent clinicians have suggested or inappropriately validated claims of child abuse in therapy sessions, thus causing harm to the parents and families of clients.

From a cross-cultural perspective, memories of satanic ritual abuse either occurring spontaneously or uncovered in therapy appear to be the North American version of dissociative disorders structured within the symbols of a premodern subcultural meaning system. Belief in Satan and Satanism are part of the American Charismatic Christian subculture, and therefore provide meaningful symbolic structures for the expression of emotional distress. Thus, dissociated memories of satanic ritual abuse or attack by satanic demons should probably be seen as idioms of distress relevant to a particular subcultural meaning system in American society and diagnosed as DTD or dissociative disorder NOS.

However, the etiological connection between dissociation and child abuse cannot be dismissed. A direct connection between documented child abuse and DID has been observed in abused children (Coons, 1994; Hornstein, 1993; Hornstein & Tyson, 1991; Peterson, 1991; Putnam, 1991). Also, there is considerable evidence that DID observed in adults had its initial onset in childhood, long before the individuals were ever exposed to hypnotherapy or psychological concepts regarding child abuse and mental illness (Bliss, 1988; Coons et al., 1988). Thus, there is a documentable connection between childhood abuse and dissociative disorders.

However, not all dissociative symptoms are attributable to child abuse. Dissociation in psychiatric patients is used as a coping or adaptive mechanism to escape many possible sources of anxiety and other associated emotional distress. Thus, the sources of stress and trauma associated with dissociative disorders are numerous. Child abuse is only one source of traumatic stress that may have a detrimental effect on mental health. Therefore, at no time should clinicians ever suggest to a patient that he or she was abused as a child, unless this can be independently documented by medical or court records, or eyewitness testimony. Nor should dissociated memories of childhood abuse uncovered in therapy be accepted at face value unless they can be reliably corroborated.

DISCUSSION AND CONCLUSIONS

The DSM-IV states that the symptoms of dissociation can be confused with the hallucinations and delusions of schizophrenia and other psychotic disorders. This point is very important because the hallucinations of trance and possession syndromes can easily be interpreted by clinicians as psychotic symptoms.

Because there is as yet no definitive understanding of the etiology of schizophrenia, and there is a poor prognosis for patients who receive this diagnosis, it is probably in the best interest of patients who show symptoms of trance or possession trance to avoid the diagnosis of schizophrenia or other psychotic disorders. In these patients, DTD (or other culturally consistent dissociative disorder) is the preferred diagnosis, and treatment appropriate to this diagnosis should be attempted before making a diagnosis of a psychotic disorder. Trance and possession syndromes generally have a better prognosis than psychotic disorders, especially when treated with culturally appropriate psychotherapy or symbolic healing.

The DSM-IV also makes the statement that the hallucinations and delusions of DTD can be distinguished from the hallucinations and delusions of schizophrenia by the *cultural congruency* of the trance, its briefer duration, and the absence of the characteristic symptoms of psychotic disorders (American Psychiatric Association, 1994). However, distinguishing dissociative hallucinations and delusions from psychotic hallucinations and delusions can be difficult, because the content of hallucinations will always be based on a person's cultural identity, whatever that is. Thus, cultural congruency is a problematic concept when talking about hallucinations and delusions. The concept of *culturally congruent hallucinations* can mean two things. First, that the hallucinations are *typical* of the culture, indicating limited cultural congruency. Second, that the hallucinations are considered to be *true* and *real* in that cultural context, indicating high cultural congruency.

This is problematic, because hallucinations and delusions are by definition *false perceptions* and *untrue beliefs*. If a hallucination is highly congruent with the culture, it may be accepted as real or true. Thus, persons can have hallucinations and yet have their hallucinations accepted as "the gospel" if the content is highly congruent with the cultural norms.

However, if the hallucinations are slightly off, and are not as congruent with the culture, they are not likely to be accepted. The person may then be seen as mentally ill or demonically possessed, depending on the cultural context. In the case of demonic possession, the hallucinations are *typical* of the culture, but not as culturally congruent as the hallucinations of a *saint* or *prophet*, whose visions or voices are accepted as coming from God.

Therefore, probably the best way to understand the notion of cultural congruency in hallucinations and delusions is how well they fit the cultural norms of beliefs and behavior. For example, in Case 3, Swami Turiyananda had hallucinations, but was not considered mentally ill in the indigenous culture. His hallucinations were highly congruent with the culture, and not considered to be hallucinations by the local population.

It is possible that with the new diagnostic criteria for DTD in the DSM-IV, persons with culturally typical spirit possession, who would have previously been diagnosed and treated for schizophrenia, will now be diagnosed with DTD rather than a psychotic disorder. This would certainly be an improvement in clinical practice.

Dissociative Trance Disorder vs. Dissociative Identity Disorder

The DSM-IV also distinguishes DTD from DID, noting that there are culture-based differences in the type of alternates in DTD and DID. Dissociative identity disorder patients typically have living human personalities, as opposed to the ghosts, demons, and deities of DTD patients. However, it should also be noted that DID patients typically have numerous alternates, while DTD patients usually only have two or three. Also, it should be noted that DID typically has a chronic course, with gradual response to treatment, while DTD can be of brief duration and highly responsive to culturally appropriate folk treatment or symbolic healing (Lewis-Fernandez, 1992).

The DSM-IV also notes that the prevalence of DTD decreases in industrialized societies where there is likely to be adherence to a modern scientific meaning system. The prevalence is likely to be higher among groups holding traditional premodern meaning systems, such as non-industrialized societies and some ethnic minorities in the United States (e.g., some Puerto Ricans and Charismatic Christians). This is consistent with the symptomatic differences between DID and DTD. Persons with a cultural identity based on a modern scientific meaning system will not usually be possessed by ghosts, demons, or deities. However, they may dissociate into separate human personalities. Just the opposite is true in traditional premodern societies.

This highlights the problem of precedence of diagnosis that exists in the diagnostic criteria for DTD in the DSM-IV. In criterion "D" for DTD, the DSM-IV states that "The trance or possession trance state does not occur exclusively during the course of a psychotic disorder (including mood disorder with psychotic features and brief psychotic disorder) or DID" (American Psychiatric Association, 1994, p. 729). Thus, the criteria for DTD indicate that if a patient's symptoms fit the diagnostic criteria for schizophrenia or DID, then schizophrenia or DID is the preferred diagnosis, even if the symptoms also fit the criteria for DTD. However, this may be an ethnocentric perspective, taking the modern forms as the normative patterns of illness and as the suggested diagnoses. This could result in misdiagnosis, inappropriate treatment, and poor outcome.

Other Premodern Syndromes

Some examples of syndromes appropriate for a diagnosis of DTD, besides the ones already mentioned, include *falling out*, a trance syndrome among Blacks in the southern United States and the Bahamas, characterized by falling down in a trance, not being able to move, yet being able to hear and understand surrounding events (Weidman, 1979).

There is a similar syndrome known as *indisposition* in Haitians, in which the person falls to the ground in a trance but is not able to understand anything said or heard (Philippe & Romain, 1979).

There is also *grisi siknis* (mentioned earlier), a trance syndrome of the Miskito Indian culture of Nicaragua. This syndrome is found almost exclusively in teenage girls and young women, is characterized by running wildly with a machete or other sharp instrument with some assaultive behavior, self-mutilation, and amnesia, and is attributed to spirit possession (Dennis, 1985).

Further, there are a number of possession trance syndromes globally characterized by the replacement of the person's usual personality by a spirit, deity, or demon from the cultural repertoire, in which the person behaves in a complex fashion as the spirit or demon (Akhtar, 1988; Bourguignon, 1976; Castillo, 1994a,b; Lewis, 1989; McDaniel, 1989; Obeyesekere, 1981; Stoller, 1989; Suryani, 1984).

It is clear from looking at dissociation cross-culturally that dissociative disorders bound-up with the belief system of the prevailing culture may include culturally formed patterns of illness experience, unique, culturally meaningful illness categories, culturally specific idioms of distress, forms of indigenous treatment that are frequently effective, and many forms of nonpathological hallucinations and culturally "bizarre" belief systems.

Nonpathological Dissociation

Institutionalized forms of trance have been identified in 437 societies, 89% of the societies for which adequate ethnographic data are available (Bourguignon, 1972). These are forms of trance that are voluntarily practiced within the context of cultural institutions, such as religious and healing rituals. These nonpathological forms of dissociation allow people in these societies access to the spiritual forces existing in their cultures, and serve many valuable functions in maintaining social structures, actualizing religious systems, providing healing and comfort to the sick and grieving, and providing meaning in life (see Case 3; Castillo, 1990, 1991, 1995; Ludwig, 1983). In the United States, common forms of nonpathological dissociation would include spiritualistic mediumship, "channeling," and glossolalia (Hughes, 1991; Lawless, 1988).

Dissociative trance disorder or any other disorder should not be considered as a diagnosis in any case of dissociation that is seen as a normal experience within the person's own culture. Dissociation in itself is not pathological. Hearing the voices of spiritual beings and forming complex, even bizarre, belief systems based on these hallucinations are normal parts of human experience going back many thousands of years, and have played a very important part in the formation and maintenance of societies and civilization in general. These experiences give meaning to life and structure to society. The divisions in consciousness at the basis of these experiences are found all over the world, and can form the normative structure of consciousness.

In general, the major categories of dissociative disorders in the DSM-IV are modern forms of dissociative experience. In premodern cultural groups there are many forms of dissociative experience that are nonpathological. These are institutionalized forms of trance behavior based in religious and healing systems. However, premodern cultural groups also have pathological forms of dissociation that differ from the major categories of dissociative disorders in the DSM-IV. These are trance and possession trance syndromes that are indigenously perceived as pathological and should be diagnosed as forms of DTD.

SUGGESTED CLINICAL GUIDELINES

1. Determine the cultural identity of the patient. Cultural identity refers to the individual's cultural or ethnic reference groups. As we have seen, dissociative disorders vary by culture, and there are normative forms of dissociation in each culture. What is normative in one culture may be exotic in another. For example, the behavior of a Taiwanese woman who is possessed by a thief-god only makes sense with reference to her cultural identity.

   Furthermore, subcultural groups have differing forms of mental illness. For example, Charismatic Christians may have greater potential for possession by satanic demons than others. Also, the Malay immigrant to the United States may or may not have the potential to run *amok*. Immigrants in North America may have varying degrees of involvement with the culture of their country of origin and Anglo-American culture in the United States. Therefore, they will behave with varying degrees of consistency to cultural norms of mental illness. The same can also be said for ethnic minorities.

   Similarly, in premodern societies, there may be modernized minority segments of the society, with individuals possessing a more modern cultural identity who may present with modern forms of dissociation. Therefore, it is vital that the cultural identity of each patient be assessed individually.

   To understand the cultural identity of the patient, the clinician must understand the individual's cultural meaning system. This involves studying the cultures of the persons clinicians are likely to see in their region's clinics and hospitals. Prior knowledge of an individual's culture will allow clinicians to know what factors to look for. However, knowing whether a particular patient fits a cultural generalization only comes from asking. Because cultural identity varies by individual, each patient should be treated as a unique case.

2. Elicit cultural explanations of dissociative symptoms. This is where the distinction between *illness* or the patient's subjective experience of being sick, and *disease*, the clinician's diagnosis, becomes crucial. If the clinician is not treating illness, but only disease, the course and outcome of the case is likely to be detrimentally affected. On the other

hand, if the clinician can simultaneously treat illness as well as disease, the course and outcome of the case are more likely to be benefitted.

Arthur Kleinman (1988) has defined what a clinician needs to do in assessing cultural explanations of an individual's illness. The clinician needs to *ask the patient* what he or she thinks is the nature of the problem. The clinician needs to ask

a. Why has the problem affected you?

b. Why has the illness had its onset now, and what course do you think the illness will follow?

c. How does the illness affect you?

d. What treatment do you think is appropriate, and what treatment do you want?

e. What do you fear most about the illness, and its treatment?

By eliciting an explanatory model, the clinician can explore the symbolism of the patient's illness, thereby highlighting sources of distress, and possible avenues of symbolic healing. This can be very important in the treatment of dissociative disorders.

3. Assess cultural and psychosocial environment. Assessing how culture is related to the psychosocial environment and levels of functioning can be very important for diagnosis and treatment of dissociation. This refers to culture-based sources of social and environmental stress, as well as social supports impacting functioning, impairment, recovery, and relapse. Clinicians need to see the patient and his or her dissociative symptoms within the total social–cultural context. This includes looking for unusual or severe stressors in the social environment affecting the patient, as well as how those stressors manifest in the dissociative symptoms of the patient.

4. Do not accept dissociative experience at face value. Cultural meaning systems contain symbolic structures that shape cognition and memory. These culture-bound symbolic structures will shape subjective experience of illness and idioms of distress. That is why dissociation can manifest in consciousness as benevolent gods, satanic demons, ghosts, spirit attack, soul loss, alternate human personalities, memories of child abuse, and so on. Dissociated memories

should be assumed to be filtered through cultural symbolic systems. Memories of child abuse need to be corroborated before being accepted. Clinicians should explore the symbolic structure of the patient's cultural meaning system in order to assess the meaning of the dissociative experience.

5. Assess cultural aspects of the clinician–patient relationship. Differences in the construction of clinical reality caused by differing cultural meaning systems in the clinician and patient can affect diagnosis and treatment. This can manifest as something simple, such as a misunderstanding of the clinician's instructions based on class or educational differences, or something more serious such as a misdiagnosis based on widely differing cultural backgrounds. For example, a clinician trained in modern psychiatry might diagnose a dissociative illness based strictly on modern conceptions of mental illness, rather than allowing for the influence of premodern concepts such as spirit possession.

6. Do not assume psychosis. Clinicians should not automatically assume the presence of a psychotic disorder because the patient presents with first-rank symptoms. First-rank symptoms are common in some forms of DTD and DID. A presumption of psychosis can contribute to misdiagnosis and less than optimal treatment and outcome.

7. Negotiate clinical reality. A negotiation of clinical reality should be made between the clinician, the patient, and, ideally, the patient's family. A plan of treatment should be drawn up that is the result of a negotiated consensus of the problem and the appropriate treatment. In this way, all the parties concerned will be operating on the same set of assumptions, and will understand and willingly agree to the course of treatment. This provides the best cognitive environment for optimal care and outcome.

REFERENCES

Akhtar, S. (1988). Four culture-bound psychiatric syndromes in India. *International Journal of Social Psychiatry, 34*, 70–74.

American Psychiatric Association. (1994). *Diagnostic and statistical manual of mental disorders—fourth edition.* (DSM-IV). Washington, D.C.: American Psychiatric Association.

Bliss, E.L. (1988). Professional skepticism about multiple personality. *Journal of Nervous and Mental Disease, 176,* 533–534.

Bourguignon, E. (1972). Dreams and altered states of consciousness in anthropological research. In F.K.L. Hsu (Ed.), *Psychological anthropology—second edition.* Homewood, IL: Dorsey Press.

Bourguignon, E. (1973). Introduction: A framework for the comparative study of altered states of consciousness. In E. Bourguignon (Ed.), *Religion, altered states of consciousness, and social change* (pp. 3–35). Columbus: Ohio State University Press.

Bourguignon, E. (1976). *Possession.* San Francisco: Chandler & Sharp.

Briere, J. & Runtz, M. (1988). Symptomatology association with childhood sexual victimization in a non-clinical adult sample. *Child Abuse and Neglect, 12,* 51–99.

Carr, J.E. (1985). Ethno-behaviorism and the culture-bound syndromes: The case of *amok.* In R.C. Simons & C.C. Hughes (Eds.), *The culture-bound syndromes: Folk illnesses of psychiatric and anthropological interest* (pp. 199–223). Dordrecht: D. Reidel.

Castillo, R.J. (1990). Depersonalization and meditation. *Psychiatry, 53,* 158–168.

Castillo, R.J. (1991). Divided consciousness and enlightenment in Hindu yogis. *Anthropology of Consciousness, 2* (3–4), 1–6.

Castillo, R.J. (1994a). Spirit possession in South Asia, dissociation or hysteria? Part 1: Theoretical background. *Culture, Medicine and Psychiatry, 18,* 1–21.

Castillo, R.J. (1994b). Spirit possession in South Asia, dissociation or hysteria? Part 2: Case histories. *Culture, Medicine and Psychiatry, 18,* 141–162.

Castillo, R.J. (1995). Culture, trance, and the mind–brain. *Anthropology of Consciousness, 6,* 17–34.

Chu, J.A. & Dill, D.L. (1990). Dissociative symptoms in relation to childhood physical and sexual abuse. *American Journal of Psychiatry, 147,* 887–892.

Coons, P.M. (1994). Confirmation of childhood abuse in child and adolescent cases of multiple personality disorder and dissociative disorder not otherwise specified. *Journal of Nervous and Mental Disease, 182,* 461–464.

Coons, P.M., Bowman, E.S., & Milstein, V. (1988). Multiple personality disorder: A clinical investigation of 50 cases. *Journal of Nervous and Mental Disease, 176,* 519–527.

Craine, L.S., Henson, C.E., Colliver, J.A., & MacLean, D.G. (1988). Prevalence of a history of sexual abuse among female psychiatric patients in a state hospital system. *Hospital and Community Psychiatry, 39,* 300–304.

Dell, P.F. & Eisenhower, J.W. (1990). Adolescent multiple personality disorder. *Journal of the American Academy of Child and Adolescent Psychiatry, 29,* 359–366.

Dennis, P.A. (1985). Grisi siknis in Miskito culture. In R.C. Simons & C.C. Hughes (Eds.), *The culture-bound syndromes: Folk illnesses of psychiatric and anthropological interest* (pp. 289–306). Dordrecht: D. Reidel.

Fink, D. & Golinkoff, M. (1990). Multiple personality disorder, borderline personality disorder, and schizophrenia: A comparative study of clinical features. *Dissociation, 3,* 127– 134.

Foulks, E.F. (1985). The transformation of arctic hysteria. In R.C. Simons & C.C. Hughes (Eds.), *The culture-bound syndromes: Folk illnesses of psychiatric and anthropological interest* (pp. 307–324). Dordrecht: D. Reidel.

Greaves, G.B. (1992). Alternative hypotheses regarding claims of satanic cult activity: A critical analysis. In D.K. Sakheim & S.E. Devine (Eds.), *Out of darkness: Exploring satanism and ritual abuse* (pp. 45–72). New York: Lexington Books.

Gussow, Z. (1985). *Pibliktoq* (hysteria) among the Polar Eskimo: An ethnopsychiatric study. In R.C. Simons & C.C. Hughes (Eds.), *The culture-bound syndromes: Folk illnesses of psychiatric and anthropological interest* (pp. 271–287). Dordrecht: D. Reidel.

Hornstein, N.L. (1993). Recognition and differential diagnosis of dissociative disorders in children and adolescents. *Dissociation, 6,* 136–144.

Hornstein, N.L. & Putnam, F.W. (1992). Clinical phenomenology of child and adolescent dissociative disorders. *Journal of the American Academy of Child and Adolescent Psychiatry, 31,* 1055–1077.

Hornstein, N.L. & Tyson, S. (1991). Inpatient treatment of children with multiple personality/dissociative disorders and their families. *Psychiatric Clinics of North America, 14,* 631–638.

Hughes, D.J. (1991). Blending with an other: An analysis of trance channeling in the United States. *Ethos, 19,* 161–184.

Kaplan, S.J. (Ed.). (1995). *Family violence: A guide for the mental health care and legal professions.* Washington, D.C.: American Psychiatric Press.

Kleinman, A. (1988). *Rethinking psychiatry: From cultural category to personal experience.* New York: Free Press.

Kluft, R.P. (1987). First-rank symptoms as a diagnostic clue to multiple personality disorder. *American Journal of Psychiatry, 144,* 293–298.

Lawless, E.J. (1988). *Handmaidens of the lord: Pentecostal women preachers and traditional religion.* Philadelphia: University of Pennsylvania Press.

Lewis, I.M. (1989). *Ecstatic religion: A study of shamanism and spirit possession—second edition.* London: Routledge.

Lewis-Fernandez, R. (1992). The proposed DSM-IV trance and possession disorder category: Potential benefits and risks. *Transcultural Psychiatric Research Review, 29,* 301–317.

Lewis-Fernandez, R. (1994). Culture and dissociation: A comparison of *ataque de nervios* among Puerto Ricans and possession syndrome in India. In D. Spiegel (Ed.), *Dissociation: Culture, mind, and body* (pp. 123–167). Washington, D.C.: American Psychiatric Press.

Ludwig, A.M. (1983). The psychobiological functions of dissociation. *American Journal of Clinical Hypnosis, 26,* 93–99.

McDaniel, J. (1989). *The madness of the saints: Ecstatic religion in Bengal.* Chicago: Chicago University Press.

Merskey, H. (1994). The artifactual nature of multiple personality disorder: Comments on Charles Barton's "Backstage in psychiatry: The multiple personality disorder controversy." *Dissociation, 7,* 173–175.

North, C.S, Ryall, J. M., Ricci, D.A., & Wetzel, R.D. (1993). *Multiple personalities, multiple disorders: Psychiatric classification and media influence.* New York: Oxford University Press.

Obeyesekere, G. (1981). *Medusa's hair: An essay on personal symbols and religious experience*. Chicago: University of Chicago Press.

Peterson, G. (1991). Children coping with trauma: Diagnosis of "dissociation identity disorder." *Dissociation, 3*, 152–164.

Philippe, J. & Romain, J.B. (1979). *Indisposition* in Haiti. *Social Science and Medicine, 13*B, 129–133.

Putnam, F.W. (1991). Dissociative disorders in children and adolescents: Developmental perspective. *Psychiatric Clinics of North America, 14*, 519–532.

Ross, C.A. & Anderson, G. (1988). Phenomenological overlap of multiple personality disorder and obsessive-compulsive disorder. *Journal of Nervous and Mental Disease, 176*, 295–299.

Ross, C.A. & Gahan, P. (1988). Techniques in the treatment of multiple personality disorder. *American Journal of Psychotherapy, 42*, 40–52.

Ross, C.A. Heber, S., Norton, G.R., & Anderson, G. (1989). Differences between multiple personality disorder and other diagnostic groups on structured interview. *Journal of Nervous and Mental Disease, 177*, 487–491.

Simons, R.C. (1985). The resolution of the *latah* paradox. In R.C. Simons & C.C. Hughes (Eds.), *The culture-bound syndromes: Folk illnesses of psychiatric and anthropological interest* (pp. 43–62). Dordrecht: D. Reidel.

Spitzer, R.L., Gibbon, M., Skodol, A.E., Williams, J.B.W., & First, M.B. (Eds.). (1994). *DSM-IV Casebook*. Washington, D.C.: American Psychiatric Press.

Steinberg, M, Cicchetti, D., Buchanan, J., Rakfeldt, J., & Rounsaville, B. (1994). Distinguishing between multiple personality disorder (dissociative identity disorder) and schizophrenia using the Structured Clinical Interview for DSM-IV Dissociative Disorders. *Journal of Nervous and Mental Disease, 182*, 495–502.

Stoller, P. (1989). *Fusion of the worlds: An ethnography of possession among the Songhay of Niger*. Chicago: University of Chicago Press.

Suryani, L.K. (1984). Culture and mental disorder: The case of *bebainan* in Bali. *Culture, Medicine and Psychiatry, 8*, 95–113.

Waldinger, R.J., Swett, C., Frank, A., & Miller, K. (1994). Levels of dissociation and histories of reported abuse among women outpatients. *Journal of Nervous and Mental Disease, 182*, 625–630.

Weidman, H.H. (1979). Falling-out: A diagnostic and treatment problem viewed from a transcultural perspective. *Social Science and Medicine, 13*B, 95–112.

CHAPTER SEVEN

Psychosis

Junji Takeshita, M.D.

CASE VIGNETTES

Case 1

Within a year after immigrating to the United States, a 21-year-old Haitian woman was referred to a psychiatrist by her schoolteacher because of hallucinations and withdrawn behavior. The patient was fluent in English, although her first language was Creole. Her history revealed that she had seen an ear, nose and throat specialist in Haiti after her family doctor could not find any medical pathology other than a mild sinus infection. No hearing problems were noted and no treatment was offered. Examination revealed extensive auditory hallucinations, flat affect, and peculiar delusional references to voodoo. The psychiatrist wondered if symptoms of hearing voices and references to voodoo could be explained by her Haitian background, although the negative symptoms seemed unrelated. As a result, he consulted with a Creole-speaking, Haitian psychiatrist.

The Haitian psychiatrist interviewed the patient in English, French and Creole. Communication was not a problem in any language. He discovered that in Haiti, the patient was considered "odd" by both peers and family, as she frequently talked to herself and did not work or participate in school activities. He felt that culture may have influenced the content of her hallucinations and delusions (i.e., references to voodoo) but that the bizarre content of the delusions, extensive hallucinations and associated negative symptoms were consistent with the diagnosis of schizophrenia.

Discussion

This case focuses on the relevance of culture to psychotic symptoms. Hearing voices is not necessarily considered pathological in some cultural contexts. Certainly in many parts of the world, including Haiti, voodoo and other beliefs in spirits are common and as a result, hearing voices or seeing things may be accepted and not maladaptive. Bizarre hallucinations combined with poor functioning, however, would be viewed universally as abnormal. In this case, perhaps because such beliefs were commonplace in Haiti, the physicians may not have been particularly concerned about the patient's symptoms. As a result, psychiatric consultation was not pursued. Negative symptom history as well as the bizarre content of the delusions was discovered only after an extensive interview. The significant deficits in current functioning, decline from previous baseline, peculiar, and culturally idiosyncratic references to voodoo, and negative symptoms are all objective factors that assist in the diagnosis of schizophrenia.

Case 2

A 47-year-old Vietnamese woman referred herself to an outpatient mental health clinic with complaints of anxiety and depression. She was interviewed by a Caucasian psychiatrist with the assistance of a Vietnamese interpreter, due to her limited command of English. During treatment she appeared paranoid, especially in her reluctance to reveal any detailed information about herself or her family.

One day, after the interpreter had left the office, the patient told the psychiatrist that she could not talk freely with the interpreter present. She stated that the Vietnamese community in the area was small, and she did not trust the interpreter to maintain confiden-

tiality. She was concerned that her family in Vietnam was being per-
secuted and stated that there were Vietnamese spies in the United
States who reported to the government in Vietnam. Furthermore,
her husband remained in a government reeducation camp and
could be subject to repercussions. In fact, she had a number of
friends whose visa and immigration statuses were in jeopardy due
to these spies. She trusted the psychiatrist because he was not a
member of the Vietnamese community. The patient was able to
effectively communicate her concerns despite her limited English.

Discussion

In this case, the psychiatrist originally suspected a paranoid psychosis due to the patient's extreme reluctance to divulge information about herself and her family. Given the difficulty in communication and the potential severity of her symptoms, it would have
been tempting to start the patient on antipsychotic medication. Fortunately, the reason for the guarded, seemingly paranoid behavior
became clear after more information was obtained. In this case, it
would be useful to obtain more information from the family and
other refugees to determine a baseline of commonly accepted ideas,
and thus tease out reality from any delusional material.

Case 3

A 45-year-old Vietnamese–Chinese male was admitted to a forensic
unit at a state hospital due to sexual assault charges and psychosis. He
had lured an elderly Chinese woman neighbor into letting him show
her a Buddhist goddess' picture, and then had attempted to rape her.
He had tried to rape his own sisters as well. When interviewed, he was
evasive and claimed not to know why he was arrested. He was vague
in answering questions regarding hallucinations and delusions.
Although he appeared to understand English quite well, a translator
was obtained. The translator, who was also his former case worker,
believed that the patient was avoiding answering questions by claiming a "language barrier." The patient denied symptoms of posttraumatic stress disorder, but refused to talk about his life in Vietnam. He
had a medical history of treated syphilis, but details were scanty.

Discussion

This case is difficult to evaluate for delusions or hallucinations due
to the patient's refusal to cooperate in an interview. The patient

claimed there was a language barrier, but his behavior was not congruent with his own cultural norms. He had violated many taboos—attempting to rape an elderly woman after luring her with a religious picture, as well as trying to rape his sisters. Posttraumatic stress symptoms are a consideration, and could possibly have contributed to the patient's behavior, but the patient had clearly violated cultural boundaries of his own or any other group. Of course, it is vital with any patient to rule out medical causes of psychosis, such as syphilis.

Case 4

A 79-year-old Filipino male was admitted to an inpatient psychiatric unit through the court system. He had a delusional belief that his wife was trying to kill him, so he decided to murder her first. When interviewed in English by a non-Filipino psychiatrist, no delusions or other odd beliefs were noted. He was cooperative and was a model patient on the ward. However, the psychiatrist felt that poor fluency in English limited the interview.

As a result, the psychiatrist asked several members of the Filipino nursing staff to serve as interpreters. They noted that the patient was fluent in Ilocano, but had significantly less understanding of Tagalog, both of which are Filipino dialects. Fixed and extensive paranoid delusions about multiple family members trying to kill him were elaborated in Ilocano, while only fragments of paranoid thoughts were revealed in Tagalog. Interestingly enough, no delusions were detected when he was interviewed in English.

Discussion

This case illustates the vital nature of communication in eliciting psychotic symptoms. Unlike Case 1, there was no decline in functioning or negative symptoms. In this case, consultation with a mental health professional of the same cultural background provided not only an insider's point of view serving as a reality check, but also a valuable second opinion.

Case 5

A 28-year-old, fourth-generation Japanese-American female with schizoaffective disorder was hospitalized for a psychotic exacerbation resulting from medication non-compliance. In addition to gross delusions and hallucinations, she displayed poor insight and denial of illness.

The interviewer assumed that mental illness was considered shameful in Asian culture and that this cultural belief was causing the patient to deny her mental illness. As a result, he organized a family meeting to help the patient and her family accept her chronic mental condition. To his surprise, he discovered that both parents not only understood the nature of mental illness, but were highly active in a local mental health group and supportive of treatment efforts. The parents expressed frustration that their daughter would not take her prescribed medications. They worried that their daughter was influenced by a cousin who eschewed medications and believed in herbal and vitamin therapy.

Discussion

In this case, a well-meaning, "culturally sensitive" clinician assumed that denial of illness and refusal of medication was due to the patient's Japanese background and a sense of shame. Fortunately, a family meeting showed that the family's attitude toward mental illness was quite to the contrary. In this case, the patient and family outwardly "looked Japanese," but were fourth-generation American citizens with Western attitudes toward mental illness. Although certain values may be associated with a particular group, it is critical to evaluate each patient as an individual and without prejudice.

INTRODUCTION

Interest in the variability of psychotic symptoms across cultures is a concept dating back prior to Kraepelin's famous visit to Java in 1904 to study schizophrenia in a non-Western country. Numerous studies since then have confirmed the existence of schizophrenia in Western and non-Western countries as well as remote islands (Lin & Kleinman, 1988). That culture is an important factor in psychotic illness is emphasized in the recently published *Diagnostic and Statistical Manual of Mental Disorders—Fourth Edition* (DSM-IV) (American Psychiatric Association, 1994). Unfortunately, determining the influence of culture on assessment is more difficult (Twemlow, 1995).

This chapter will review the literature regarding the role of culture and ethnicity in the development, assessment and prognosis of schizophrenia. Practical guidelines relating to assessment for the clinician will be suggested.

PHENOMENOLOGY OF PSYCHOSIS

Hallucinations and Delusions

The influence of culture on the specific content of symptoms serves as a good introduction for discussion. Al-Issa (1977) contends that culture often determines whether hallucinations are considered pathological. In developed countries, psychotic hallucinations are viewed negatively and attempts are made to differentiate them from imagery, dreams, and dissociative states. Efforts are generally made to ignore, eliminate, and deny such hallucinatory experiences. Of course, there are significant exceptions, such as those individuals who choose to enhance such sensations with the use of psychotomimetic drugs. On the other hand, in many developing societies such experiences can be viewed as being spiritual, positive, and acceptable and as a result are encouraged in various ceremonies.

The content of delusions and hallucinations is clearly influenced by the background and life experiences of the patient (Tseng & McDermott, 1981). As an example, it would have been difficult to have delusions of control involving computers prior to the invention of computers. Similarly, persecutory delusions in the United States might involve the police, whereas, in Africa, a sorcerer might be the villain (Leff, 1988). Katz et al. (1988) evaluated psychotic symptoms in Nigeria and India. They noted that in both countries psychosis is expressed as a breakdown of culturally sanctioned norms with subsequent release of behavior that otherwise would be kept in check.

Religion frequently affects the presentation of psychosis. Hindu and Buddhist religions favor withdrawal and isolation as a coping mechanism. Interestingly, Indian, Japanese, and Okinawan patients, from those respective religions, with schizophrenia, have a higher frequency of social withdrawal than their Western counterparts. Of course, it would be incorrect to state that religion causes psychotic symptoms; rather, delusions reflect the religious background of the patient (Murphy et al., 1963). Bar-El et al. (1991) note that about 50 tourists every year are hospitalized after visiting Jeruselum. The specific content of the delusions reflects the religious background of these patients.

Culture can therefore serve as a reference point for psychotic behavior. Indeed, although the DSM-III-R views talking to a dead person as a delusion (American Psychiatric Association, 1987), the DSM-IV emphasizes that delusions need to be considered from the standpoint of culture. The DSM-IV also notes that, after bereavement, hallucinations of the deceased person are common (American Psychiatric Association, 1994). It would be incorrect to make a diagnosis of psychosis purely on the basis of hallucinations and delusions.

PROGNOSIS OF SCHIZOPHRENIA

Given the problems in assessment, researchers have wondered whether schizophrenia could be diagnosed consistently using standard nosology throughout the world. In other words, would a common cluster of symptoms be present in all patients with schizophrenia? Some studies have suggested that Schneiderian symptoms were not specific for Malay and Nigerian patients (Salleh, 1992; Pela, 1982).

The World Health Organization has investigated similarities and differences in the presentation and prognosis of schizophrenia in two studies. In the first project, the International Pilot Study of Schizophrenia, psychiatrists evaluated 1202 patients in Colombia, Czechoslovakia, Denmark, India, Nigeria, Taiwan, the former USSR, the United Kingdom and the United States using the Present State Examination, a semistructured interview. Countries were chosen to represent varying levels of social and industrial development. Obvious organic psychoses were excluded. Common symptoms across sites included lack of insight, delusions, flat affect, auditory hallucinations and experiences of control. Follow-up at two and five years showed a higher percentage of favorable outcomes in the less developed countries as represented by Nigeria (57%) and India (48%) compared to developed countries (the United Kingdom, the United States, and Denmark) in which favorable outcomes ranged from 6% to 23%. The incidence of poor-outcome schizophrenia in Nigeria and India was 5% and 15%, respectively, compared with poor-outcomes of 11% to 31% in the developed countries. Outcome measures involved length of psychotic episode, social impairment and extent of remission (Sartorius et al., 1978; Lin & Kleinman, 1988; Karno & Jenkins, 1993).

The second study, Determinants of Outcomes of Severe Mental Disorders, involved incidence-based sampling of 1379 patients from

Denmark, India, Colombia, Ireland, the United States, Nigeria, the former USSR, Japan, the United Kingdom and Czechoslovakia (Jablensky et al., 1992). This study confirmed the conclusions of the earlier study, namely, the existence of core symptoms and better prognosis in developing countries.

Although problems in methodology have been reported (Karno & Jenkins, 1993; Edgerton & Cohen, 1994), the conclusion of better outcomes in less developed countries was quite unexpected. One would not anticipate that patients from developed countries, with a greater expenditure for mental health, would have poorer prognoses. Better outcomes were compared between Mainland China and Taiwan, and rural and industrialized parts of India (Lin & Kleinman, 1988), suggesting that urbanization may result in a more severe form of schizophrenia. Birchwood et al. (1992) noted that in the United Kingdom, psychotic patients who were immigrants from developing countries suffered a less insidious disease, as indicated by a lower readmission rate.

Industrialized societies emphasize individualism, competition and self-reliance. Employment and housing are frequently unavailable. Indeed, for a patient with schizophrenia, life in an urban, industrialized area is difficult. On the other hand, in developing countries, the emphasis on the village structure, long-term relationships, stability, supportiveness, and interdependence fosters recovery. Such characteristics are not unlike the milieu of a long-term psychiatric hospital.

The extended family structure may also contribute to a better outcome in developing countries. The extended family system appears to be a protective factor in schizophrenia. In Qatar, schizophrenic patients residing in extended families had a better outcome than individuals in nuclear families (Lin & Kleinman, 1988). Families in the developing countries may also have a greater tolerance for mental illness and aberrant behavior because of their reliance on supernatural causes to explain illness and bizarre behavior. High "expressed emotion," more prevalent in developed countries, may be correlated with a worse outcome (Karno & Jenkins, 1993).

MIGRATION AND PSYCHOSIS

Studies of immigrant populations illustrate the complexities and controversies in defining a cause and effect for psychosis. Increased incidence of paranoid disorders have long been observed among many different refugee groups, from Eastern European refugees in

Norway and England to Southeast Asian refugee groups (Westermeyer, 1989). Verdonk (1979) notes that not only did immigrants
tend to have a higher rate of psychosis, but also the incidence
increased with the distance from the home country. The rationale
for this disparity is quite controversial.

Some have attributed these differences to a pre-immigration phenomenon; that is, the increased incidence of psychotic disorders is
merely due to selection bias. In other words, the immigrants, even
prior to their move, had greater psychopathology compared to their
nonimmigrant counterparts in the home country. The incidence
among refugees may be even higher. For example, in recent history,
many Cuban psychiatric patients were forcibly exiled from their
home country; obviously the prevalence of mental illness in these
Cuban refugees would be high. Thus, symptoms are an expression
of an underlying diathesis to mental illness exacerbated by the
stress of immigration, rather than the immigration process itself
causing mental illness.

Others view such a development as a post-immigration event.
Newhill (1990) elaborates the concept of *healthy cultural paranoia*,
which she defines as a defense mechanism for a minority immigrant to deal with prejudice, oppression, discrimination, and other
stressors. Such *paranoia* is increased with greater disparity between
cultures. This lack of trust and suspiciousness ultimately increases
to such an extent that the immigrant develops a paranoid delusion.
Westermeyer (1989) suggests that problems in acculturation and
paranoid symptoms are synergistic. Successful acculturation is
associated with diminished paranoid symptoms. Of course,
although all immigrants may face such stressors and have distrust,
only a minority develop paranoid disorders. Obviously there is quite
a jump from "suspiciousness" to paranoid delusions. That stress
exacerbates mental illness is generally accepted. That stress by itself
causes mental illness is debatable.

It is important to realize that among immigrant groups, particularly refugees, a paranoid defense may be reasonable and quite adaptive. The government in the home country may use torture, spies, and
other means of controlling and tracking its citizens. Mental health
"treatment" may be used for such torture. Even after arrival in a new
country, such individuals will likely continue to be mistrustful, and,
with the problem of poor communication, be mistakenly characterized as mentally ill. Assessment of such a "paranoid" patient frequently reveals other illnesses, such as depression and anxiety disorders. Post-traumatic and dissociative disorders may be especially
prevalent and can be confused with psychotic symptoms.

Interestingly, increased rates of psychotic disorders persist among minorities generations after the initial immigrant group. The increased rate of diagnosis of schizophrenia in the African-American population in comparison with similar Caucasian patients has been well-documented using older data with less stringent criteria for schizophrenia as well as recent studies using current nomenclature (Strakowski et al., 1993; Jones & Gray, 1986; Simon et al., 1973; Sugarman & Craufurd, 1994). Dunn and Fahey (1990) note that the rate of schizophrenia for African Caribbeans in Britain appeared to be 14 times the general population, but no difference was noted after correction for age, sex, and socioeconomic status. Twemlow (1995) suggests the existence of subcultures, which may be quite different from the dominant national culture. Some researchers (Flaskerud & Hu, 1992) believe that differences in schizophrenia among African Americans, a group with a subculture, are due to differences in symptoms and expression rather than diagnosis.

DIAGNOSIS OF PSYCHOSES

Diagnostic Problems

Problems in classification may be responsible for some of the problems in assessment. Although nosology has increased greatly with DSM-IV and *International Statistical Classification of Diseases and Related Health Problems—Tenth Revision* (ICD-10) (World Health Organization, 1992) nomenclature, schizophrenia may still be diagnosed without stringent adherence to diagnostic criteria. American hospital clinicians gave the diagnosis of schizophrenia much more commonly among African Americans, but rates were equal when research criteria were used (Jones & Gray, 1986; Strakowski et al., 1993). However, a prospective study of 54 African Caribbeans and 49 White British psychotic inpatients did not support the idea of misdiagnosis (Harvey et al., 1990). The more restrictive criteria for schizophrenia in the "culture" of British psychiatry may have influenced the rates of diagnosis.

Jones and Gray (1986) state that the African-American patient's language, behavior, and interpersonal style may be viewed as foreign and so misunderstood that differences may be seen as evidence of a thought disorder, affective disturbance, and bizarre behavior, respectively, resulting in a misdiagnosis of schizophrenia. Strakowski et al. (1993) suggest that epidemiological differences may be caused by racial bias, cultural misunderstanding, differences in symptoms, biology, and confounding diagnoses, including drug psychosis. Adebimpe (1994) states that rates are affected by a number of differences, which include treatment-seeking behavior (e.g., African Americans seek help from non-mental health workers), involuntary commitment, research sampling errors, differences in psychopathology, problems with psychological testing, stressors of minority status, and treatment differences. Racial stereotypes may be particularly contributory. For example, clinicians were presented with clinical vignettes in which the variables were solely race and sex. African Caribbeans were thought of as more violent with more appropriate use of criminal proceedings than their Caucasian counterparts (Lewis et al., 1990). Given the negative connotation of the diagnosis of schizophrenia, it becomes difficult to determine whether these differences are real or due to other factors. Other psychotic diagnoses, such as bipolar disorder and psychotic depressions, may be misdiagnosed as schizophrenia among minority groups. A longitudinal history as well as assessment of level of functioning may assist in diagnosis.

Psychiatric diagnosis may be influenced or concealed due to the culturally based stigma of mental illness. Machizawa (1992) notes that in Japan the term *neurasthenia* continues to be used as a euphemism for serious mental disorders, typically schizophrenia, because it lacks stigma. In fact, she noted that 70% of practitioners did not reveal the diagnosis of schizophrenia to their patients. Okada and Kinoshita (1995) report a Japanese term, *shinshinsho*, that refers to psychosomatic illness but is more often a label that conceals serious mental illness. The stigma of mental illness may also influence help-seeking behavior, so that the patient may not present for treatment until symptoms are quite severe.

Of course, one should not assume that the culture or ethnic group determines individual values or beliefs. Indeed, it is increasingly difficult to determine the "culture" of an individual and the extent of identification with a cultural group. It becomes even more complicated in instances of mixed ethnicity and varying levels of assimilation, even within the same immigrant cohort.

The Interview

Good communication is critical for any psychiatric interview, although to some degree, negative symptoms can be assessed through observation. Language barriers complicate the evaluation of the culturally different patient. The use of an interpreter has its own problems. In a busy clinical setting, the interpreter is frequently a bilingual family member rather than a clinician or a neutral third party. Important clinical data may be intentionally or unintentionally filtered out. Del Castillo (1970) relates several interesting cases in which psychotic symptoms were evident in the patient's native language but not in the second language. During psychotic exacerbations, otherwise bilingual patients may be unable to communicate adequately in English, their second language. It appears that with increased disorganization in thinking, patients revert to their primary language.

Newhill (1990) suggests that a paraprofessional of the same ethnicity or cultural background may provide critical information despite a lesser amount of training. In addition, the therapeutic alliance may be better. Of course, there may be other problems, such as the patient over-identifying with the interviewer and vice versa.

SUGGESTED CLINICAL GUIDELINES

1. Good communication and understanding of language is critical. Although negative symptoms can be observed to some extent, elaboration of delusions and hallucinations requires excellent communication in the patient's primary language. The ideal consultation involves a clinician of the same language and cultural background, who can provide an insider's point of view and a valuable second opinion. A clinician needs to be aware of the limitations of a standard interpreter, especially if he or she is a family member. The interpreter may minimize or even aggravate the patient's symptoms.

2. There are common features in the presentation of schizophrenia despite varying cultures. Schneiderian symptoms can be particularly helpful. The diagnosis of schizophrenia cannot be made on just one symptom, such as delusions or hallucinations, however. Other characteristics, such as negative symptoms and poor functioning, are necessary for diagnosis.

3. Psychotic symptoms are not fixed to a reference point and are influenced by past experiences and the identified cul-

ture. Common beliefs of family members can serve as a practical baseline to determine normal behavior versus pathology. For example, a paranoid style of coping may be adaptive and expected for an individual with a history of oppression and torture.

4. The data suggest that minorities may be particularly prone to overdiagnosis of schizophrenia. Diagnosis should be based on strict criteria and not used indiscriminantly. Other psychotic illnesses, such as bipolar disorder and psychotic depressions, need to be considered. Culture-bound syndromes, dissociative disorders, and posttraumatic stress disorders can be confused with psychotic symptoms. In some areas, euphemisms such as neurasthenia may be used as a cover for a psychotic illness, typically schizophrenia. At the same time, one should not underdiagnose schizophrenia with claims that psychosis is culturally congruent.

5. There are cultural differences in help-seeking behavior for a mental health problem. The patient may see a number of other individuals prior to referral for formal mental health treatment. Stigma of mental illness can result in complete avoidance of mental health services until symptoms become seriously disruptive.

6. The general characteristics of a cultural group may not reflect individual beliefs. The external appearance (i.e., ethnic/racial category) may be unrelated to the values of the patient, especially with increasing heterogeniety of the population. It is critical to evaluate each patient carefully as an individual.

REFERENCES

Adebimpe, V.R. (1994). Race, racism and epidemiological surveys. *Hospital and Community Psychiatry, 45*, 27–31.

Al-Issa, I. (1977). Social and cultural aspects of hallucinations. *Psychological Bulletin 84*, 570–586.

American Psychiatric Association. (1987). *Diagnostic and statistical manual of mental disorders—third edition revised*. (DSM-III-R). Washington, D.C., American Psychiatric Association.

American Psychiatric Association. (1994). *Diagnostic and statistical manual of mental disorders—fourth edition.* (DSM-IV). Washington, D.C., American Psychiatric Association.

Bar-El, I., Witztum, E., Kalian, M., & Brom, D. (1991). Psychiatric hospitalization of tourists in Jerusalem. *Comprehensive Psychiatry, 32,* 238–244.

Birchwood, M., Cochrane, R., Macmillan, F., Copestake, S., Kucharska, J., & Cariss, M. (1992). The influence of ethnicity and family structure on relapse in first episode schizophrenia. *British Journal of Psychiatry, 161,* 783–790.

Del Castillo, J.C. (1970). The influence of language upon symptomatology in foreign-born patients. *American Journal of Psychiatry, 127,* 242–244.

Dunn, J. & Fahey, T.A. (1990). Police admissions to a psychiatric hospital: Demographic and clinical diffferences between ethnic groups. *British Journal of Psychiatry, 156,* 373–378.

Edgerton, R.B. & Cohen, A. (1994). Culture and schizophrenia: The DOSMD challenge. *British Journal of Psychiatry, 164,* 222–231.

Flaskerud, J.H. & Hu, L. (1992). Relationship of ethnicity to psychiatric diagnosis. *The Journal of Nervous and Mental Disease, 180,* 296–303.

Harvey, I., Williams, M., McGuffin, P., & Toone, B.K. (1990). The functional psychoses in Afro-Caribbeans. *British Journal of Psychiatry, 157,* 515–522.

Jablensky, A., Sartorius, N., Ernberg, G., Anker, M., Korten, A., Cooper, J.E., Day, R., & Bertelsen, A. (1992). Schizophrenia: Manifestations, incidence and course in different cultures—A World Health Organization Ten-Country Study. *Psychological Medicine,* Monograph Supplement *20,* 1–97.

Jones, B.E. & Gray, B.A. (1986). Problems in diagnosing schizophrenia and affective disorders among blacks. *Hospital and Community Psychiatry, 37,* 61–65.

Karno, M. & Jenkins, J.H. (1993). Cross-cultural issues in the course and treatment of schizophrenia. *Psychiatric Clinics of North America, 16,* 339–348.

Katz, M.M., Marsella, A., Dube, K.C., Olatawura, M., Takahashi, R., Nakane, Y., Wynne, L.C., Gift, T., Brennan, J., Sartorius, N., & Jablensky, A. (1988). On the expression of psychosis in different cultures: Schizophrenia in an Indian and in a Nigerian community. *Culture, Medicine and Psychiatry, 12,* 331–355.

Leff, J. (1988). *Psychiatry Around the Globe.* London: Gaskell.

Lewis. G., Croft-Jeffreys, C., & David, A. (1990). Are British psychiatrists racist? *British Journal of Psychiatry, 157,* 410–415.

Lin, K.M. & Kleinman, A.M. (1988). Psychopathology and clinical course of schizophrenia: A cross-cultural perspective. *Schizophrenia Bulletin, 14,* 555–567.

Machizawa, S. (1992). Neurasthenia in Japan. *Psychiatric Annals, 22,* 190–191.

Murphy, H.B.M., Wittkower, E.D., Fried, J., & Ellenberger, H. (1963). A cross-cultural survey of schizophrenic symptomatology. *International Journal of Social Psychiatry, 9,* 237–249.

Newhill, C.R. (1990). The role of culture in the development of paranoid symptomatology. *American Journal of Orthopsychiatry, 60,* 176–185.

Okada, F. & Kinoshita, S. (1995). Shinshinsho: clinical entity or pseudoscience? *Lancet, 346,* 66–67.

138   *Psychosis*

Pela, O. (1982). Cultural relativety of first rank symptoms in schizophrenia. *International Journal of Social Psychiatry, 28,* 91–95.
Salleh, M.R. (1992). Specificity of Schneider's first rank symptoms for schizophrenia in Malay patients. *Psychopathology, 25,* 199–203.
Sartorius, N., Jablensky, A., & Shapiro, R. (1978). Cross-cultural differences in the short-term prognosis of schizophrenic psychoses. *Schizophrenia Bulletin, 4,* 102–113.
Simon, R. J., Fleiss, J.L., Gurland, B. J., Stiller, P.R., & Sharper, L. (1973). Depression and schizophrenia in hospitalized Black and White mental patients. *Archives of General Psychiatry, 28,* 509–512.
Strakowski, S.M., Shelton, R.C., & Kolbrener, M.L. (1993). The effects of race and co-morbidity of clinical diagnosis in patients with psychosis. *Journal of Clinical Psychiatry, 54,* 96–102.
Sugarman, P.A. & Craufurd, D. (1994). Schizophrenia in the Afro-Caribbean community. *British Journal of Psychiatry, 164,* 474–480.
Tseng, W.S. & McDermott, J.F. (1981). *Culture mind and therapy. An introduction to cultural psychiatry.* New York: Brunner/Mazel.
Twemlow, S.W. (1995). DSM-IV from a cross-cultural perspective. *Psychiatric Annals, 25,* 46–52.
Verdonk, A. (1979). Migration and mental illness. *International Journal of Social Psychiatry, 25,* 295–305.
Westermeyer, J. (1989). Paranoid symptoms and disorders among 100 Hmong refugees: A longitudinal study. *Acta Psychiatric Scandinavica, 80,* 47–59.

CHAPTER EIGHT

Posttraumatic Stress Disorder

Gary H. Cohen, M.D.

CASE VIGNETTES

Case 1

A 32-year-old African-American male was seen in the emergency room (ER) of a large public city hospital. The patient was arrested by the police following an incident in which he ran shouting and yelling in a "wild" fashion through a crowded downtown shopping district. The patient was disheveled, pushing and randomly assaulting people as he proceeded. In the ER, the patient was restrained and his workup evaluation was begun. His blood pressure, pulse rate, and respiration were all elevated, but his pupil size was normal, equal, round, and responded to light. There were no positive neurological signs. The patient soon calmed down, but remained confused and had no memory of the incident. The toxicology reports were negative for alcohol and for illicit drugs. Later, the patient admitted having been under considerable work and family stress, but denied any other problems. However, he did give a history of several previous acute admissions to psychiatric wards for "crazy" behavior. He had been given antipsychotic drugs, but he was not consistently taking the medication. Historically, the admissions always occurred during February and March. After eight hours of observation in the ER, the man was discharged and referred back to his local mental health clinic with a diagnosis of schizophrenic reaction.

Discussion

This case, unfortunately all too typical, involves the inappropriate use of the diagnosis of schizophrenia with concomitant use of phenothiazine medication to control symptoms, which under closer exam were part of Posttraumatic Stress Disorder (PTSD) and not an underlying thought disorder. Besides failure to prescribe treatment for the specific disorder, this patient was being exposed to potentially untreatable side effects of phenothiazines such as tardive dyskinesia. Culturally, symptoms of anxiety and/or depression may present in an atypical manner in African-American, Hispanic, and Jewish patients, and might be perceived by clinicians of other backgrounds as paranoid, psychotic, and/or hysterical-dissociative symptoms. This can lead to misdiagnosis. In this case, the patient was eventually able to verbalize what had happened to him during the incident. Careful questioning in the ER would have elicited the details of a combat-related "flashback," initiated by the backfire of a car exhaust, in which the patient thought he was back in the crowded streets of Saigon, during the TET offensive period of February to March 1968. The history of repetitive episodes always occurring during the same time of year in the absence of substance abuse or thought disorder should have led to consideration of an anniversary reaction.

Case 2

A 46-year-old married, Chinese-Hawaiian American Vietnam veteran was seen in a local mental health clinic, having been referred by his wife, who felt her husband might be suffering from PTSD. The veteran stated that over the years since he participated in combat in Vietnam with the United States Army, he had been gradually, but consistently withdrawing from life. He had almost no friends or social life. "I prefer to be alone. I don't want to be around people, but otherwise I am okay. There is nothing wrong with me." On further questioning, however, the man admitted to marked problems with keeping a job, especially if his supervisors, fellow workers, or customers were Caucasians. His average job length was less than a year, despite his claiming to have good skills and training. On three separate occasions, fights or other altercations with White males had required police intervention. When he was questioned about this, the man stated, "I don't like Whites, I don't trust them, I don't feel like an American." He gave a history of consuming three to five beers per night to "help me sleep," as well as frequently using marijuana, all since returning from the armed forces.

Discussion

The family referral of victims of trauma, where the victim denies problems, is a common occurrence since it is the family who has the most experience living over time with a loved one who has PTSD. Despite this man's denial, the presence of chronic insomnia, isolation, difficulty relating with people, as well as work problems and self-medication with alcohol and drugs, are important indications that PTSD may be present. Further workup is necessary to make an accurate diagnosis. This man's sense of alienation from American society and specifically his unconscious resentment for Caucasians had already interfered with his social and work life. The patient admitted that his dislike of Caucasians started with the Vietnam War, where colleagues in his own company called him a "gook." He never felt accepted by the other American soldiers. "I felt that I had to fight and shoot my own people, sometimes it was terrible." This latter conflict was a core issue in his treatment and would make treatment by a Caucasian clinician difficult unless acknowledged and dealt with early in the course of therapy.

Case 3

A 72-year-old Japanese-American World War II veteran was seen by his primary care physician in a health maintenance organization clinic for chronic fatigue and insomnia. The onset was dated about 10 years before, following the patient's retirement. The patient stated he had plenty of energy before retirement, but since then, he had been going downhill. He reported many vague aches and pains, in conjunction with fatigue and insomnia. The physical exam and laboratory tests were within normal limits, and essentially noncontributory to making a diagnosis. The primary care physician was unclear about diagnosis and referred the patient to a sleep clinic and for a magnetic resonance imaging (MRI) test. The MRI was within normal limits, but the sleep studies showed disruption in sleep continuity, trouble falling asleep, and disturbance in rapid eye movement (REM) sleep. Stage II sleep was decreased, and REM time was increased with overall duration of sleep being only 4.5 hours. There was no stage IV sleep. Finally, the patient was referred to the VA Mental Health Clinic, where a routine Minnesota Multiphase Personality Inventory (MMPI) was done. The MMPI demonstrated increases in anxiety and paranoia. During intake, this elderly veteran admitted to repetitive and frequent nightmares and reliving a combat incident in World War II, in which a close friend was killed. "The thoughts just come into my mind. I can't stop them."

Discussion

The physical presentation of anxiety and depressive symptoms through fatigue and vague somatic symptoms for which no organic etiology can be found is common among the elderly, but in this case also represents a typical manifestation in certain Asian cultures, especially the Japanese. The sudden onset of the patient's symptoms postretirement is an important clue. For that reason, a psychophysiologic disorder should be included in the differential. Additional clues such as insomnia, nightmares, and intrusive thoughts clearly point the way to a diagnosis of PTSD. In this particular case, the expense and discomfort of sleep tests were quite unnecessary. Even the lengthy MMPI could probably have been avoided by taking a careful history with emphasis on PTSD (although helpful, the MMPI takes about four hours to complete and could have been replaced by quicker and more patient-friendly screening tests for PTSD). The sleep test disclosed one of the common patterns in PTSD, that is, shortened sleeping time, frequent awakening, and loss of stage IV sleep (Ross et al., 1984).

INTRODUCTION

Ubiquitous, pervasive, and historically constant, stress disorders brought about by the cruel vulgarities of nature and of people seem to be consistent scourges on human existence. Prominently imprinted on our minds because of the large number of returning combat veterans from the Vietnam conflict who presented with traumatic stress symptoms, it is now recognized that this disorder has long historical precedents and tragic contemporary equivalents in everyday modern life, ranging from the sequelae of childhood and spousal abuse, rape and assault, to natural disasters, such as fires, earthquakes, and tornadoes. Furthermore, new research increasingly suggests that trauma not only can produce PTSD, but can precipitate the development of other psychopathologies, such as borderline personalities, substance abuse, and depression. Therefore, the accurate identification and early treatment of the disease is crucial for a favorable patient outcome.

The purpose of this chapter is to examine PTSD, and its manifestations in different ethnic and cultural groups as it relates to the *Diagnostic and Statistical Manual of Mental Disorders—Fourth Edition* (DSM-IV) (American Psychiatric Association, 1994) criteria, in order to assist the clinician in making an accurate diagnosis and treatment plan when working with diverse population groups.

PHENOMENOLOGY

By definition, the symptoms of the disorder arise after exposure to an extreme traumatic stressor, involving direct personal experience of an event that involves actual or threatened death or serious injury or threat to physical integrity; or witnessing an event that involves death, injury, or threat to the physical integrity of another person; or learning about the unexpected or violent death, serious harm, or threat of death or injury experienced by a family member or other close associate (American Psychiatric Association, 1994). The importance of the traumatic experience cannot be underestimated and is essential to the diagnosis; indeed, monozygotic twin studies (Goldberg et al., 1990) confirm that this illness is clearly stress-related and independent of genetic loading.

Inherent in making the diagnosis is a combination of symptoms. This combination involves reexperiencing the traumatic event, avoidance of stimuli associated with the trauma, and persistent symptoms of increased physiologic arousal. Symptoms of reexperiencing include such phenomena as recurrent and intrusive thoughts, recurrent dreams of the event, reliving the experience, and intense psychological or physiological distress at exposure to internal or external cues that resemble the event. Symptoms of avoidance include efforts to avoid thoughts, activities, places or people associated with the event, inability to recall the event, diminished interest or participation in significant activities, feelings of detachment from others, restricted affect, and sense of a foreshortened future. Symptoms of hyperarousal include difficulty falling or staying asleep, irritability or outbursts of anger, difficulty concentrating, hypervigilance, and exaggerated startle reaction. Despite some controversy (O'Donohue & Elliot, 1992; Wilson, 1994) regarding the exclusiveness, scientific validity, and shortcomings of the DSM-IV criteria, it is these criteria that will be used by most American clinicians to make the diagnosis of PTSD. Furthermore, Carlson and Rosser-Hogan (1994) point out the remarkable consistency of the symptoms regardless of the source of the trauma. Symptoms have been reported not only in Vietnam veterans (e.g., Sonnenberg, 1985), but also victims of concentration camps (Arthur, 1982), kidnapping (Terr, 1983), rape (Kilpatrick et al., 1985), natural disasters (Green et al., 1990), and prisoners of war (Arthur, 1982; Beebe, 1983).

EPIDEMIOLOGY

Posttraumatic stress disorder has been with the human race nearly as long as there has been recorded history. Evidence of the illness has been traced to the sixth century B.C. In more modern times, there are written descriptions of the illness from the American Civil War, World War I, and World War II, in which diagnostic labels such as war neurosis or combat shock were used to label the stress symptoms. The DSM-III gave legitimacy to the term *Posttraumatic Stress Disorder*, to cover a syndrome that can arise after exposure to severe or life-threatening trauma.

After every war, the diagnosis of PTSD or its equivalent condition is remade, almost as if it were a new syndrome freshly discovered. In reality, however, the illness has been consistent over time. In general, the public has become most aware of the illness after a war, but in fact, there are many examples of civilian PTSD, related to a number of different stressors. The prevalence of the disorder (Helzer et al., 1987), is about 1% of the general population. This figure is misleading, however, when the data for the prevalence in individuals who have had a life-threatening trauma is examined. The prevalence rate for these individuals goes from about 25% (Davidson et al., 1991) to 50% (Norman, 1988) to even higher in some studies of Southeast Asian refugees from Cambodia (Mollica et al.,

1987). Depending on life history, several factors influence the prevalence rate, such as age (children and aging victims have higher prevalence rates), and the specificity of the trauma itself. For example, Sutker et al. (1994) found lifetime prevalence rates as high as 65% in service personnel who did grave registration duty during the Persian Gulf War. The whole area is an active research concern at the present time (Foy et al., 1987). It is these latter prevalence rates that are relevant to the health provider. The client seeking help will, by definition, have had a trauma and therefore fall into a high risk group. The combat veteran, the abused spouse, the rape victim, the burn patient, and so forth, all will have a significantly high risk for development of PTSD.

Probably the most heavily studied group of PTSD patients has been the American combat veteran from the Vietnam conflict. The National Vietnam Veterans' Readjustment Study (Kulka et al., 1990) reports a lifetime prevalence of 30%. According to this study, 15.2% of Vietnam veterans will have the syndrome at any given time. This value represents about 480,000 individuals. Schlenger et al. (1992) found differential rates among racial/ethnic subgroups of veterans who served in combat in Vietnam. For example, the current prevalence was found to be 27.9% among Hispanic males, 20.6% among Black males, and 13.7% among White males. Adjusting for predisposing factors, the difference between White and Black veterans became statistically insignificant, but the Hispanic prevalence rate remained statistically significant.

In addition to United States combat veterans, a second major population for research of PTSD has been the large number of political refugees who have come to the United States since the 1960s from Central and South America, Europe, and Asia, following changes in the United States immigration laws that made it easier to obtain political asylum. Prevalence and incidence rates of PTSD differ considerably depending on the group studied and the site of the study. For example, Cheung (1994) found a 12.1% prevalence rate among Cambodian refugees, a figure similar to the 15% current prevalence found among American Vietnam veterans. However, patients presenting with either physical or mental illness can be expected to show very high incidence rates. Kinzie et al. (1990) surveyed 322 Indochinese refugees at a psychiatry clinic and found a 93% rate of PTSD in the Mein Laotian Hill people and 54% in the Vietnamese. Interestingly, often as high as 25% of the children of victims of PTSD will have symptoms of the disorder as well.

Depression, as a comorbid illness, is very common and needs to be identified, as the presence of a clinical depression could change the treatment plan. Other factors that are very important in refugee groups are acculturation, adjustment to a new environment, and grief over losses suffered because of immigration to a new country. Generally, the most frequent symptom is recurrent intrusive thoughts, although, as noted above, the comorbidity of depression might change the clinical presentation. Frequently, isolation and withdrawal, often accompanied by anger, are also symptoms. These symptoms can be manifest through a refugee's lack of interest in maintaining cultural ties and general isolation from his or her own community at a time when he or she might need the support most (Abe et al., 1994). This complicates the course of treatment, and often means that the refugee with PTSD is cut off from traditional support systems while at the same time he or she has not acculturated to Western medicine and treatment practices. The result is an intractable PTSD, which not only handicaps the victim but affects the spouse and children as well.

Similar rates, sometimes approaching the 80% level in the literature, occur with other man-made trauma such as the Holocaust, refugees from war torn areas, victims of assault, rape, and torture. Natural disasters, like man-made trauma, can also produce high levels of PTSD sequelae. Generally, the literature reflects a lower incidence with natural disasters than with man-made trauma, but the percentages can range from 10% to 80% and therefore are clinically important. For example, a mud slide in Colombia that killed 30,000 people resulted in a prevalence rate of 78% in survivors (Lima et al., 1991). An important variable in controlling PTSD sequelae appears to be the level of community response; that is, the faster rehabilitation and return to normality occurs, the less the negative sequelae and psychological morbidity. Indeed, the community support of a collective disaster probably distinguishes this type of trauma from an isolated trauma of assault or rape.

Generally speaking, a natural disaster is accepted more readily by the victim than a man-made trauma, and as a result produces less secondary anger and hostility. This is especially true in cultural groups, such as Hawaiians and Native Americans, where a belief in nature's basically good intent is an inherent part of the culture. Similarly, individuals from a Buddhist culture are more apt to accept a natural disaster with resignation and fatalism. Although such belief systems probably decrease the incidence of PTSD after a trauma, they also heighten denial as a psychological function and make diagnosis difficult.

Man-made trauma is seen as preventable, with someone or something responsible. Anger is greater and denial symptoms are less. Worst of all is personal trauma in which there is a direct attack on a individual's person, self-respect, image, integrity, social roles, and safety.

In general, the chances of developing PTSD depend on a number of genetic, social, psychological, and demographic factors. Unequivocally, the literature in the area of trauma points toward the relative strength of the stressor as being the single most important factor in predicting morbidity; that is, the greater the trauma, the more likely it is that there will be long-term psychiatric morbidity. Factors related to the trauma itself include such things as duration of trauma, degree of threat to life, repetition of trauma, and reawakening of earlier similar traumatic experiences. In addition to the nature of the trauma, other factors that have been found to increase morbidity include: inexperience with the stressor; past history of mental illness, trauma, and childhood abuse; dependent personality traits; age and infirmity; children under age 12; low level of education; history of alcohol and drug abuse; and lack of a support system.

It is important, however, for the clinician to also be aware of the factors and personality strengths that preclude or limit the occurrence of morbidity after a trauma. The fact that 30% or more of victims exposed to trauma do not develop residual psychiatric symptoms presents a rich area for research, which may lead to methods that will limit the sequel in other less fortunate victims of trauma. A key factor appears to be the degree of control the victim feels he or she has during the trauma, even if the "control" is only psychological. Among the factors that have been found to heighten the perception of control in a victim of trauma are leadership (e.g., taking charge during a disaster), competency (knowing what to do during the disaster), ability to join others in group cohesiveness, and motivation to survive or help others survive. In this context, being "prepared" and well trained are important in survival. Conversely, in battle, a poorly trained, non-cohesive, substance-using group of soldiers is going to be at high risk not just for trauma but for development of long-term psychiatric disability secondary to the traumatic event.

SKILLFUL ASSESSMENT

Assessment of a patient with PTSD begins with the most essential ingredients for a successful diagnostic interview, that is, establishing sufficient rapport with the patient to get maximal information to make an accurate diagnosis and to begin a functional treatment plan. Secondary goals of any initial examination include assessment of the patient's current danger to himself or others, assessment of physical factors that might be affecting the psychiatric disorder, an estimate of current social and work functioning, and an evaluation of the patient's strengths and weaknesses.

Because establishment of rapport may be difficult with the PTSD patient, and yet is so important in achieving all the other goals of a first interview, some basic concepts of interviewing will be reviewed as they apply to a multiethnic population. The setting of the interview should be private and confidential, with emphasis placed on making the patient comfortable and willing to talk freely. The interview should be structured, with the examiner carefully explaining to the patient, in a concrete and direct fashion, why the interview is being held, the rules of confidentiality, and what will happen during the course of the interview. It should not be assumed that the patient from a cultural background not familiar with Western psychiatry understands or feels comfortable with a traditional psychiatric interview. Very often, the interview will symbolize to the patient that he or she is considered "crazy," and as a result the patient will not disclose significant information to the examiner. In many Asian cultures, for example, having a mental disorder is considered a weakness that results in marked lack of status and "face" for the victim. Male patients, especially, will go to great lengths to hide this information, even from themselves. Women victims often interpret the traumatic event as something shameful and will not speak of the incident outside of the immediate family constellation. In addition to differing cultural expectations and feelings about mental illness and psychiatry, issues of transference and countertransference are always potential roadblocks to open and free communication of information from the patient. For example, a Black patient might be hesitant to disclose problems to a White interviewer, and a female trauma victim may be reluctant to talk to a male interviewer. The issue here, of course, is trust, and until at least partial trust is established the interviewer will not be able to get all the information needed to make an accurate diagnosis.

Diagnostic Interview: General Considerations

A psychiatric interview for PTSD should follow a traditional psychiatric protocol for intake interviews, realizing that it may take several sessions to get all the information necessary to design a good treatment plan. It is important to be as comprehensive as possible in the examination to assure that all the biological, psychological, and social aspects that might be contributing to the symptoms are elucidated. This is especially important in transcultural evaluations, in which symptoms could easily be misunderstood or stereotypes could interfere with accurate diagnosis. An example of this might be the clinical interpretation of "voices" in different cultures; the same symptoms may have markedly different etiologies and implications in different cultures. Only by taking a very careful and comprehensive history can the interviewer assure that the diagnosis and treatment plan will be accurate. Thorough medical and substance abuse histories are mandatory because of the strong impact they can have on the presentation of symptoms and the course of treatment.

The most important areas of the assessment will be the "present illness" and the "past history" (sometimes called pre-trauma history). The presenting complaints are essential for making the diagnosis, of course, but they are not always clear-cut. For example, the patient may emphasize somatic symptoms such as fatigue and insomnia, but not spontaneously bring up nightmares or intrusive thoughts. The pre-trauma history is important to help the examiner understand why the patient is responding in a given way to a trauma and should include exploration of childhood abuse and coping mechanisms for stress.

Exploring the Trauma

In addition to information obtained in a routine psychiatric evaluation, the clinical assessment for PTSD should include a number of specific questions related directly to the traumatic event. This writer prefers to begin the history of the present illness with open-ended questions, allowing the patient to tell in his or her own words what symptoms have been most troublesome, and only asking closed-ended questions for purposes of clarification or emphasis. However, some cultural groups may be reluctant to discuss emotional and traumatic events spontaneously and will need to be encouraged through direct questions. For example, Lum's (1974) study of Chinese in San Francisco's Chinatown, clearly indicated that their belief pattern was that mental health was maintained by the avoidance of bad thought and the exercise of willpower. For this group of Asian-Americans to "talk out" their problems with a counselor or physician would be perceived as counterproductive by the patient, and information could only be obtained through structured and direct questioning. A somatic complaint, such as insomnia, may be easier for the patient to talk about, and often allows the examiner to obtain crucial data that is not spontaneously given by the patient. The examiner can then gradually explore the complaint, moving the questions from relatively "safe" topics to increasingly more emotionally laden ones. For example, when doing an insomnia workup, the examiner should begin with data such as sleep patterns and gradually proceed to more emotionally tinged areas, such as nightmares and the content of the nightmares.

Whatever the technique for data collection, the examiner should get as much information about the traumatic event as possible, including the emotional content and meaning of the event to the victim. Some helpful directions and questions for the patient are:

1. Ask the patient to describe the traumatic event in as great detail as possible.

2. Inquire about what occurred directly before the event and how the victim was feeling.

3. Ask about what happened during the event. Explore all the senses as they relate to the event (touch, taste, olfactory, hearing, sight).

4. Ask about what happened after the event. How did other people respond?

5. Are there things that the patient might have forgotten?

6. What was going on in the patient's life when the traumatic event occurred?

7. How did the event affect the patient's life? How does he or she feel talking about it?

8. How could the event have been avoided? Who is to blame?

9. What will make things better? What has the patient done that makes things better?

The process of obtaining a history of the trauma also invariably initiates the treatment process. For example, the last question noted

(What will make things better?), begins to move the victim into the area of recovery and reorients both the patient and the examiner to the practical purpose of the examination.

Gathering Additional Data

As noted, the past history is important in understanding how the patient became the sort of person he or she is, and the genetic, behavioral, environmental, psychological forces that contributed to his or her adult personality and response to stress. In addition, the past history will give important clues as to how the patient will react in the future, as well as the ultimate prognosis. Special attention should be given to childhood abuse, history of previous psychiatric illness, substance abuse in the patient or patient's family, and the strength and weaknesses of the patient. If the trauma is related to military combat, a thorough military history should be taken. The military history should include the branch of service, dates of the service time, job description or primary duty while in service, the area of service (war zone), unit of service, type of discharge (honorable or dishonorable), and rank at the time of discharge.

A careful medical review and physical exam are mandatory in any workup of trauma-related mental disorders for both medical and legal reasons. It has been known for several decades that both acute and chronic stress can have physiological consequences, which may result in organic changes in both animal and human organisms. More recent research is beginning to conceptualize PTSD as a multisystem disorder that affects a number of neurochemical transmission systems, including noradrenergic, dopaminergic, and serotoninergic systems. Also included are benzodiazepine receptors, and the hypothalamic–pituitary–adrenal axis (Southwick et al., 1995). In addition, Litz et al. (1992) suggested that victims of combat-related PTSD tend to complain of symptoms that are possibly related to sympathetic hyperactivity, especially cardiopulmonary and gastrointestinal complaints, such as ringing in the ears, rapid breathing, racing heart, sexual disinterest, butterflies in the stomach, and nausea. These changes are complicated by a wide range of physical problems can arise directly from a trauma such as rape or an assault, or result from chronic nutritional deprivation and mistreatment, as in a prisoner of war situation.

If the physical sequelae of trauma are ignored in the treatment plan it will markedly alter the efficacy of any psychological approaches in treatment. Special attention should also be given to evaluating comorbidity. The two most common comorbid conditions with PTSD are depression and substance abuse. Depression is easily treated by traditional approaches, and use of antidepressive medications has a high rate of favorable response, although the efficacy of treatment of the depression is independent of treatment for PTSD. Nonetheless, successful treatment of a comorbid depression will often give the patient significant relief and more energy to work on underlying PTSD problems. "Self-medication" by the excessive use of alcohol or other abusive substances can lead to comorbidity of PTSD with substance abuse, a frequent problem in combat-related PTSD. Kulka et al. (1990) found a 75% co-occurrence between substance abuse and PTSD in Vietnam War veterans. Whether this is also true in victims of other kinds of trauma is still controversial, but the data clearly indicates that the clinician working with PTSD victims must be prepared to identify and handle comorbid substance abuse problems. These drugs, in themselves, can produce physiological and behavior changes that may mimic and worsen PTSD symptoms (for example, the early morning awakening of long-term alcohol abuse can both mimic and worsen the insomnia of PTSD). Detoxification can be an especially difficult time because of the reemergence of flashbacks and other PTSD symptoms and for that reason, hospitalization is often preferable to social or outpatient detoxification. Three psychological evaluations that may be helpful in screening patients for comorbidity are the Structured Clinical Interview for DSM-III-R (SCID) (Spitzer & William, 1990), the Symptom Check List-90 (SCL-90) (Derogatis, 1983), and the Minnesota Multiphasic Personality Inventory-II (Butcher et al., 1989).

Standardized psychological testing can be helpful in the routine evaluation and diagnosis of PTSD. A number of different instruments have been developed in the last decade, especially in the area of assessing combat PTSD. The Mississippi Scale (Keane et al., 1988), the SCL-90 (Saunders et al., 1990), and the Impact of Events Scale (Horowitz et al., 1979) are all useful in different areas of assessment. The Mississippi Scale is useful in distinguishing veterans with or without PTSD, while the SCL-90 is quite helpful in criminally related trauma such as rape or assault. A number of structured interviews also exist, such as the SCID, which may be helpful in the assessment. The utility of these and other assessment and diagnostic instruments in different cultural and ethnic groups is a question of ongoing discussion (Westermeyer, 1985), but the weight of evidence seems to be toward the universal utility of the scales across different cultures, often accompanied with one of several acculturation scales in different research settings.

Finally, the clinician should utilize all possible outside resources for information, such as spouse, family, employers, or significant community leaders.

SUGGESTED CLINICAL GUIDELINES

As noted above, the management of the clinical interview can determine, in a very real sense, whether or not the patient shares sufficient information for a diagnosis to be made and whether or not he or she is willing to make the crucial decision to join in a therapeutic relationship with the care provider. This is true, of course, in any initial diagnostic interview, but is especially important when working in a transcultural setting. It is important, therefore, to reemphasize the value of cultural sensitivity in the medical setting.

1. Consideration of the patient's gender, age, and level of acculturation should be early in the interview. All members of a given minority group are not the same. There may in fact be wide variations in life experiences and level of acculturation that can impact the interview process. Accommodations should be made in setting, manner of interview, and testing tools utilized in order to help the patient feel at ease in order to obtain scientifically relevant information from the patient.

2. Orient the patient. Be clear about what the patient can expect to happen in an interview. Do not assume the patient will understand the rules of confidentiality. Assuring confidentiality will help the patient to feel safe.

3. Consider alternative settings for the interview. For example, some cultural groups may feel uncomfortable within a traditional hospital/clinic setting depending on their culture's attitudes toward hospitals. Other groups may see the hospital or clinic as an extension of the majority group oppression (e.g., Russian immigrants might perceive a mental health clinic as a potential prison). Many minority groups will feel more comfortable within their own neighborhood, for example, at a local medical clinic or church.

4. Align yourself with the trauma victim against the trauma. This will help alleviate feelings of shame and will allow the patient to give a more complete history.

5. Give the patient "control" over the interview. Use open-ended questions initially and let the patient know that he or she will not be forced to talk about anything that he or she does not wish to talk about.

6. Give the patient "control" over the trauma. This is difficult, particularly since victims of trauma in actuality have very little control over what happened to them. One of the best ways to give this feeling of control is through education, an important part of the interchange between the patient and the provider during a first interview.

7. Be open about transference/countertransference issues. You may not get an honest response from the patient, but the very fact you acknowledged and are able to openly talk about countertransference feelings will assist the interview.

REFERENCES

Abe, J., Zane, N., & Chun, K. (1994). Differential responses to trauma: Migration-related discriminants of post-traumatic stress disorder among Southern Asian refugees. *Journal of Community Psychology, 22*, 121–135.

American Psychiatric Association. (1994). *Diagnostic and statistical manual of mental disorders—fourth edition*. (DSM-IV). Washington, D.C.: American Psychiatric Association.

Arthur, R. J. (1982). Psychiatric syndromes in prisoner of war and concentration camp survivors. In C.T. Freeman & R.A. Faguet (Eds.), *Extraordinary disorders of behavior* (pp. 99–174). New York: Plenum Press.

Beebe, G. W. (1983). Follow-up studies of World War II and Korean War veterans. *American Journal of Epidemiology, 101*, 400–422.

Butcher, I. N., Dahlstrom, I. R., Graham, J. R., Tellegen, A. & Kaemmer, B. (1989). *Minnesota Multiphasic Personality Inventory (MMPI-2): Manual for administration and scoring*. Minneapolis: University of Minnesota Press.

Carlson, E. & Rosser-Hogan, R. (1994). Cross-cultural response to trauma: A study of traumatic experiences and post-traumatic symptoms, in Cambodian refugees. *Journal of Traumatic Stress, 7*, 43–58.

Cheung, P. (1994). Posttraumatic stress disorder among Cambodian refugees in New Zealand. *International Journal of Social Psychiatry, 40*, 17–26.

Davidson, J. R. T., Hughes, D., Blazer, D. G., & George, L. K. (1991). Posttraumatic stress disorder in the community: An epidemiological study. *Psychological Medicine, 21*, 713–721.

Derogatis, L. R. (1983). *SCL-9OR: Manual I*. Baltimore: Johns Hopkins University.

Everly, G. & Lating, J. (1995). *Psychotraumatology.* New York and London: Plenum Press.

Foy, D. W., Carroll, E. M. & Donahoe, C. P. (1987). Etiological factors in the development of post-traumatic stress disorder in clinical samples of Vietnam veterans. *Journal of Clinical Psychology, 42,* 17–27.

Goldberg, J., True, W. R., Eisen, S. A. & Henderson, W. G. (1990). A twin study of the effects of the Vietnam War on post-traumatic stress disorder. *Journal of the American Medical Association, 263,* 1227–1232.

Green, B., Grace, M., Lindy, J., & Leonard, A. (1990). Race differences in response to combat stress. *Journal of Traumatic Stress, 3,* 379–393.

Green, B., Grace, M., Lindy, J., Leonard, A., Korol, M., & Winget, C. (1990). Buffalo Creek survivors in the second decade: Stability of stress symptoms. *American Journal of Orthopsychiatry, 60,* 43–54.

Helzer, J., Robins, L., & McEvoy, L. (1987). Post-traumatic stress disorder in the general population. *New England Journal of Medicine, 317,* 1630–1634.

Horowitz, M., Wilner, N. & Alvarez, W. (1979). Impact of events scale: A measure of subjective stress. *Psychosomatic Medicine, 41,* 209–218.

Keane, T. M., Caddell, J. M., & Taylor, K. L. (1988). The Mississippi Scale for combat related post-traumatic stress disorder. *Journal of Consulting Psychology, 56,* 85–90.

Kilpatrick, D., Vernon, L., & Best, C. (1985). Factors predicting psychological distress among rape victims. In C. Figley (Ed.), *Trauma and its wake: The study and treatment of post-traumatic stress disorder* (pp. 113–141). New York: Brunner/Mazel.

Kinzie, J., Boehnlein, J., Leung, P. K., Moor, L. J., Riley, C., & Smith, D. (1990). The prevalence of post-traumatic stress disorder and its clinical significance among Southeast Asian refugees. *American Journal of Psychiatry, 147,* 913–917.

Kulka, R. A., Schlenger, W. E., Fairbanks, J. A., Hough, R. L., Jordan, B. K., Marmar, C. R., & Weise, D. S. (1990). *The national Vietnam Veterans readjustment study.* New York: Brunner/Mazel.

Leavitt, L. & Fox, N. (1993). *The psychological effects of war and violence on children.* Hillsdale, New Jersey: Lawrence Erlbaum Associates.

Lima, B.R., Shaila, P., Santacruz, H., & Lorano, J. (1991). Psychiatric disorders among poor victims following a major disaster: Armera, Colombia. *Journal of Nervous and Mental Disease, 179,* 420–427.

Litz, B. T., Keane, T., Fisher, L. Marx, B., & Monaco, V. (1992). Physical health complaints in combat related post-traumatic stress disorder. *Journal of Traumatic Stress, 4,* 131–141.

Lum, R. (1974). *Issues in the study of Asian American communities.* Paper presented at meeting of the Western Psychological Association, San Francisco, April.

Mollica, R. F., Wyshank, G., & Lavelle, J. (1987). The psychosocial impact of war trauma and torture on Southeast Asian refugees. *American Journal of Psychiatry, 144,* 1567–1572.

Norman, E. M. (1988). Post-traumatic stress disorder in military nurses who served in Vietnam during the war years. *Military Medicine, 153,* 238–242.

O'Donohue, W. & Elliot, A. (1992). The current status of post-traumatic stress disorder as diagnostic category problems and proposals. *Journal of Traumatic Stress, 5,* 421–435.

156   *Posttraumatic Stress Disorder*

Ross, R.J., Ball, W.A., Sullivan, K.A. (1984). Sleep disturbances as the hallmark of posttraumatic stress disorder. *American Journal of Psychiatry, 146*, 697–707.

Saunders, B. E., Mandoki, K. A., & Kilpatrick, D. G. (1990). Development of a crime related post-traumatic stress disorder scale within the Symptom Checklist-90. *Journal of Traumatic Stress, 3*, 439–448.

Schlenger, W. E., Kulka, R. A., Fairbanks, J. A., Jough, R. L., Jordan, K., Marmar, C. R., & Weise, D. S. (1992). The prevalence of post-traumatic stress disorder in the Vietnam generation: A multimethod, multisource assessment of psychiatric disorder. *Journal of Traumatic Stress, 5*, 333–363.

Sonnenberg, S. (1985). Introduction: The trauma of war. In S. Sonnenberg Ed.), *Stress and recovery in Vietnam veterans* (pp. 3–12). Washington, D.C.: American Psychiatric Press.

Southwick, S., Krystal, J., Johnson, D., & Charney, D. (1995). Neurobiology of post-traumatic stress disorder. In G. Everly & J. Lating (Eds.), *Psychotraumatology* (pp. 49–66). New York and London: Plenum Press.

Spitzer, R. L., & William, M. (1990). *Structured clinical interview for the DSM-III-R. Patient edition (SCID-P version 1.0)*. Washington, D.C.: American Psychiatric Press.

Sutker, P., Uddo, M., Brailey, K., Vasterling, J., & Errera, P. (1994). Psychopathology in war-zone deployed and non-deployed Operation Desert Storm troops assigned graves registration duties. *Journal of Abnormal Psychology, 103*, 383–90.

Terr, L. C. (1983). Chowchilla revisited: The effects of psychic trauma four years after a school bus kidnapping. *American Journal of Psychiatry, 140*, 1543–1550.

Westermeyer, J. (1985). Psychiatric diagnosis across cultural boundaries. *American Journal of Psychiatry, 142*, 798–805.

William, M.B. & Sommer, J. (1994). *Handbook of post-traumatic therapy*, Westport, Connecticut: Greenwood Press.

Wilson, J. P. (1994). The need for an integrative theory of post-traumatic stress disorder. In M. B. William, & J. Sommer (Eds.), *Handbook of post-traumatic therapy* (pp. 3–18). Westport, Connecticut: Greenwood Press.

CHAPTER NINE

Suicidal Behavior

Patricia Harrison, M.D.

CASE VIGNETTES

Case 1

A 29-year-old African-American male, an inmate of a maximum security prison, was brought to a hospital emergency room after attempting to hang himself. The patient had been convicted on charges of the rape and murder of an 18-year-old Caucasian girl. He was serving a life sentence without parole. Subjected to considerable abuse and harassment for more than a year at the hands of both inmates and guards, most of whom were Caucasian like his victim, he had become increasingly depressed. Prison records documented poor sleep, decreased appetite, and weight loss during the previous two months. The psychiatrist on call, a female Caucasian, was consulted. Examination revealed a medium-build Black man in wrist and leg shackles. There were rope marks around his neck. Eye contact was poor, but he was cooperative. He presented with psychomotor retardation, slow, soft speech, and blunted affect. His mood was depressed and hopeless. There was no evidence of psychosis. He appeared to regret that his suicide attempt had failed. The psychiatrist was asked to make a determination of the seriousness of his suicidal intent.

Discussion

This case illustrates the importance of isolation and lack of a support group in the etiology of depression and suicidality. The patient committed a particularly heinous crime, was incarcerated for life, and was thereby alienated from mainstream society. Nevertheless, many people serve long sentences in prison and do not kill themselves. This man, however, by the nature of his crime and his minority status, was denied a means of establishing a group identity and obtaining social support. There were few Blacks in his prison, and he experienced considerable prejudice. Additionally, cut off from family members, all of whom lived far away, the patient's sense of isolation, helplessness, and hopelessness was complete.

It is well-known that antisocial behavior and depression are not mutually exclusive. This patient presented with clear-cut symptomatology, partially documented by prison resources. The careful clinician must always factor in his or her own personal responses to a patient. The stereotype of the violent, young Black man is a powerful one among some Whites in American society, one that arouses considerable fear and hostility. When confronted with a living example of this stereotypical "Other," the evaluator is all too likely to diagnose malingering and to overlook signs of genuine affective disorder. There is a temptation, no matter what the person's ethnicity, to label anyone who has committed a violent crime as antisocial. By assuming that the patient is malingering for the sake of some kind of primary gain, such as time out of prison, the evaluator avoids having to empathize with someone whose actions are repugnant. This is a defense that effectively isolates the evaluator's own unconscious aggression and undoes its potency. The more alien the person thus categorized, the easier the unconscious process.

In this case, the female Caucasian psychiatrist had to separate racial stereotypes and gender-related fears of sexual assault from the assessment of the patient's psychopathology. She then had to proceed to a determination of suicidality as objectively as possible.

Case 2

A 68-year-old White male was brought to a hospital emergency room by his son. The patient, whose wife of 40 years had died 3 months prior, had become increasingly depressed and was convinced that his children were going to put him in a nursing home. He took several sleeping pills in the morning before his son was scheduled to visit him. In the emergency room, the patient was distraught, struggling to hold back tears. Despite reassurances from his son to the contrary, he remained fixed in his belief that he would be taken from the hospital to a nursing home.

Discussion

This case is a typical example of a high-risk patient in American culture. Factors contributing to increased chance of completed suicide include age greater than 65, male gender, Caucasian race, widowed status, and retirement. On the other hand, there was a high likelihood of discovery, and the pills were unlikely to be fatal. Significant issues arise regarding discharge, for very little in the patient's profile will have changed. Although depressive symptoms may be treatable with medication, he will still reside in an increasingly fragmented culture that prizes youth over age. The extended family is disappearing from American culture, replaced at first by the nuclear family and, more recently, by increasing numbers of single-person households. Where once the elderly were respected for their wisdom and experience, they are now more often perceived as having little or no contribution to make to society. Growing numbers are sequestered in retirement communities and nursing homes.

In assessing this patient, the clinician must determine the relative importance of the various risk factors. The majority of people with similar high-risk profiles will actually never kill themselves, and the epidemiology of large groups cannot predict the behavior of individuals. However, this patient presents some clinical and cultural clues about the seriousness of his attempt. For example, while it is not unusual for a middle-class White family to place an aging parent in a nursing home, for a man the patient's age, who is in reasonably good health, it is unlikely. Until contact with the children is established to determine the validity of the patient's fears, one can assume that his concern is unrealistic, even slightly paranoid, and may be evidence of a developing psychotic depression. The presence of vegetative signs reinforces this speculation. A major depressive episode could certainly evolve from a normal grieving process, especially in a society in which elderly couples often live in relative isolation. The absence of an extended family makes the loss of a spouse that much more catastrophic. In addition, older men may feel particularly overwhelmed when forced to deal with household tasks that traditionally were the purview of women. The apparent lack of seriousness of the suicide attempt, as evidenced by the rapid discovery and the small number of pills taken, can be somewhat misleading. The gesture is likely to appear dramatic to clinicians who have become inured to dealing with borderline character disorders. However, when the act is considered in the context of a society that discourages older men from expressing their feelings, it can be seen as a desperate cry for help, directed primarily at the patient's children. Unless they are willing and able to respond, the patient will remain at very high risk.

Case 3

A 16-year-old Micronesian male was brought to a hospital emergency room after a neighbor found him attempting to hang himself. The young man had become involved in a loud argument with his parents when his father refused to give him money for beer to share with his friends at a weekend evening gathering. The neighbors called an ambulance when they saw the man slumped near a window with one end of a rope around his neck and the other end around a curtain rod. In the emergency room, he was calmed, and then admitted that he had intended to end his life because his father had refused to give him money for beer. When his parents arrived, he was able to tell them how important it was to him to participate in his peer group by contributing beer. They agreed and said they were ready to take him home. The evaluator found no history or sign of depression associated with the suicidal act, and was uncertain about ongoing suicidality. He recommended hospitalization for several days, but the patient and his parents declined. They did not even want outpatient follow-up treatment.

Discussion

In Micronesia, the suicide rate has risen sharply among young men since the 1960s. The ratio of completed male to female suicides is a phenomenal 11:1 and partially reflects the role confusion of young men in this largely matriarchal society. In contrast to women and older men, whose status has not significantly changed with the introduction of Western technology and services, adolescent males have found themselves in an increasingly unsupportive and unstructured environment. In the past, young people had access to a much larger family and social network. Conflicts could be mediated by relatives or community elders. After World War II, however, the economy changed from agrarian to cash-based, and more people began moving into cities. The nuclear family became the primary source of interaction. The traditional values of respect for one's elders, humility, and avoidance of expressed anger persisted, but the support system had shrunk. In addition, young men made fewer contributions to the family's subsistence, because unemployment was high and traditional means of food collection were no longer useful. Courage in battle became anachronistic. Alcohol use increased. Therefore, substance abuse, loss of identified male tasks and bonding rituals, and destabilization of the family all contributed to the rise in suicide rates among young men. The same crisis does not appear to have arisen among young women, presumably because they maintained their high status in the society (Rubinstein, 1992).

It is noteworthy that suicidal behavior among the young men is usually not associated with major depression, is often triggered by minor stress, and occurs rather impulsively. Once the person is rescued, the prognosis is fairly good that there will be no further attempts.

Case 4

A 24-year-old, married, Japanese female tourist traveling with her young son, was brought to a hospital emergency room after being prevented from jumping off the balcony of her hotel room. She had cut her wrists severely, leading to significant blood loss. She had then written a message in Japanese on the walls with her blood. She shouted loudly for the hotel manager to call the police. In broken English, she begged the police to take care of her son after her death and attempted to jump from the balcony.

Discussion

Parent–child suicide (*oyako shinju*), which usually involves mother and child, appears to be specific to Japan, Korea and China (Ohara, 1963). Interestingly, although the rate of double suicide has declined, that of parent–child suicide has not decreased markedly since the 1930s and has been present in Japanese literature since 1302. Studies have generally found mental illness in the mother, usually depression, as well as a strong enmeshment between parent and child. This has been felt to be consistent with Japanese culture, which may allow a mother to become over-involved with her children and which sometimes views offspring as possessions (Ohara, 1963, Yoshimatsu, 1992). The cultural aspects of this case presented a diagnostic puzzle. First, clinicians in the United States tend to see wrist-cutting as borderline behavior that is rarely a serious suicidal gesture. On the other hand, the patient had lost enough blood that the physician in the emergency room considered a transfusion. The patient appeared electively mute in the emergency room whereas history indicated that she had been speaking at least broken English earlier. This type of behavior is sometimes felt to be hysterical. Smearing blood on the hotel walls was highly dramatic, but could also represent a psychotic thought process.

Traveler's psychosis has been documented in people who cross multiple time zones (Young, 1995; Langen et al., in press). It was also noted to be unusual for a young Japanese matron to be traveling without her husband. A diagnosis of major depression, ruling out psychotic features, was made, and the patient was admitted to the hospital. At that time, the evaluators were unaware of *oyako shinju*, but later, in formulating the case, they found this culture-specific tradition quite pertinent. Though deeply depressed, the patient *might* have unconsciously managed to avoid a parent–child suicide, which might have resulted from her illness had she remained in Japan. Her unconventional trip to the United States and her dramatic cry for help in the form of blood-writing served as a life-saving rebellion against a centuries-old tradition.

INTRODUCTION

While suffering is a universal feature of human existence, the means of dealing with it vary from person to person and culture to culture. The act of suicide is strongly influenced by cultural values, and a stressor that may seem trivial in one society may be worth dying for in another.

Several questions have been asked about suicide, including who commits suicide, why they do it, by what means and under what circumstances. The literature reveals certain cross-cultural consistencies. For example, it appears generally true that women attempt suicide more often, but men are more likely to successfully complete it (DesJarlais et al., 1995). Men tend to use more violent methods. Suicide rates usually decrease during times of war and in very poor countries. Additionally, suicide is positively correlated with mental illness (Fombonne, 1994; Kok & Tseng, 1992). Otherwise, suicide appears to be strongly culturally shaped.

VARIATIONS IN OBSERVED SUICIDAL BEHAVIOR

Who Commits Suicide?

Recent studies indicate that suicide rates are increasing worldwide (Diekstra, 1993; Fombonne, 1994; Aldridge, 1992; Bille-Brahe, 1993; DesJarlais et al., 1995). Nevertheless, the 1989 World Health Statistics Annual documented rates ranging from 6 per million women in Malta to 581 per million men in Hungary (World Health Organization, 1989). This large variation indicates that significant sociocultural factors are at work, not all of which are readily explainable. For instance, the Scandinavian countries of Denmark and Sweden have very high rates of suicide; but Norway, which is ethnically and culturally very similar, has substantially lower rates. The reasons are not known, although religious beliefs, child-rearing practices, and national record-keeping have all been hypothesized to contribute to the difference. Interestingly, the combined rates of accident and suicide are about the same for all three countries (Retterstol, 1975).

During the past 20 years, suicide rates of adolescents and young adults have generally increased in Western societies (Diekstra, 1993). This trend is dramatically apparent in Micronesia, where suicide among young men has reached almost epidemic proportions—nearly 100 per 100,000 population for the 20-24 age group (Rubinstein, 1986, 1992; DesJarlais et al., 1995). The hypothesis is that the increasing suicide rate reflects the growing turmoil of modern society and the loss of defined roles, particularly for men. Most studies indicate that suicide rates among women have remained stable; one exception is the cohort in Bille-Brahe's (1993) review, which reveals significant increases in female completed suicides in Denmark.

How Do People Commit Suicide?

Obviously, people use the tools that are available. Countries with rigorous gun control have very few suicides by gunshot. Those that have ready access to medications show increasing rates of drug overdose. Rural, agrarian communities may demonstrate ingestion of toxic chemicals. Additionally, methods of suicide vary over time in any given society. Historically, hanging and drowning have been favored means in many cultures, but these appear to be declining. Jumping from tall buildings is now a common method in urban areas.

Interestingly, acculturation affects methods of suicide. For instance, Japanese Americans in Los Angeles who committed suicide by traditional Japanese methods, such as hanging, were more likely to have Japanese rather than American first names than Japanese Americans who committed suicide by common American means, such as gunshot or overdose (Yamamoto, 1974). What remains unclear is whether or not increased availability (i.e., guns, skyscrapers, and medication) contributes to increased rates of suicide.

Ethnic-Related Patterns of Suicidal Behavior

In 1976, the World Health Organization released its epidemiological report describing four patterns of suicide based on age. Type A, the Czechoslovakian pattern, revealed rates increasing progressively with age. Type B, the Finnish pattern, showed a steady increase until age 50-60, followed by a decline. Type C, the Berlin pattern, mirrors the Finnish except for an increase in rates after age 75. Finally, Type D, the Japanese pattern, shows a double peak, one for ages 15-24 and another after age 45 (World Health Organization, 1976). Additionally, a Pacific pattern has been described (Kok & Tseng, 1992), in which there is a sharp increase of suicide in the young, followed by a decline with age. This is the siutation in Micronesia, Samoa and Hawaii. These different suicide patterns are associated with age-related periods of distress among different ethnic groups.

It is interesting to note that the Japanese type of suicide curve no longer applies in Japan. During the past three decades, life may have become less stressful to the young, and the formerly high rate of suicide in youth has declined. Instead, the rates for the middle-aged and aged are rising (Wen, 1974). Thus, in Japan, the age-related suicide curve has changed to the Czechoslovakian type, with a steady increase in suicide rate relative to age (Yoshimatsu, 1992).

SOCIOCULTURAL UNDERSTANDING OF SUICIDAL BEHAVIOR

Social Determinants of Suicide

Suicide, which apparently contradicts the primary evolutionary drive for self-preservation and preservation of the species, is in some ways the most aberrant of human behaviors. Massive pressures, either individual, social, or cultural, must be present to override the biological urge for life.

In 1897, Emil Durkheim described three types of suicide: altruistic, anomic, and egoistic. He was among the first to view suicide as a reflection of specific societal values. He believed that social solidarity was inversely correlated with suicide rates. This theory continues to have merit, as indicated by Farberow (1975), who demonstrated that historically, cultures with rigid moral and religious stances tend to have lower suicide rates than rationalistic, liberal societies. Where individual freedom is prized, suicide is more common; where society is valued over the individual, it is rare. This theory is not universally agreed upon, as evidenced by Iga and Tatai (1975), who state that the severe authoritarianism of Japanese culture has led to high suicide rates, particularly among women, resulting from their socially imposed sense of helplessness.

Apparently only in China do women commit suicide more frequently than men (DesJarlais et al., 1995), but the numbers are high in Japan as well. Females have been noted to use more lethal means in Japan than in some other countries. For both China and Japan, the high rates of female suicide are thought to be due in part to the low status of women, and the highly restrictive environment in which they have had to live (Iga & Tatai, 1975; DesJarlais et al., 1995). Rates may decline as they gain more personal freedom.

Farberow (1975) divided suicide into two broad categories: social or institutional and individual or personal. These seem to correspond to Durkheim's in that altruistic or institutional suicide is prescribed, even demanded, by the society and contains a heavy component of duty and obligation. Examples would include *suttee* in India and *seppuku* in Japan. Durkheim's anomic and egoistic suicide can be subsumed under Farberow's heading of personal suicide. Personal suicide of the anomic type may represent a statement to society, as in the "death before dishonor" of a defeated Roman commander, or *fun-shi*, a Japanese expression of indignation against authority (Farberow, 1975; Kok & Tseng, 1992). Egoistic personal suicide reflects the narcissistic crisis of the modern world. Either through illness, isolation or loss, the individual can no longer endure his existence. Those people for whom the basic human needs of food, clothing, shelter, and personal safety are consistently met may have nothing tangible to struggle for and thus find themselves overwhelmed by existential despair.

Freud postulated the existence of the death instinct, or Thanatos, which could result in either suicide or homicide, depending on whether the aggression was internalized or externalized (Freud, 1949). This theory was quite applicable to a society in the industrial era, when weapons were becoming increasingly effective. At the time, aggression was becoming less highly prized for its survival value, and the recognition of its destructive potential was growing. Such concerns are even more valid in a postindustrial society, in which nuclear power makes irreversible mass destruction possible.

SOCIOCULTURAL FACTORS INFLUENCING ATTITUDES TOWARD SUICIDE

Religion

As mentioned above, attitudes toward suicide vary widely among different cultures and are influenced by a number of factors, including religion, economy, and social strife. Not surprisingly, ambivalence is often the result. For example, Confucianism reveres family obligations; the suicide of a healthy individual would thus be seen as an abandonment of familial duties. On the other hand, the considerable skepticism regarding life after death eliminates the fear of punishment that is inherent in many religions, as well as the sense of escaping to something better. In general, Eastern religions, in which reincarnation and circularity are prominent, do not condemn suicide too vigorously (Kok & Tseng, 1992).

The monotheistic religions of the West (Judaism, Christianity, and Islam) are essentially linear, and function on the presumption of eternal redemption or damnation based on the actions of a single lifetime. Suicide has generally been seen as a moral crime in these societies. This makes sense in light of the Judeo–Christian–Moslem triad, which arose among people who were oppressed by larger, more powerful populations. Suicide would not be condoned by a group that needs every individual to survive. Premature death would need to serve a purpose for the greater good of the group. Martyrdom for the sake of one's religious beliefs would be acceptable, but not suicide over one's private pain. On the other hand, in China, Japan, and India, where overpopulation has long been an issue, an individual's survival has less relevance for the long-term survival of the group. The Western corollary to this is the rise of Protestantism, in which there is a much higher rate of suicide than in Catholicism. Although the concept of heaven and hell still exerts a powerful influence, as environmental resources have become increasingly strained, suicide has become less of a sin and more of a weakness for which forgiveness is possible.

Socioeconomic Status

Social class and economic standing appear to have a counter-intuitive effect on suicide rates, at least in some cultures (Fombonne, 1994). The *samurai* of Japan had a strong tradition of honorable suicide. After the Roman Republic became an empire under the rule of the Caesars, the nobility began killing themselves with increasing frequency. Suicide also peaked in the upper classes of eighteenth century Europe (Aldridge, 1992). Currently, Caucasians, the dominant ethnic group in the United States, kill themselves more frequently than African Americans (DesJarlais et al., 1995; Reynolds et al., 1975), a finding which is consistent with the collective nature of Black culture and with the identification of an external negative force against which African Americans must fight. As with the oppressed groups mentioned earlier, the underprivileged in modern society must maintain their group solidarity in order to survive. They cannot afford the luxury of flight from individual suffering.

War and Oppression

With some exceptions, suicide rates decline when there is an identified external force against which a group of people can align themselves. This is true in times of war as well as oppression (Noomen, 1975; Kok & Tseng, 1992). However, a question arises when one considers the fact that suicide rates actually *increased* in Japan during World War II (DesJarlais et al., 1995). Does the decline that is usually seen in cultures that are intolerant of suicide represent a genuine decrease in suicidal ideation, or an increase in indirect suicide that goes unrecognized, that is victim-precipitated homicide or self-sacrifice? The epic tales of many cultures are filled with heroes who die fighting against overwhelming odds. The adventure film, the modern American equivalent of the epic poem, consists of protagonists in highly ritualized battles against vastly superior forces. Death in combat is almost universally seen as heroic (for males). Even when it occurs without hope of victory, it serves the purpose of altruistic suicide. Conflict can therefore be seen as serving two purposes; it provides an external enemy against which the individual may direct his aggression, and it allows a purposeful suicide for those whose aggression is predominantly internal.

CULTURAL CONSIDERATIONS IN ASSESSMENT OF SUICIDE

Ambiguities of Suicidal Action

One of the major challenges facing mental health professionals is the determination of suicidal intent. Many cases are ambiguous, and in some instances conservative treatment (i.e., hospitalization) is not in the best interests of the patient (Beahrs and Rogers, 1993). Cultural factors can both assist and impede the clinician in his or her evaluation. Cultural differences between patient and clinician can interfere with an accurate assessment of the severity of a given situation. What may appear to be a serious suicide attempt to one evaluator may seem more of a dramatic cry for attention to another. Accurate history-taking becomes crucial in order to determine the patient's motives (despair, anger, guilt, or shame), expectations (death, discovery, or revenge), and feelings about survival (relief, embarrassment, or disappointment).

Sometimes it is unclear if a suicide attempt has been made, even when death ensues. Accidental overdoses with prescription and recreational drugs are not uncommon, and can be difficult to distinguish from impulsive suicidal acts. Fatalities from automobile collisions are usually recorded as accidental, but it is thought that a significant number are, in fact, suicides. Certain countries appear to underreport suicides. Records may avoid the term suicide, and describe cause of death in terms of the physical etiology (gunshot wound, ingestion of toxic chemicals, etc.) (Ladrido-Ignacio & Gensaya, 1992).

Suicidal Behavior that Follows Known Patterns

As described previously, different populations are at different risk for suicidal behavior. The profiles have changed somewhat during the past 20 years, but generally, older White males continue to be at high risk (as in Case 2). The existence of mental illness also increases a person's chance of completed suicide (as demonstrated in Case 4).

Of growing concern is the danger posed to young men in rapidly changing societies (as shown in Case 3). Issues of masculinity and role confusion are currently quite prominent. It is tempting to attribute these findings to an idiosyncratic reaction of one culture. However, examining other societies in similar situations reveals the same pattern. Certain Native American tribes also show an increase in suicide rates among young men. As with the Micronesians, a large percentage (75%) are associated with substance abuse. Other contributing factors include the breakdown of traditional values, geographical isolation, unemployment, and a history of abandonment by caretakers (Shore, 1975). These risk factors correspond to the experience of the Micronesians who live on small islands in the Pacific and who usually kill themselves as a direct response to rejection by a parent. In addition, both groups demonstrate a marked degree of contagion, in that one suicide in a community will often set off a rash of others (Rubinstein, 1992; Shore, 1975). The groups differ in that Native Americans often kill themselves in jails or boarding schools, a pattern that has not been found in Micronesia, possibly because of the absence of a significant number of such institutions (Shore, 1975; Tousignant & Mishara, 1981).

Elsewhere, suicide rates among young men are also rising. The Inuit may have a tradition of the elderly taking their own lives, but, in actuality, more than 50 percent of suicides are men under the age of 25 who have been ingesting alcohol (Tousignant & Mishara, 1981). Substance abuse also figures in the suicides of young Hawaiian men, who kill themselves five times more often than women. They tend to present with motives centering around family conflict and social disruption as well (Tseng et al., 1992). Although documented mental illness does not figure prominently in the suicides of any of these groups, it is apparent that substance abuse and social destabilization are important factors in the increasing mortality rates among young men.

The Solitary Nature of Suicidality

The case of the young African-American inmate illustrates the importance of individualizing one's assessment, for although the patient was in an epidemiologically low-risk group, his circumstances had placed him at high risk.

While all of the above case vignettes have been used to demonstrate cultural issues in suicidal behavior, it must be remembered that, ultimately, suicide is the act of an individual. Society may encourage or discourage the act; it may dictate the means or shape the motives. But the final choice resides within the person, and it is with this person that the clinician must engage. Cultural differences must be transcended in order to deal help with an all-too-private pain.

SUGGESTED CLINICAL GUIDELINES

1. The clinician should be familiar with any special suicidal behavior that may exist in a cultural group. Obviously, this is not always possible; for example, *oyako shinju* is not well-known outside of Japan. However, broad patterns of suicidal behavior are recognizable, and correlative history obtained from family members and friends can be invaluable in the assessment of specific cases.

2. The clinician should explore the meaning of suicide from the patient's cultural point of view. Is it an act of sacrifice, a social statement or an attempt to end personal suffering? It is important to avoid the projection of one's own value system onto the patient and to recognize that a seemingly trivial stressor, such as an argument with a parent, can lead to serious consequences.

3. The clinician should be aware of the cultural context of help-seeking behavior. The expectations of patients differ as to the role of the clinician. Some people will look to the evaluator for advice and guidance; others will need a safe

place for expression of emotions. Again, avoid the assumption that the patient wants what the clinician would want in similar circumstances.

4. The clinician should be able to distinguish between suicidal behavior that is culturally sanctioned and that which is pathological. Treatable mental illness is strongly associated with suicide, and even in societies that are tolerant of suicide, there will be individuals who, if prevented from killing themselves, will be grateful for the intervention.

REFERENCES

Aldridge, D. (1992). Suicidal behaviour: A continuing cause for concern. *British Journal of General Practice, 42*, 482–485.

Beahrs, J.O. & Rogers, J.L. (1993). Appropriate short-term risk in psychiatry and the law. *Bulletin of the American Academy of Psychiatry and the Law, 21*, 53–67.

Bille-Brahe, U. (1993). The role of sex and age in suicidal behavior. *Acta Psychiatrica Scandinavia, Suppl 371*, 21–27.

DesJarlais, R., Eisenberg, L., Good, B., & Kleinman, A. (1995). *World Mental Health: Problems and Priorities in Low-Income Countries*. New York, Oxford: Oxford University Press.

Diekstra, R.F.W. (1993). The epidemiology of suicide and parasuicide. *Acta Psychiatrica Scandinavia, Suppl 371*, 9–20.

Durkheim, E. (1897). *Le Suicide*. 1951 Translation. New York: Free Press of Glencal.

Farberow, N.L. (1975). Cultural history of suicide. In N. Farberow (Ed.), *Suicide in Different Cultures* (pp. 1–16). Baltimore: University Park Press.

Fombonne, E. (1994). Increased rates of depression: Update of epidemiological findings and analytical problems. *Acta Psychiatrica Scandinavia, 90*, 145–156.

Freud, S. (1949). *An Outline of Psychoanalysis*. London: Hogarth Press.

Iga, M. & Tatai, K. (1975). Characteristics of suicides and attitudes toward suicide in Japan. In N. Farberow (Ed.), *Suicide in different cultures*. (pp. 255–280). Baltimore: University Park Press.

Kok, L. & Tseng, W. (1992). Introduction: Orientation to cross-society comparison. In L. Kok & W. Tseng (Eds.), *Suicidal behavior in the Asia-Pacific region* (pp. 1–14). Singapore: Singapore University Press.

Ladrido-Ignacio, L., & Gensaya, J. P. (1992). Suicidal behaviour in Manila, Philippines. In L. Kok & W. Tseng (Eds.), *Suicidal behavior in the Asia-Pacific region* (pp. 112–126). Singapore: Singapore University Press.

Langen, D., Streltzer, J., & Kai, M. (in press). "Honeymoon psychosis" in Japanese tourists to Hawaii. *Cultural Diversity and Mental Health*.

172   *Suicidal Behavior*

44

Noomen, P. (1975). Suicide in the Netherlands. In N. Farberow (Ed.), *Suicide in different cultures* (pp. 165–178). Baltimore: University Park Press.

Ohara, K. (1963). Characteristics of suicides in Japan especially of parent–child double suicide. *American Journal of Psychiatry, 120,* 382–385.

Retterstol, N. (1975). Suicide in Norway. In N. Farberow (Ed.), *Suicide in different cultures* (pp. 77–94). Baltimore: University Park Press.

Reynolds, D.K., Kalish, R., & Farberow, N.L. (1975). A cross-ethnic study of suicide attitudes and expectations in the United States. In N. Farberow (Ed.), *Suicide in different cultures* (pp. 35–50). Baltimore: University Park Press.

Rubinstein, D. (1986). Micronesian suicide. In W.S. Tseng (Ed.), *Culture and mental health in Micronesia* (pp. 170–188). Honolulu: Department of Psychiatry, School of Medicine, University of Hawaii.

Rubinstein, D. (1992). Suicidal behavior in Micronesia. In L. Kok & W. Tseng (Eds.), *Suicidal behavior in the Asia-Pacific region* (pp. 199–230). Singapore: Singapore University Press.

Shore, J.H. (1975). American Indian suicide—fact and fantasy. *Psychiatry, 38,* 86–91.

Tousignant, M. & Mishara, B. (1981). Suicide and culture: A review of the literature (1969–1980). *Transcultural Psychiatric Research Review, XVIII,* 5–33.

Tseng, W., Hsu, J., Omori, A., & Mclaughlin, D. (1992). Suicidal behaviour in Hawaii. In L. Kok & W. Tseng (Eds.), *Suicidal behavior in the Asia-Pacific region* (pp. 231–248). Singapore: Singapore University Press.

Wen, C.P. (1974). Secular suicidal trend in postwar Japan and Taiwan—An examination of hypotheses. *International Journal of Social Psychiatry, 20,* 8–17.

World Health Organization. (1976). Special subject—suicide 1950–1971. *World Health Statistic Report, 29,* 396–413.

World Health Organization (1989). *World health statistics annual.* Geneva: World Health Organization.

Yamamoto, J. (1974). Japanese and American suicides in Los Angeles. *Transcultural Psychiatric Research Review, 11,* 197–199.

Yoshimatsu, K. (1992). Suicidal behavior in Japan. In L. Kok & W. Tseng (Eds.), *Suicidal behavior in the Asia-Pacific region* (pp. 15–40). Singapore: Singapore University Press.

Young, D. (1995). Psychiatric morbidity in travelers to Honolulu, Hawaii. *Comprehensive Psychiatry, 36,* 224–228.

CHAPTER TEN

Violent Behavior

R. Andrew Schultz-Ross, M.D.

CASE VIGNETTES

Case 1

A male Caucasian inmate is sent from prison to a hospital for psychiatric evaluation. The patient is over six feet tall, highly muscular, and heavy. He has pasty white skin and an angry glare. His voice is slow, but loud; he has a thick accent from the southern United States. Officials bring him from the prison in shackles to be evaluated by a diminutive and bespectacled African-American psychologist. The patient just glares at the evaluator, refusing to answer any questions with a demeaning, "Not to you," and is ushered away. In reviewing the records, the psychologist finds that the patient is serving a sentence for murdering an elderly woman. The patient did not know the woman, but tackled her, football style, on a city sidewalk, lifted her in the air, and dumped her some yards away. She later died of her injuries. The patient had difficulties in the most secure section of the state's highest security prison. He is convinced that the correctional officers mean him harm. He believes that they make noises on the loudspeaker, spy on him, poison him, and plan to kill him. According to unconfirmed reports from the prison, some of the officers responded to the patient's beliefs by acting them out—actually announcing his name on the loudspeaker for no reason or whispering threats a few feet away from his room. He spends his days lifting weights, writing grievances and praying. He is a devout Christian. He shows no remorse for the murder, as he believes that the victim was part of a plot against him. During times of increased agitation, he threatens the prison officers with violence. The records indicate that the patient was brought up in Alabama, and worked for years in a series of warehouses. He was a loner, with few friends. Little is known about his family or his personal beliefs, but the evaluator believes that the man is a racist, probably due to the long history of racism in the southern United States. He suspects that the patient is unwilling to be examined by an African-American professional.

Discussion

Indeed, there is a racial issue between the patient and the evaluator. The patient distrusts and disrespects the evaluator because of his race, but is less dominated by this issue than the evaluator suspects. The patient's refusal is more substantially based on paranoia of the evaluation itself. He believes anyone working for the state is part of an elaborate plot against him, and he is unwilling to "feed" the plot by providing information. To some extent, the evaluator assumed a reason based on the patient's accent and the history of racism in Alabama. The evaluator continued to try to meet with the patient and listen to the patient's concerns. Eventually, enough of a bond was formed that the patient cooperated with the evaluation. After being committed to the institution where the evaluator worked, the patient asked to be seen by the evaluator on several occasions, ostensibly to discuss grievances and complaints, but it was clear that an increased level of trust and respect had developed.

Case 2

A part-Hawaiian man lived in a group home with many other men of various ethnic groups. He was convicted of murdering his ex-wife's father, a man who had always disapproved of the marriage. His wife's family was Portuguese American and Catholic. The father believed that the patient was a "heathen" and was unfit to marry his daughter. The patient killed his ex-father-in-law by punching him to death. Prior to the murder, the patient had been an amateur boxer with many victories. At the time of the murder, he was paranoid and had been using cocaine in large amounts. In prison, he stopped using drugs (although they were available within the institution). He was placed on anti-psychotic medication and became less paranoid. Mild to moderate diffuse cognitive deficits were found on examination, and were felt to be due to the heavy drug use and boxing.

After the expiration of his prison sentence, the man was placed in a half-way house for individuals with substance abuse and/or mental illness difficulties. In most ways, he was considered to be a "model citizen," but he would hit others if he were called one of a limited number of pejorative names. These names were either racial insults given by residents of other ethnic backgrounds, or words of various dialects implying or alleging homosexuality. Although the patient remained on anti-psychotic medication, these insults would be followed by a limited degree of paranoia. The patient would believe that the other man meant him harm, and would begin to suspect that the insults were escalating beyond the level observed by the staff at the house.

The staff were afraid of the potential for serious injury because of his history of murder and boxing training. At times, he would strike others forcefully, but the staff were able to intervene prior to any serious injury. After each assault, he would express remorse to the victim and staff. Some of the staff members thought that he was trying hard to be nonviolent, and believed his remorse. Their position was supported by the patient's many pledges not to harm anyone and excellent attendance and participation in nonviolence groups. Others thought that he was manipulating the staff and believed that he did not feel that his violence was wrong. This position was supported by the patient's reports that his reason for pursuing nonviolence was to avoid a return to prison, and by his total lack of remorse for telling another resident to hit someone who had failed to pay a debt.

Discussion

On close examination, the patient's remorse seemed to be genuine, but partial. The Native Hawaiian people, as a group, are socioeconomically disadvantaged. Many have noted their degree of disenfranchisement, felt to be due to their domination by other cultures. There was a huge decline in the population of the native people due to imported diseases, an overthrow of the Hawaiian government in

1893, and a massive reorganization of the religious, political, and economic life of the Islands by missionaries and foreign business-men. The patient grew up as a member of this disenfranchised culture, and kept his shame inside until he was given a label that, in his perception, made him less valued than other men. This sensitivity seemed to relate to the loss of power of the native people in Hawaii, and perhaps to the cultural tradition of several distinct groups with different roles, powers, and rights. In time sequence, it seemed that the aggravation of the man's shame led to markedly increased anxiety and subsequent aggravation of his paranoia.

In a sense, his remorse seemed to be less about violence than about obedience and respect. He was upset with himself for disobeying the staff's request for him to avoid violence. His recommendation of violence to a peer, among other events, seemed to indicate that he still believed he could resolve his problems by being violent.

In pursuing new modalities of treatment, staff at the halfway house started a group that emphasized understanding of Hawaiian culture. In this way, he seemed to be able to replace some shame with self-respect. In addition, individual work included a focus on specific reasons for owning nonviolence, rather than trying to follow it as potentially resented obedience. His rate of violence declined, although as he used talking more as a means of coping, the depth of his shame and violent thinking was further revealed.

Case 3

While in college, a woman of Puerto Rican descent married her boyfriend, who was from Argentina. His family in Buenos Aires was wealthy and aristocratic; her family members were recent immigrants to New York City and were in the American lower middle class. After the couple wed, they moved to Los Angeles, near the husband's older brother. Shortly after the move, the husband began beating his wife when he was drunk. She appealed to her husband, who would apologize but repeat the behavior. Eventually, she asked for assistance from her husband's brother, who said that she was doing something wrong. She sensed that the brother also did not approve of her. After the birth of a child, the beatings worsened. Afraid and angry, the woman took a California friend's advice and filed for divorce. The litigation was protracted and angry. For economic and social support, she moved back with her family in New York. There, she received lukewarm support from her family, who believed that divorce was wrong. She nonetheless stayed in New York and eventually was divorced. Several years later, she married a man of Puerto Rican descent. After about two years, he also began to beat her. She refused to tell anyone for three years, but eventually sought assistance at a counseling center. Despite escalation of the violence, she refused to consider separation. After her husband left her for several months, she allowed him to move back into the home.

Discussion

Cultural and family support (or rejection) is a powerful force. Although there are broad cultural norms for family violence, this example may reveal how a microcultural norm may be set up in one family or group. This woman may have been taught that her physical safety and comfort are lesser values than the bond of marriage and family support. These family values may not be the norm for American or Hispanic culture, but they are abetted by larger social forces that support victimization of women.

INTRODUCTION

On a clinical, investigative, and even political level, psychiatrists are becoming more involved in the assessment of violence. Whether viewed as the symptom of an individual or a social phenomenon, violence involves culture. Every cultural group sanctions some violence, albeit not always in a formal manner. Societal responses to violence, and more specifically the law, also reflect cultural values. The assessment of violence for the purpose of legal decisions introduces morality and legality into clinical issues; such evaluations can lead to potentially incorrect consequences if cultural issues are ignored. Thus, the assessment of violence requires more than cultural acknowledgment; such assessment is a complex, uncertain, and intrinsically cultural exchange.

LITERATURE REVIEW

A Symptom of Illness?

It is becoming less odd to view violence as a possible symptom of mental illness. Indeed, research by Lewis et al. (1989) indicates that highly violent juveniles have a high proportion of often undiagnosed psychiatric and/or neurological impairment. Similarly, data from the Epidemiologic Catchment Area study (Swanson et al., 1990) indicated that more than half of the subjects who reported violence in the preceding year met criteria for a psychiatric disorder. A number of psychiatric diagnoses are associated with violence. Appelbaum and Gutheil (1991) noted that disorders such as delusional disorder of the paranoid and erotomanic types, and neuropsychiatric conditions such as intermittent explosive disorder are associated with violence. Temporolimbic epilepsy and schizophrenia have a more controversial association, as noted by Treiman (1986, 1994), Tardiff (1994), and O' Shaughnessy (1994). In a recent development, Fava et al. (1990, 1993) have described a variant of mood disorders called "anger attacks," which appear to respond to serotonergic agents. Although this syndrome is not yet accepted as an official diagnosis, this area of inquiry indicates that psychiatric researchers are exploring violence and considering it, at least in some forms, to be within the purview of psychiatry. Of diagnostic categories accepted by the American Psychiatric Association (1994), substance use has a clear association with violence (Appelbaum & Gutheil, 1991; Gottlieb et al., 1988; Bushman & Cooper, 1990). Of course, antisocial personality disorder contains violence as a diagnostic criterion and is part of the behavior of many individuals with this disorder (Reid, 1985).

Nonetheless, the issue of whether violence is sometimes or even always a symptom of mental illness tends to provoke discomfort in practitioners. There has always been a "mad versus bad" viewpoint; if violence is caused by an illness, then the violent individual is viewed somewhat less as a perpetrator and more as a victim of illness, at least from a Western viewpoint. Perhaps violence is more likely to be considered a symptom when the act occurs on a psychiatric ward, but even then, there is much discomfort (Davis, 1991). There is often disagreement about when and if patients should be charged for assaults in the hospital (Phelan et al., 1985). Clearly, there is even less consensus about the behavior of violent people outside the hospital, in the general community. The labeling of violence as a symptom in this group has generated great discomfort, because of the role psychiatry and other disciplines play in the insanity defense—the "mad versus bad" issue again, this time in the courtroom. The fear is that psychiatric attempts at understanding could lead to legal attempts at acquittal by reason of mental illness.

Realizing these difficulties, let us nonetheless assume (at least for the moment) that violence can be viewed in a manner similar to other symptoms. If so, then we know that the experience of acting violently and the nature of the expression of the violent behavior is likely to vary across cultures (Tseng & McDermott, 1981), although it tends to be committed by young males of low socioeconomic status across cultures (Messner, 1988). The tolerance of violence is also likely to vary. Furthermore, the form of the violence also differs across cultures. For example, *amok* (nondiscriminate, massive homicide) is a well-known, culture-bound form of sudden, severe violence described in Malaysia, the Philippines, and other cultures (Westermeyer, 1973).

The Culture of Violence

Indeed, even if we lay aside the issue of the role of illness, violence can still be viewed as a culturally relevant or culturally determined behavior. Cultural determination is perhaps clearest in the case of war. Nonetheless, it appears likely that every major culture sanctions violence either formally and/or informally to varying degrees. These issues are not new. There has always been a difficulty in training warriors to be violent, and then protecting the warrior's own citizenry, an issue most recently experienced in the United States in the aftermath of the war in Vietnam. Indeed, Archer and Gartner (1984) found that violent crime increased in nations after their involvement in war, with the most increase in victorious nations.

While cultures clearly vary in the tolerable expression of violence, it is less than clear whether certain cultures themselves are more violent. In this regard, the definition and tools used to measure violence are important considerations. Lester (1990) encountered difficulty in attempting to compare violence in different nations; methodological limitations were also noted by Gartner (1995).

Nonetheless, there are many reports that the United States has a much higher homicide rate than other industrialized nations (Goldstein, 1994). Emde (1993) has argued that the United States has a culture of violence, and that the love of violence must be appreciated to be changed. Perhaps the culture of violence is passed from generation to generation, and through the media. In contrast, O'Nell (1986) reported that the Zapotec, a nonviolent tribe in Mexico, appears to teach nonviolence to its children. It also allows some acceptable violence.

Perhaps more controversial than the behavior of the larger group is the violence of subcultures (Singer, 1986). Attempts to explain subcultural violence have a long history in the United States, where researchers have tried to understand many decades of increased violence in the southern United States. The history of the American Civil War, slavery, and high gun ownership have been included in the many varied attempts at explanation (Goldstein, 1994). In recent years, rates of violence in other regions have risen to approach that in the southern region. Subcultural groups are often the most violent and the least sanctioned by the larger group. Representatives of a larger culture may be more forgiving of violent behavior that is in accord with the cultural values of the larger group, and more rejecting of similar behavior exhibited by a member of a smaller, more unusual group (Messner, 1988).

One of the difficulties is determining what is meant by culture and cultural group. Some might only include ethnicity as a determining factor. Using this factor alone, an inner city gang might be considered a cultural group if the members were all members of the same ethnicity. What if the values of the gang were different from the values of others of the same ethnicity who are not gang members? What about gangs that have mixed ethnicity, but similar values (albeit values that are repugnant to many)? Indeed, as will be discussed further below, violence may result from cultural conflict. Many observers have noted an elevated rate of violence among African Americans in the United States. There have been many attempts to understand and explain this observation. Although there is a strong perception of fear among other groups (especially European Americans), the vast majority of African-American violence is against other African Americans (Blue & Griffith, 1995). Ucko (1994) has argued that the increased rate of spousal abuse in African-American families may relate to the conflict between African values that include strong women in a more reciprocal relationship and more the macho values brought to America from Europe.

Indeed, domestic violence may be an area that involves the most difficulties in cross-cultural assessment. Korbin (1981), discussing child abuse, noted that acceptable care from the viewpoint of one culture may be deemed abusive in another. This finding may be easy to see through Western eyes, but, according to Korbin, some non-Western cultures find accepted Western practices (such as scheduled feeding and allowing a child to cry) abusive. However, Korbin also asserts that each culture has a set of acceptable behaviors; it may be possible to at least define abuse within the cultural group. The variance of forms of abuse is not insignificant; for example, Japanese mothers may find it more tolerable to abandon or even kill their infants than mistreat them in other ways (Wagat-suma, 1981). Wilson and Daly (1995) describe one attempt at understanding male violence against women through evolutionary psychology; cultures that do not support such violence may have other cultural means to control female sexuality (and therefore the genome). Domestic violence also begets domestic violence. It is often believed that victims of child abuse may become victimizers. It seems likely that women are usually violent against their abusive mates; women who commit murder usually do it within the household, although this pattern may be most true in the United States (Kruttschnitt, 1995).

It is tempting to "use" culture to explain behavior that is, in some way, forgivable, and to exclude gangs on that basis. But, even the sense of forgiveness is cultural; we routinely forgive the fictionalized versions of Robin Hood and his merry "gang" as they display historical versions of behavior remarkably similar to modern gangs. Indeed, the larger culture might be more forgiving of violence against a rejected, hated, or radical sub-group (Razack, 1994).

Society's organized forgiveness is cultural, because laws have a cultural basis. Morals, values, and judgments are not absolute, but vary across cultures. Even within a culture, as social movements change the mainstream of the opinion held by the culture, the law changes. These changes can be seen in the civil and women's rights movements and in the slower changes of laws affecting homosexual behavior.

Similarly, psychiatrists and other mental health practitioners increasingly appreciate the role of culture in illness, including the variability of symptoms among cultural groups (Leff, 1988). As noted in the work of Kleinman (1978, 1980, 1987; Kleinman et al., 1978), Tseng and McDermott (1981), and Comas-Diaz and Griffith (1988), symptoms are to be interpreted within a cultural context, and cultural cause excluded before the label of psychopathology is given. According to the *Diagnostic and Statistical Manual of Mental Disorders—Fourth Edition* (DSM-IV) (American Psychiatric Association, 1994), many clinical psychiatric syndromes first require the exclusion of cultural explanations. In areas with great cultural diversity, these issues are even more relevant in diagnosis (McDermott, 1980).

A Systemic View

Some practical pointers regarding violence as a symptom of illness and culture can be arranged from a systemic point of view, beginning with the small and ascending to the larger systems. On a microscopic level, we must consider neurological abnormalities, and recall that such deviations may not necessarily cause violence but contribute to it, since violence is often considered to be multifactorial and overdetermined. Recent research by Raine et al. (1994) suggests that murderers may have an abnormality in prefrontal metabolism on a PET (positron emission tomography) scan. Similarly, frontal lobe lesions were associated with violent incidents in a study of psychiatric patients by Heinrichs (1989). Serotonin has been noted to be an important factor (Apter et al., 1990; Marazziti & Conti, 1991; Eichelman, 1988). Violence is strongly associated with drug and alcohol use, which varies among cultural groups. Obviously, mental disorders must be considered. Whether there are genetic causes of violence is not yet clear. The concept of genetic selection for aggressiveness is accepted in animal breeding. Theoretically, if this type of breeding occurred in humans, it could lead to neurochemical differences among groups. In a study using a Danish cohort, Kandel et al. (1989) found that minor physical anomalies (purported to be associated with developmental defects of the central nervous system) were associated with recidivistic adult violence.

On the next level up, we look at the individual. Here, the psychodynamics of violence play a role. Violence can be seen as a universal impulse that most of us successfully inhibit most of the time. All too often, it represents a repetition of past trauma. Shame and a lack of empathy are often felt to be powerful factors with a rich cultural basis. The presence and presentation of shame differs. Sexual fears, inadequacies, and addictions may play a role in paraphilic violence, and perhaps in domestic abuse as well.

Ascending another level, we consider the dyad of the perpetrator and the victim. Violence may often represent, or at least be allowed, by a failure of the perpetrator to see the victim as a similar, equal, or worthwhile being. Retribution plays a role, and while violence is not the answer for violence, consideration must be given to the possibility that the victim was also violent (Widom, 1989; Singer, 1986).

On still another level, family issues may play a vital role. The role and history of violence in the perpetrator's family can set the stage for later reenactments of childhood traumas, a repetition noted in the work of Lewis et al. (1989). In Farrington's (1989) prospective study of 411 men in London, economic deprivation, a family history of crime, parental problems, school problems, hyperactivity, and antisocial behavior were the best predictors of aggression and violence. Thus, developmental and family issues both play a role. Similarly, Busch et al. (1990) found that homicidal adolescents had a higher proportion of violent family members, gang involvement, serious educational problems, and alcohol use. These are socioeconomic, but also subcultural issues. An unclear percentage of abused children go on to become abusive and violent adults.

Moving up a level, we encounter the subcultures and cultures themselves, and their values and identities, issues that were explored by Freud (1953). An important factor here is the relationship of the individual to his culture, or cultures. Many of us have split allegiances, and we may even have a complex set of inconsistent beliefs that spring forth from the interaction of distinct cultures with each other. Aspects of violence that vary across cultures include the definitions of spouse and child abuse, and the acceptability, whether legal or societal, of murder for the sake of honor.

On the final level we find the dyad of the violent perpetrator and the evaluator. Violence has the potential to result in powerful countertransference. Like the patient or defendant, the professional has a culture, a family, and personal opinions and experiences related to violence. The interaction between the perpetrator and the doctor is a dynamic interchange of these likely conflicting values. While we cannot excuse violence, it is arguably necessary for a treating clinician to have some understanding of how and why it occurred. Unexplained violence is unfathomable, but a close examination of the individual usually provides a sense of the factors that led to the behavior, although such an explanation of a historically human interaction is rarely reassuring.

DISCUSSION

Immigrants and subcultures may have different values than those contained in the legal statutes. Thus, an offender's cultural values may differ from the legal requirements of the society in which he lives. In addition to immigration, law is affected by the political history of a nation, and may not completely reflect the values of the majority of its citizens if it was imposed by outside forces. Many societies that were colonies have imported law. It is frightening to consider the possibilities of a law without cultural acceptance. At times, law enforcement officials may act according to cultural beliefs that are different from those of the people they arrest. If this situation occurs for the majority of citizens, it may perhaps be termed cultural injustice, but what if it affects only a small group of

people or a single defendant? Such issues may arise in our attempts
to understand gang or other subculture behavior.

Thus, psychiatry and law each have (professional) cultural issues.
These issues come to bear in one of the most important arenas for
the assessment of violence—the insanity defense (Reid, 1988). The
mental health examination for the insanity defense can be used as a
model for discussing all assessments of violence, since even if the
assessment is never used in court, it often forms the basis of others'
judgments of a patient's behavior. It can be argued that an insanity
assessment expands the role of the practitioner to the arena of
morality, because most of these evaluations require an assessment of
the defendant's sense of right and wrong. What if the cultural values
of right and wrong are different for the evaluator and defendant? Is
criminal behavior (something against the law) always also against
cultural values? Clearly not, and violence is no exception.

Violence arouses strong feelings, which may reflect cultural differences and judgment. The examiner's morality and values are culturally based, whether or not they are in accordance with the prevailing law. These feelings and values may affect the assessment in a
number of ways. The examiner who finds the patient to be capable
and "wrong" may tend to diagnose a personality disorder and lean
away from treatment. Another examiner seeing the same patient
may see him as more of a victim of his situation, and therefore ill.
Since the behavior of violent people is often a result of a variety of
factors, both examiners may be correct. The point is that cultural
factors may lead them to emphasize one aspect or another.

Morality itself is cultural. Indeed, perhaps expressions and even
definitions of remorse differ among cultures. Remorse has been the
focus of remarkably little research, but it is probably the basis for
much of our sense of forgiveness. Thus, a potentially culturally
biased judgment of the presence of remorse may subtly affect our
diagnosis. Similarly, other aspects of attitude and behavior with cultural bias, such as likability and understandability, may be affected.
Perhaps the scientific evaluator should ignore such issues, but it
seems likely that potentially subjective perceptions of remorse color
attempts at objective inquiry. Thus, it is not only mental health that
is affected by culture, the law is also affected. Moreover, their intersection, the interpretation of psychological issues for the courtroom, is also subject to cultural uncertainty (Stone, 1984).

To further complicate this situation, communication between the
examiner and the defendant (or the lack of it) may change the balance. An examination is a cultural exchange that may result in clarity or confusion. Of course, the examiner tends to have the legal

power, and his opinion may hold great sway in court, potentially influencing life or death decisions. The ability of the examiner to understand the cultural issues, and use them to promote understanding rather than prejudice, is vital.

SUGGESTED CLINICAL GUIDELINES

1. Recognize that violence is multifactorial; it rarely has a singular cause. Culture affects many of these factors, including neurological and neurochemical factors, psychosis, mood disorders, personality disorders, and substance abuse. Individual psychological factors, such as shame, also vary in presentation among cultures.

2. Consider perpetrator–victim issues. There may have been previous violence in either direction, although it is often assumed that the victim has always been the victim. Cultural values, such as fidelity in a romantic or marital relationship, may differ, as may values about violence. Variability can even occur between two individuals of the same nominal culture, due to differences in acculturation, family differences, or personal allegiance.

3. If possible, assess family and developmental factors, including abuse and family violence. Realize that the definition of abuse differs across cultures, although it can be strongly argued that immigrants must adapt to the expectations of their new homes.

4. Consider subcultural values. Subcultures include gangs, smaller ethnic subgroups within a larger group, and the citizens of regions within a larger land mass. Subcultural membership and affiliation may be clear and acknowledged or hidden. Similarly, the shared values of the subgroup may not be codified. Subcultures, such as gangs or immigrant groups, may not be tolerated or respected by the larger culture in which they reside. Subcultural values may not excuse behavior, but they often help to explain it.

5. Note the values of the larger cultural group. It is important to realize that there may be complications in this assess-

ment, such as differences in acculturation or allegiance, and family or subcultural differences. Historically, there have often been smaller groups of warriors in which violence is more accepted than in the larger group.

6. Consider intercultural issues—concerns that arise at the intersection of cultures. Immigration is one example that was discussed in subcultures. Other issues include cross-cultural relationships and children of mixed cultural background, split allegiances, and generational differences. These issues complicate the cultural understanding of violence by creating more areas to examine. They may also lead to violence, as the intersection of cultural values (such as status or gender roles) may lead to stress and violence.

7. Perform a cultural check on yourself as the evaluator—what are your values, and those of the agency or agencies that you represent? How do they compare with those of the patient? We must realize that it is not only violence that is culture-bound, but also the law and the interaction between evaluator and patient itself. Cultural awareness or acknowledgment is not enough. Instead, when we examine a violent person, we need to be aware that the cultural differences between us create uncertainty regarding the meaning, role, and justification of violence, and the appreciation and communication of responsibility. Moreover, cultural issues can enter into the evaluation through our emotional reaction to these differences. The dynamic interaction creates enormous uncertainty. The best that we can do is to struggle within the limits of uncertainty by being aware of them.

REFERENCES

American Psychiatric Association. (1994). *Diagnostic and statistical manual of mental disorders—fourth edition.* (DSM-IV). Washington, D.C.: American Psychiatric Association.

Appelbaum, P.S. & Gutheil, T.G. (1991). *Clinical handbook of psychiatry and the law, second edition.* Baltimore: Williams and Wilkins.

Apter, A., van Praag, H.M., Plutchik, R., Sevy, S., Korn, M., & Brown, S.L. (1990). Interrelationships among anxiety, aggression, impulsivity, and mood: A serotonergically linked cluster? *Psychiatry Research, 32,* 191–199.

Archer, D. & Gartner, R. (1984). *Violence and crime in cross-national perspective*. New Haven, CT: Yale University Press.

Blue, H.C. & Griffith, E.H. (1995). Sociocultural and therapeutic perspectives on violence. *Psychiatric Clinics of North America, 18*, 571–587.

Busch, K.G., Zagar, R., Hughes, J.R., Arbit, J., & Bussell, R.E. (1990). Adolescents who kill. *Journal of Clinical Psychology, 46*, 472–485.

Bushman, B.J. & Cooper, H.M. (1990). Effects of alcohol on human aggression: an integrative research review. *Psychological Bulletin, 107*, 341–354.

Comas-Diaz, L. & Griffith, E.E.H. (1988). *Clinical guidelines in cross-cultural mental health*. New York: John Wiley & Sons.

Davis, S. (1991). Violence by psychiatric inpatients: a review. *Hospital and Community Psychiatry, 42*, 585–590.

Eichelman, B. (1988). Toward a rational pharmacotherapy for aggressive and violent behavior. *Hospital & Community Psychiatry, 39*, 31–39.

Emde, R.W. (1993). The horror! The horror! Reflections on our culture of violence and its implications for early development and morality. *Psychiatry: Interpersonal & Biological Processes, 56*, 119–123.

Farrington, D.P. (1989). Early predictors of adolescent aggression and adult violence. *Violence & Victims, 4*, 79–100.

Fava, M., Anderson, K., & Rosenbaum, J.F. (1990). Anger attacks: Possible variants of panic and major depressive disorders. *American Journal of Psychiatry, 147*, 867–870.

Fava, M., Anderson, K., & Rosenbaum, J.F. (1993). Are thymoleptic-responsive anger attacks a discrete clinical syndrome? *Psychosomatics, 34*, 350–355.

Freud, S. (1953). *Civilization and its discontents, vol. 21, The standard edition of the complete psychological works of Sigmund Freud*. Strachey, J., Freud, A., Strachey, A., & Tyson, A. (Tr.). London: Hogart Press.

Gartner, R. (1995). Methodological issues in cross-cultural large-survey research on violence. In R.B. Ruback & N.A. Weiner (Eds.), *Interpersonal violent behaviors: Social and cultural aspects* (pp. 7–24). New York: Springer.

Goldstein, A.P. (1994). *The ecology of aggression* (pp. 67–79). New York: Plenum Press.

Gottlieb, P., Gabrielsen, G., & Kramp, P. (1988). Increasing rates of homicide in Copenhagen from 1959 to 1983. *Acta Psychiatrica Scandinavica, 77*, 301–308.

Heinrichs, R.W. (1989). Frontal cerebral lesions and violent incidents in chronic neuropsychiatric patients. *Biological Psychiatry, 25*, 174–178.

Kandel, E., Brennan, P.A., Mednick, S.A., & Michelson, N.M. (1989). Minor physical anomalies and recidivistic adult violent criminal behavior. *Acta Psychiatrica Scandinavica, 79*, 103–107.

Kleinman, A. (1978). Clinical relevance of anthropological and cross-cultural research: concepts and strategies. *American Journal of Psychiatry, 135*, 427–431.

Kleinman, A. (1980). *Patients and healers in the contest of culture: An exploration of the borderland between anthropology, medicine and psychiatry*. Berkeley: University of California Press.

Kleinman, A. (1987). Anthropology and psychiatry: The role of culture in cross-cultural research on illness. *British Journal of Psychiatry, 151*, 447–454.

Kleinman, A., Eisenberg, L., & Good, B. (1978). Culture, illness, and care: clinical lessons from anthropologic and cross-cultural research. *Annals of Internal Medicine, 88*, 251–258.

Korbin, J.E. (1981). Introduction. In J.E. Korbin (Ed.), *Child abuse and neglect: Cross-cultural perspectives* (pp. 1–12). Berkeley: University of California Press.

Kruttschnitt, C. (1995). Violence by and against women: a comparative and cross-national analysis. In R.B. Ruback & N.A. Weiner (Eds.), *Interpersonal violent behaviors: Social and cultural aspect* (pp. 89–108). New York: Springer.

Leff, J. (1988). *Psychiatry around the globe: A transcultural view, Second Edition*. London: Gaskell—The Royal College of Psychiatrists.

Lester, D. (1990). Suicide, homicide and the quality of life in various countries. *Acta Psychiatrica Scandinavica, 81*, 332–334.

Lewis, D.O., Lovely, R., Yeager, C., & Della Femina, D. (1989). Toward a theory of the genesis of violence: A follow-up study of delinquents. *Journal of the American Academy of Child & Adolescent Psychiatry, 28*, 431–436.

Marazziti, D. & Conti, L. (1991). Aggression, hyperactivity and platelet imipramine binding. *Acta Psychiatrica Scandinavica, 84*, 209–211.

McDermott, J.F., Jr. (1980). Introduction. In J.F. McDermott, Jr., W.S. Tseng, & T.W. Maretski (Eds.), *People and cultures of Hawaii: A psychocultural profile* (pp. 1–4). Honolulu: University of Hawaii Press.

Messner, S.F. (1988). Research on cultural and socioeconomic factors in criminal violence. *Psychiatric Clinics of North America, 11*, 511–525.

O'Nell, C.W. (1986). Primary and secondary effects of violence control among the nonviolent Zapotec. *Anthropological Quarterly, 59*, 184–190.

O'Shaughnessy, R.J. (1994). Violent adolescent offenders. In R. Rosner (Ed.), *Principles and practice of forensic psychiatry* (pp. 357–366). New York: Chapman & Hall.

Phelan, L.A., Mills, M.J., & Ryan, J.A. (1985). Prosecuting psychiatric patients for assault. *Hospital and Community Psychiatry, 36*, 581–582.

Raine, A., Buchsbaum, M.S., Stanley, J., Lottenberg, S., Abel, L., & Stoddard, J. (1994). Selective reductions in prefrontal glucose metabolism in murderers. *Biological Psychiatry, 36*, 365–373.

Razack, S. (1994). What is to be gained by looking white people in the eye? Culture, race and gender in cases of sexual violence. *Signs, 19*, 894–923.

Reid, W.H. (1985). The antisocial personality: a review. *Hospital and Community Psychiatry, 36*, 831–837.

Reid, W.H. (1988). Clinical evaluation of the violent patient. *Psychiatric Clinics of North America, 11*, 527–537.

Singer, S.I. (1986). Victims of serious violence and their criminal behavior: subcultural theory and beyond. *Violence & Victims, 1*, 61–70.

Stone, A.A. (1984). *Law, psychiatry and morality: Essays and analysis*. Washington D.C.: American Psychiatric Press.

Swanson, J.W., Holzer, C.E. III, Ganju, V.K., & Jono, R.T. (1990). Violence and psychiatric disorder in the community: evidence from the Epidemiologic Catchment Area surveys. *Hospital & Community Psychiatry, 41*, 761–770.

Tardiff, K. (1994). Violence: Causes and nonpharmacological treatment. In R. Rosner (Ed.), *Principles and practice of forensic psychiatry* (pp. 438–443). New York: Chapman & Hall.

Treiman, D. (1994). Aggressive behavior and violence in epilepsy: guidelines for expert testimony. In R. Rosner (Ed.), *Principles and practice of forensic psychiatry* (pp. 451–460). New York: Chapman & Hall.

Treiman, D.M. (1986). Epilepsy and violence: Medical and legal issues. *Epilepsia, 27* (suppl. 2), S77–S104.

Tseng, W.S. & McDermott, J.F. (1981). *Culture, mind and therapy: An introduction to cultural psychiatry.* New York: Brunner/Mazel.

Ucko, L.G. (1994). Culture and violence: the interaction of Africa and America. *Sex Roles, 31,* 185–204.

Wagatsuma, H. (1981). Child abandonment and infanticide: A Japanese case. In J.E. Korbin (Ed.), *Child abuse and neglect: Cross-cultural perspectives* (pp. 120–138). Berkeley: University of California Press.

Westermeyer, J. (1973). On the epidemicity of amok violence. *Archives of General Psychiatry, 28,* 873–876.

Widom, C.S. (1989). Does violence beget violence? A critical examination of the literature. *Psychological Bulletin, 106,* 3–28.

Wilson, M. & Daly, M. (1995). An evolutionary psychological perspective on male sexual proprietariness and violence against wives. In R.B. Ruback & N.A. Weiner (Eds.), *Interpersonal violent behaviors: social and cultural aspects* (pp. 109–133). New York: Springer.

CHAPTER ELEVEN

Personality Disorders

Alan Buffenstein, M.D.

CASE VIGNETTES

Case 1

A 45-year-old Japanese-American man visited a university-associated mental health clinic with a chief complaint of anxiety attack. As part of an educational activity, the patient was interviewed for clinical assessment by a group of psychiatric residents of different ethnic backgrounds. The patient revealed that he was still single, lived alone, and was financially dependent on his 55-year-old brother. He had been laid off as a carpenter five years before, and had not worked since then, other than at odd jobs here and there. He felt that such unskillful work did not fit him. His elder brother, who was approaching retirement, had told him that he should seek a regular job, so that he could support himself in the future.

Personal history revealed that he had lost his mother at the age of three. His father was cold and distant, and it was his elder brother, acting as a father, who took care of him. After finishing high school, he decided to enlist in the army. He adjusted well to the structure of army life. When he was young, he was interested in girls, but he never dated, and throughout his life he seldom socialized other than occasionally going fishing with a couple of friends from high school. He lived by himself in a small house, and spent his time doing housework and taking care of the yard.

During the interview, he appeared to be a quiet person. He did not initiate any conversation, and answered questions in a yes or no fashion. He was concerned about his future, and agreed with his elder brother that he needed a job, so that he could save money for his own retirement. Unfortunately, each time he picked up the paper he found that he became nervous, and was afraid that he might be turned down from any application for employment.

The residents were in agreement that the patient suffered from an anxiety disorder, but they were divided in diagnosing a personality disorder. Some residents, mostly of Caucasian background, felt that the patient was suffering from a personality disorder, with problems of being inadequate, asocial, passive, or dependent; others, mainly of Asian background, felt that even though he was not a typical Asian American, his behavior pattern was not abnormal to the extent of being pathological.

Discussion

The concept of normal or abnormal is very much influenced by sociocultural attitudes, particularly in relation to whether a person is independent or dependent, adequate or inadequate, or active or passive. A middle-aged person, depending on his elder brother for financial support, may be seen as inadequate and dependent according to the norms of American culture, but this may not necessarily be true for other cultures. This patient's behavior may not be desirable, but it might be considered acceptable, based on the cultural assumption that it was the elder brother's duty to take care of his brother, if the latter had difficulty taking care of himself. Indeed, the elder brother never criticized the patient's behavior as "inadequate" or "dependent." He was merely concerned about the patient's security from a financial point of view. While it was clear that the patient needed some kind of help to improve his life situation, it was not clear that the patient deserved a diagnosis of personality disorder.

Case 2

An attractive Italian-American female patient was seen in the intensive care unit for psychiatric consultation following a mild overdose of pills. The patient had a long psychiatric history with several suicidal gestures and multiple psychiatric hospitalizations. She had previously been diagnosed as having prominent borderline and histrionic personality features, including seductiveness, manipulativeness, and rapid shifts from idealizing to denigrating her relationships. A new psychiatric resident from a Middle Eastern country interviewed the patient, observed by an experienced psychiatric nurse. The resident was very taken by the patient's story of being misunderstood and mistreated by men. He caressed her forehead and her hair in an attempt to soothe her and sympathize with her. He promised to do everything he could to help the patient. Following the interview, the nurse attempted to discuss the case with the resident. She talked about the patient's personality traits, and discussed disposition and follow-up considerations. She gently pointed out the need to carefully maintain doctor–patient boundaries with this manipulative patient. The resident listened quietly, and then finally spoke up: "In my country, women do not tell men what to do."

Discussion

Norms for interpersonal behavior may vary widely across cultures, genders, and age groups. The patient's histrionic traits of emotionality, seductiveness, drama, and novelty-seeking must be carefully evaluated in relation to degree of distress or impairment. In this case, the new psychiatric resident was flattered by the patient's response to him, and, perhaps because of his own cultural background, did not recognize the patient's personality disorder, and the risk that she would become increasingly demanding and provoking if he became overly sympathetic. At the same time, he was not culturally prepared to accept supervision from a female, even if she were more knowledgeable and experienced.

INTRODUCTION

This chapter will focus on the impact of culture on the assessment of personality disorder. The relationship between culture and personality will briefly be reviewed, including: the theory of ethnic character; the impact of migration and acculturation in personality assessment;

and issues regarding the assessment of personality disorders in general. Finally, cultural aspects within the assessment of personality disorders will be presented, including suggestions for clinical practice.

The diagnosis of personality disorder is particularly susceptible to evaluator bias, and inter-evaluator agreement is relatively low. Personality disorder occurs at a deeper and more profound level compared with symptom or behavior, and is not usually perceived by the person as the source of their distress. Culture obviously impacts powerfully on the formation of the structure of personality and the choice of symptom manifestation.

CULTURE AND PERSONALITY

Concept of Self and Society

In psychoanalytic theory, the two most critical periods for normal development of personality are birth through the oedipal conflict, and adolescence. It is during these periods that the individual's ego develops by integrating psychosexual, psychosocial, and identity elements. Growth, maturation and individuation are all terms used to imply a process of self-realization and mutual recognition. One's identified culture and subculture provide a forum in which the individual self can transcend into identity consciousness. Early and core identifications are formed, initially, through the relationship with the mother, and later extend to the family, relatives, and eventually outsiders through school and other sources.

Personality is shaped by culture through a process of conflict resolution surrounding the individual self and value systems as the individual adapts to the realities of a larger societal reality (Erikson, 1960). The goal of individuation is for the individual to establish a degree of cohesiveness and integration surrounding the tasks of identity formation and the ability to deal with intimacy with others. Failure to achieve these tasks means that relationships will be distorted and are loaded in the direction of fascination and imagination (Hall, 1983). Flexibility within the individual, in terms of social responsiveness, becomes limited, and there is a loss of underlying stability (Menninger, 1967).

Specific subcultures subsume value systems that differ so that the concept of self changes in terms of ego boundaries. The concept of self may include the family and extended kin group in some cultures, but not in others. Individuals will accept a gradation of intimacy from family to stranger, and there exists a psychosocial homeostasis so that all members within a given subculture understand the rules of interaction (Hsu, 1985). The concept of self and society is relevant to the clinician in the assessment of issues such as ego boundaries, enmeshment, selfishness, and emotional dependency.

Society and Personality

Individuals behave differently when they become part of a group. Freud (1922) hypothesised that, in becoming part of a group, an individual is pushed to regress to a communal set of values that is inherently more primitive in nature. Groups, therefore, need to maintain a high degree of internal structure, as well as external sets of rules, such as taboos against incest and exogamy, in order to avoid fragmentation and maintain group cohesiveness.

Within the group context it is seen that individuals with personality disorders experience symptoms and display behaviors that reveal their underlying problems. Maladaptive behavior associated with personality disorders almost always occurs in the interpersonal realm and is characterized by merging of personal boundaries (Perry & Vaillant, 1989). Borderline individuals are especially likely to substitute identifications for object choice and get caught up in the culture of the group.

Culture influences the particular pathoplasty or shape of symptom formation, as well as acting as a direct pathogenic influence on the development of personality. Child-rearing practices with significant differences across cultures, family-based experiences such as over-conformity to social expectations in Asian cultures, and societal influences between cultural subgroups, may function as pathogenic/pathoplastic factors of personality disorder. For example, Eastern Jews in Israel tend toward hysterical expressiveness compared to Western Jews who are more introspective and obsessional (Alarcon & Foulks, 1995).

Without cultural and subcultural validation, the individual becomes alienated and unable to find meaning in life (Opler, 1967), and will experience prolonged insults to identity. These individuals may join a gang, cult, or other such fringe group, seeking self-validation, and these groups may be over represented with individuals who are personality disordered (Wallace, 1961).

Ethnic Character

Ethnic or national character in a given society is a composite mirror of the world view, values, and ethos of that society. National character reveals the values of the culture and subsumes patterned differences for various status components, such as male or female, or older and younger son. Repressive authoritarian societies reproduce their cultural ethos in their citizenry, such that oppressor groups show lack of creativity and conformism. Minorities are often anxious, frightened, and hostile. Oppressed groups have the most unequivocal perception of their surroundings. Enlightened societies may produce more resilient and flexible people (Dommisse, 1983).

From an academic point of view there are different ways to conceptualize and define ethnic character:

Ideal Personality

According to anthropologist Ruth Benedict (1934), each society has a more or less clear idea of what constitutes the "good man" or the "good woman"—the kind of person an individual ought to be. Through reward and punishment, the ideological contours of a culture are impressed upon its individuals in terms of an ideal personality type. Consequently, the personalities of the majority in any society are largely reflections of the ideal personality presented by that society's culture.

Basic Personality

Abram Kardiner (1945), a psychoanalyst by training, proposed that certain culturally established techniques of child rearing shape basic attitudes toward life, form the basic personality structure characteristic of that society, and are also reflected in the society's mythology, religion, and social organization. Thus, culture and personality are dynamically interrelated systems.

Modal Personality

This term is closely related to basic personality. It represents the most common personality type in a given community (DuBois, 1944).

Migration, Acculturation, and Personality Disorders

Immigrants pose a unique group within which personality disorders are especially likely to be misdiagnosed. Presumably, there is some selection *a priori* of the type of persons who leave their native land, or of those forced out by war, poverty, and persecution. Migration and minority status place heavy cultural burdens on individuals. Those with personality disorders may tend to look for answers in the outside world as opposed to being introspective, and such individuals may find it easier to live behind a facade in a foreign country.

Issues such as language barriers, lack of knowledge of rules and regulations, limited financial means, and lack of adequate reference groups might lead to guarded behaviors, which may be misperceived as suspicious, tense, hyperserious, detached, and unemotional, and may lead to the erroneous assumption of personality disorder. Paranoid traits such as distrustfulness, rigidity, a sense of oppressiveness, anger, and adversarialism can be misapplied to minority groups and individuals.

Furthermore, the pace of acculturation may vary greatly among social groups. Groups slow to acculturate may behave in ways subject to misjudgment and criticism by the host culture. Protective behaviors, such as social isolation, may also be "medicalized" or considered pathological (Alarcon & Foulks, 1995).

The evaluation of the acculturation process can be especially revealing in the understanding of personality disorders, particularly if the individual can be referenced against a group. Personality disordered individuals will often demonstrate acculturation that deviates from the individual's reference group. This may not be readily apparent as, for example, the individual could actually appear to have assimilated very well on the surface.

METHODOLOGICAL ISSUES— DIAGNOSTIC PARADIGMS

The categorical approach to personality is symptom and behavior oriented, as in the *Diagnostic and Statistical Manual of Mental Disorders—Fourth Edition* (DSM-IV) (American Psychiatric Association, 1994), a descriptive nosology. The dimensional paradigm, in contrast, tends to ground illness within the context of life experiences and involves the interpretation of life events. Psychodynamic theories, such as ego and object relations theories (Hartman, 1958), are relevant to this approach. Within the dimensional paradigm, normality and abnormality imperceptibly merge, and personality disorder is viewed in part as a maladaptive resolution in terms of contradictory societal–cultural relations.

A third paradigm involves the psychobiology of personality disorder based on genetic selection for dominant traits and temperaments (Siever & Davis, 1991). Using this paradigm, personality disorders correspond to categorical conditions on a continuum of psychopathology. Recognized categories with genetic predisposition include: cognitive–perceptual, impulsivity–aggression, affective, and anxiety–inhibition.

PREVALENCE OF PERSONALITY DISORDERS

Ideally, cross-cultural comparison could provide an argument for social factors contributing to the etiology of various psychopathologies. In reality, cross-cultural comparisons are complicated by issues such as age, race, educational level, socioeconomic status, and other factors, such that no population within a stated cultural boundary can be assumed to be uniform. Heterogeneity within cultural groups makes a true determination of the cultural differences in frequency of personality disorders exceedingly difficult.

Antisocial personality disorder (ASPD) and borderline personality disorder (BPD) are well-defined impulse control disorders with clear behavioral pathology, which makes them reliable for research (Paris, 1992). Impulsivity and suicide appear to be related. Cross-cultural studies of suicide show that the rate of suicide in the young is highest in areas where there is the most social disintegration. Since suicidality is often related to BPD, Moriya et al. (1993) hypothesize that BPD could be more common in societies undergoing rapid change. Denmark has a low incidence of murder, a high incidence of suicide, a high normative for anger turned inward, and a basic or modal character, which includes depressive traits and passive aggression. Burma, on the other hand, has a high murder rate and its modal personality includes externalization, paranoia, and antisocial trends. Perry and Vaillant (1989), however, report that there is no firm data to link any personality disorder with any specific culture.

Dahl (1986), using the DSM-III (1980), reported that in 231 psychiatric admissions in Norway, 45% had been diagnosed with personality disorder, of which 44% had one diagnosed, 36% had two, and borderline and schizotypal were present in 20% each. Oldham and Skodol (1991), using similar criteria, evaluated 129,000 patients in New York state mental health facilities and found a prevalence rate for personality disorder of 10.8%, of which one-sixth had BPD. Surveys in Germany and the United States in nonpsychiatric populations put the prevalence rate for any personality disorder equally at about 10%. Casey and Tyrer (1986), in a primary care setting in Britain with non-psychiatric patients, found a rate of 34%, and a high correlation with alcohol abuse and anxiety states.

SPECIFIC PERSONALITY DISORDERS

Borderline Personality Disorder

Borderline personality disorder is the most common personality disorder seen in clinical settings in Western countries, perhaps because of the tendency toward help-seeking. Studies put the prevalence rate in an oupatient sample at about 1% to 2%. The diagnostic entity of borderline personality disorder has only recently been adopted in the *International Statistical Classification of Diseases and Related Health Problems—Tenth Revision* (ICD-10) (World Health Organization, 1993) classification of disease. The construct has been included in the DSM-III since 1980.

Only rarely has BPD been examined for cross-cultural validity. In one study, 85 female Japanese outpatients were diagnosed using Gunderson's diagnostic index for borderlines and a Japanese version of the same with proven reliability. These were compared to Japanese and American patients evaluated in three studies done in the United States (Moriya et al., 1993). It was found that Japanese patients were less likely to be substance abusers but had higher scores for depersonalization and derealization. They were also more likely to have intense masochistic dependent relationships, less likely to be socially isolated, and more likely to be living at home. They scored similarly on anger and self-mutilation. It was also found that Japanese patients were more likely to have been previously diagnosed with neurotic or reactive depression, and that this was similar to results from Britain. The authors felt that the entity of BPD had cross-cultural validity, and that it was not confined to North American culture.

Antisocial Personality Disorder

Leighton et al. (1963) reported the prevalence of ASPD to be 11% in men and 5% in women in the general population. Weissman et al. (1978), in an eight year follow-up of a systematic survey of households in New Haven, reported a prevalence rate of 0.2%, although the follow-up sample had a higher proportion of Whites and was under-represented for the lowest social class. Antisocial personality disorder was examined in the Epidemiological Catchment Area Study (Nestadt et al., 1994) and also in Taiwan (Compton et al., 1991) using the same strict methodology. The rates in nonclinical samples ranged from 0.2% in Taiwan to 3% in the United States. In both studies, similar rating instruments and sampling populations were involved. The investigators speculated that the differences obtained may reflect true differences in the prevalence rates or other more subtle things like the tendency to give socially acceptable answers in the Taiwan culture. Additionally, there may have been differences within the tests given cross-culturally in terms of equivalency. In clinical samples reported by Widiger (1991), the median prevalence rate was 7%. Prevalence rates vary according to the demographics of the population under study more than by country or type of interview employed.

In a paper evaluating the validity of "psychopathy" in Black and White male prisoners, Kosson et al. (1990) point out that 45% of prisoners in the United States are Black. They conclude that psychopathy, as measured by the psychopathy checklist, an instrument used with Whites and Blacks, is a valid construct in Black inmates. In general, they suggest that unless race is taken into account, the psychopathy checklist is less valid and that personality factors may play a smaller part in scores assigned to Blacks compared to Whites, because of the relatively greater importance of social factors in Blacks. They question whether Blacks are overdiagnosed with ASPD. Lopez (1989) also suggests that there exists an overpathologizing bias toward Blacks and lower-class individuals relative to Whites and women for ASPD, and that clinicians are more likely to be biased in their recall of these patients. As many as half of inner city youth may have this diagnosis misapplied, as the criteria are inappropriate for settings in which value systems and behavioral rules make learning to be violent a protective and survival strategy (Alarcon & Foulks, 1995).

There may be differences in the associated features of ASPD. In a study by Lewis et al. (1983), there was an association between alcoholism and ASPD in Whites but not in Blacks. Kosson et al. (1990) found that there were racial differences in associated features, such as Blacks having less anxiety compared to their White counterparts.

Dependent Personality Disorder

The construct of dependent personality disorder would appear to overlap with borderline, histrionic, avoidant, and schizotypal personality disorders. Hirschfeld et al. (1991) reported that dependent personality disorder was diagnosed more frequently in females when standardized instruments were not used, and suggested that physicians may be responsible for the differing gender rates. The style of passivity, politeness, deferential treatment, and acceptance of others' opinions is normative in Asian and Arctic societies. Some religious groups and strongly paternalistic societies may also appear outwardly passive. Similarly, self-blame and self-deprecation may exist as conventionally acceptable means for gain in the larger social context (Alarcon & Foulks, 1995).

Other Personality Disorders

Paranoid personality disorder tends to be more frequently diagnosed in men. Immigrants, ghetto populations, and minorities may have this label misapplied because they may tend to be secretive and mistrustful of institutional agencies.

Histrionic personality disorder may be confused with the hyperemotionality seen in late adolescence and early adulthood in some ethnic communities, and with flamboyant style, for example, in persons of Mediterranean origin. The disorder is also powerfully influenced by age, and is over-represented in separated and divorced populations. The diagnosis is especially prone to gender bias from the point of view of the examiner.

Obsessive-compulsive personality disorder may be more prevalent in Caucasians than in Blacks. It is also more likely in those employed and married. The disorder might be confused with cultural values, for example, religious conservatism and overadherence to rules, as found among Orthodox Jews, or the work ethic of the Japanese.

Avoidant personality overlaps with social phobia. It may be mistaken for the quiet demeanor in Asian Americans, or in populations experiencing the migration acculturation process. It may reflect strong family-oriented values that tolerate an avoidant–dependent behavior pattern.

Narcissistic personality disorder may be misapplied more commonly to minorities, especially those that are more alienated from the mainstream, and those that hold "machismo" as a cultural value, such as younger members of Latin descent.

One might suspect that cultures with different modal personalities would vary in the prevalence of certain personality disorders. Cultures in which emotionality is prominent might be more susceptible (or less?) to histrionic personality disorder, for example. The paranoid subtype of schizophrenia is much more common in the United States compared to some other cultures. Whether paranoid personality is also more common is unknown. Unfortunately, there is insufficient data with which to resolve such hypotheses.

CLINICAL ASSESSMENT OF PERSONALITY DISORDER

History

Information is gathered through a review of the history of a patient. Record review should precede the clinical interview, particularly in the assessment of ASPD, since self-reports from such patients may not be reliable. The interview may be structured or semi-structured, and may involve the use of rating scales or questionnaires. Zimmerman et al. (1986) administered the Structured Interview for DSM-III Personality to compare groups in which there was additional informant involvement. In their clinical sample, the rate of personality disorder went from 34% to 57% when there was an additional informant, except in the case of ASPD, where there was better reliability on the subjective interview alone. While a collateral history may not be necessary for the diagnosis of ASPD, it would seem that it must be helpful to confirm specific facts stated in the history by the patient.

The Interview

Semi-structured interviews would seem to provide the best yield in the diagnosis of personality disorder, however, it may be best to use a selection of questions taken from multiple inventories. These should be applied consistently over time, and may include self-report inventories. Clinicians are more likely to give higher adaptive ratings to members of their own cultural group and more pathological stereotypical ratings to the racial outgroup. The use of culturally sensitive interpreters may be helpful in assessing personality disorder.

Personality Inventories and Psychological Testing

Psychological tests can increase the misdiagnosis of personality disorders unless cultural modifiers are employed. There may be cultural differences in the attitudes toward test-taking as well as cultural variability in responses, for example, in acquiescence or the provision of socially desirable answers. For a test to have validity, it should have cultural isomorphism to the population under scrutiny, as tests tend to reflect the relative values of the society. In Americans, for example, values of competition, independence, and achievement may be implicitly built into the test situation.

Okozaki and Sue (1995) investigated cultural considerations regarding psychological assessments of Asian Americans. In their discussion on methodology, they emphasized the need for discriminating between the etic and emic approaches; the etic perspective referring to the assumption of universality or culture-freeness of the construct, whereas the emic perspective refers to the cultural-specific point of view. Studies that apply Western-derived measures involving Asians have to maintain not only equivalence in translation, but must also accurately convey the concept. Caution has to be taken in the interpretation of trait personality tests such as the Minnesota Multiphase Personality Inventory (MMPI). Asian patients for example show more introversion, depression, self-abasement, and lack of self-confidence if results are tabulated using traditional Western norms. However, from the Asian perspective, these traits may reflect more positive attributes such as filial piety, modesty, and respect for authority.

When evaluated by means of projective testing, Chinese Americans tended to have themes of shame, and attitudes toward authority figures that were qualitatively different from those of non-Asians (Okazaki & Sue, 1995). These could be interpreted as either conflicts over authority, or as reflecting cultural ideals with adaptive solutions to conflict. The fact that Chinese attach different meanings to colors such as red and white is an example of the need for culturally appropriate interpretations of projective tests.

In a court-ordered correctional program, Blacks compared to Whites had higher scores on the narcissistic, paranoid, and hypomanic scales (Hamberger & Hastings, 1992). Such characteristics may actually reflect a realistic adaptation to living in an oppressive and prejudicial society. These findings serve to reinforce the need to contextualize these abnormal profiles to reference groups.

The affiliation felt by individuals within different cultures for their value systems has to be understood in order for trait analyses to hold validity. Yang and Bond (1990) combined both emic and etic approaches to give a derived trait scale to 2000 Chinese students, and identified five basic emic dimensions of Chinese personality. These were social orientation/self-centeredness; competence/impotence; expressiveness/conservatism; self-control/impulsiveness and optimism/neuroticism. They compared these to five derived American traits: extraversion, agreeableness, conscientiousness, emotional stability, and culture. Overall, Western-derived trait inventories might lead to erroneous misdiagnosis of personality disorder in Chinese.

SUGGESTED CLINICAL GUIDELINES

1. Learn the history of the patient's particular culture and subculture, and the degree of acculturation for that individual. This is particularly important when evaluating immigrants, persons of minority status, and cases where there may be gender discrimination.

2. Accurate and comprehensive history-taking, a complete interview and interpretation of tests from both an etic and an emic perspective are essential if one is to appreciate the nuances of personality disorder.

3. The clinician should consider the social, occupational, and personal context in which the patient must function, giving careful attention to how the patient has handled sentinel events and decisions in the past, and paying attention to the patient's entire personality, including adaptive, as well as maladaptive traits.

4. Maximal usage should be made of collateral information from family, neighbors, and others who know the person, his or her past life pattern, and the subculture with which he or she identifies him or her self. An interpreter or a member of the reference group may provide invaluable assistance in the evaluation, provided this can be done without breaking confidentiality or inhibiting the patient.

5. Culture should not be a synonym for poorly understood behavior or personality traits. Patients with personality disorders may attempt to conceal their difficulties under the guise of culture, and cultural differences may be misinterpreted as personality disorders.

6. Guard against distortion or bias in assessment due to one's own social, ethnic, and cultural background. Signs such as emotional overinvolvement or underinvolvement, fantasies of rescuing or abandoning the patient, and paranoid fears and fantasies about the patient, should alert the clinician to countertransference attitudes.

REFERENCES

Alarcon, R. & Foulkes, E. (1995). Personality disorders and culture: Contemporary clinical views (Part A). *Cultural Diversity and Mental Health*, *1*, 3–17.

American Psychiatric Association. (1980). *Diagnostic and statistical manual of mental disorders—third edition*. (DSM-III). Washington, D.C.: American Psychiatric Association.

American Psychiatric Association. (1994). *Diagnostic and statistical manual of mental disorders—fourth edition*. (DSM-IV). Washington, D.C.: American Psychiatric Association.

Benedict, R.F. (1934). *Patterns of culture*. New York: Houghton Mifflin.

Casey, P.R. & Tyrer, P. (1986). Personality, functioning and symptomatology. *Journal of Psychiatric Research*, *20*, 673–681.

Compton, W., Helzer, J., Hwu, H.G., Yeh, E.K., McEvoy, M., Tipp, M., & Spitznagel, E. (1991). New methods in cross-cultural psychiatry: Psychiatric illness in Taiwan and the U.S. *American Journal of Psychiatry*, *148*, 1697–1704.

Dahl, A. (1986). Some aspects of DSM-III personality disorders illustrated by consecutive sample of hospitalised patients. *Acta Psychiatrica Scandinavica*, *73* (Suppl 328), 61–66.

Dommisse, J. (1983). *The case of South Africa: The mental health effects of apartheid*. Portsmouth, VA: J. Dommisse.

DuBois, C. (1944). *The people of Alor*. Minneapolis: University of Minnesota Press.

Erikson, E. (1960). The problem of ego identity. In M. R. Stein (Ed.), *Identity and anxiety*. Glencoe: The Free Press.

Freud, S. (1922). Other accounts of collective mental life. *Group psychology and the analysis of the ego*. New York: Liveright.

Hall, J. (1983). Basic concepts in Jungian Psychology. *Jungian dream interpretation* (pp. 9–19). Toronto: Inner City Books.

Hamberger, L.K. & Hastings J.E. (1992). Racial differences on the MCMI in an outpatient clinical sample. *Journal of Personality Assessment*, *58*, 90–95.

Hartmann, H. (1958). *Ego psychology and the problem of adaptation*. New York: International Universities Press.

Hirschfeld, R., Shea, M., & Weise, R. (1991). Dependent personality disorder: Perspectives for DSM-IV. *Journal of Personality Disorder*, *5*, 135–149.

Hsu, F. L. K. (1985). The self in cross-cultural perspective. In A.J. Marsella, G. DeVos, & F.L.K. Hsu (Eds.), *Culture and self: Asian and Western perspectives*. New York: Tavistock Publications.

Kardiner, A. (1945). The concept of basic personality structure as an operational tool in the social science. In R. Linton (Ed.), *The science of man in the world crisis* (pp.107–122). New York: Columbia University Press.

Kosson, D., Smith, S. S., & Newman, J. P. (1990). Evaluating the construct validity of psychopathy in Black and White male inmates. *Journal of Abnormal Psychology*, *99*, 250–259.

Leighton, D., Harding, J., Macklin, M., Hughes, C., & Leighton A. (1963). Psychiatric findings of the Stirling County Study. *American Journal of Psychiatry*, *119*, 1021–1026.

Lewis, C., Cloninger, C., & Pais, J. (1983). Alcoholism, antisocial personality and drug use in a criminal population. *Alcohol and Alcoholism, 18,* 53–60.

Lopez, S. (1989). The assessment of psychopathology in racial and ethnic minorities. In J. N. Butcher (Ed.), *Clinical personality assessment* (pp. 145–146). New York: Oxford University Press.

Menninger, K. (1967). *The vital balance.* New York: The Viking Press.

Moriya, N., Miyake,Y., Minakawa, K., Ikuta, N., & Nishizono-Maher, A. (1993). Diagnosis and clinical features of borderline personality disorder in the East and West: A preliminary report. *Comprehensive Psychiatry, 34,* 418–423.

Nestadt, G., Samuels, J., Romanoski, A., Folstein, M., & McHugh, P. (1994). DSM-III personality disorders in the community. *American Journal of Psychiatry, 151,* 1055–62.

Nuckolls, C. (1992). Toward a cultural history of the personality disorders. *Social Science and Medicine, 35,* 37–47.

Okazaki, S. & Sue, S. (1995). Cultural considerations in psychological assessment of Asian Americans. In J. N. Butcher (Ed.), *Clinical personality assessment* (pp. 107–119). New York: Oxford University Press.

Oldham, J. & Skodol, A. (1991). Personality disorders in the public sector. *Hospital Community Psychiatry, 42,* 481–487.

Opler, M. (1967). *Culture and social psychiatry.* New York: Atherton Press.

Paris, J. (1992). Social risk factors for borderline personality disorder: A review and hypothesis. *Canadian Journal of Psychiatry, 37,* 510–515.

Perry, C. & Vaillant, G. E. (1989). Personality disorders. In Kaplan, H. I. & Sadock, B. J. (Eds.). *Comprehensive textbook of psychiatry/V* (p. 1352). Baltimore: Williams & Wilkins.

Robins, L. & Regier, D. (1991). *Psychiatric disorders in America.* New York: The Free Press.

Siever, L. & Davis, K. (1991). A psychobiological perspective on the personality disorders. *American Journal of Psychiatry, 148,* 1647–1658.

Wallace, A. (1961). *Culture and personality, second edition.* New York: Random House.

Weissman, M., Myers, J., & Harding, P. (1978). Psychiatric disorders in the United States urban community. *American Journal of Psychiatry, 135,* 459–462.

Widiger, T. A. (1991). DSM–IV reviews of the personality disorders: Introduction to special series. *Journal of Personality Disorders, 5,* 122–134.

World Health Organization, Division of Mental Health. (1993). *International classification of diseases* (ICD-10). Geneva: WHO.

Yang, J. & Bond, M. (1990). Cultural considerations in psychological assessment of Asian-Americans. In J. N. Butcher (Ed.), *Clinical personality assessment* (p. 112). New York: Oxford University Press.

Zimmerman, M., Pfohl, B., Stangl, D., & Corenthal, C. (1986). Assessment of DSM-III personality disorders: The importance of interviewing an informant. *Journal of Clinical Psychiatry, 47,* 261–263.

CHAPTER TWELVE

Adolescent Psychopathology

Danilo E. Ponce, M.D.

CASE VIGNETTES

Case 1

A 15-year-old Filipino female was admitted to an adolescent psychiatric inpatient unit because of lack of sleep, not eating, withdrawal, isolation, inability or refusal to communicate, "bizarre behaviors" such as turning up the television in the "wee" hours of the morning, "hearing voices," and threats of killing herself if she were removed from home and placed elsewhere, such as in a hospital.

The patient and her family had migrated from the Philippines to the United States four years prior to admission. She was reportedly doing quite well until two years prior to admission when she abruptly refused to go to school. She had menarche during the summer of that school year, but other than that there were no significant events that might have precipitated her refusal to go to school. With mounting pressure from the school for her to return, her parents sent her back to the Philippines. While in the Philippines she also refused to go to school and continued her pattern of with-drawal, isolation, uncommunicativeness; she just watched televi-sion. She came back to the United States after a year, in time for the start of school, but she still refused to attend school. Instead, she stayed in her small room (which she shared with siblings), and did not venture outside the house. The school requested mental health services, and the workers who saw her on home visits (as she absolutely resisted any efforts to take her out of the house) vari-ously diagnosed her as having major depression, elective mutism, agoraphobia, psychotic disorder, or schizophrenia. There were ini-tial speculations that she might have been severely physically or sexually abused, but this was quickly ruled out. Despite pressure from the school, the courts, mental health workers, and well-mean-ing relatives, the patient remained steadfastly in her room. She was placed on sertraline (an antidepressant) with no noticeable effect, and this was eventually discontinued. Her parents finally agreed to hospitalize her when her behavior became intolerably irritating, worrisome, and unintelligible to them.

While in the hospital, she initially assumed a catatonic posture—sitting in a corner, totally uncommunicative, not acknowledging the presence of anybody else, and refusing medications. On the second day of hospitalization, she surprisingly opened up to the treating male Filipino psychiatrist, who spoke to her in her dialect. She admitted to being very scared about being hospitalized, and recounted a tale of being publicly *shamed*, and *humiliated* by a teacher two years prior to admission (coinciding with the beginning of the symptoms) because "I could not hear what she was saying . . . something is wrong with my ears . . . I hear sloshing sounds . . . I vowed after that I will never go to school again, ever." A subsequent ear examination revealed a chronic middle ear infection, and a review of records also showed that she had had the ear infection more than two years earlier but that it was never adequately treated because the parents had no insurance and feared the expense. With this information, a treatment plan was developed that was success-ful in returning the girl to school.

Discussion

Shame (*hiya*), and *face* (*amor propio*) are very important and power-ful dynamics in explaining psychosocial phenomena in Filipino cul-ture. They are even more so in the adolescent girl struggling with developmental issues of identity formation. In this case, shame and loss of face were powerful enough to cause the youngster not to attend school for two years, to withstand pressure from her school, mental health workers, the courts, and her parents; and to eventually and inappropriately be diagnosed as having a psychiatric disorder(s), hospitalized, and treated with psychotropic medications.

Case 2

A 16-year-old Laotian male was taken to the emergency room of a hospital by his father because for the past few weeks he had become increasingly isolated and withdrawn, staying up late, staring at the ceiling for hours on end, talking to himself, and muttering about a "lady inside my head"; throwing objects at nonexistent persons; and not eating, consequently losing a lot of weight. After signing admission papers, the father changed his mind at the last minute, and took his son home with no explanation. Two weeks later, the youngster was back at the emergency room, this time brought by his mother and uncle.

The patient's father believed that "evil spirits" were responsible for his son's inexplicable behaviors, and he was ambivalent about seeking Western medical help. The family sought the help of local Laotian indigenous healers (shamans) but there was no noticeable improvement. The father then grudgingly instructed the mother and uncle to take the youngster back to the hospital. While in the hospital, the youngster admitted to abusing methamphetamines and being a member of a youth gang. The parents had a difficult time believing what their son told the treating psychiatrist, and admitted to being at a loss as to what to do.

Discussion

Drugs and gangs further complicate an already complicated and confusing picture in discussing cultural considerations of psychopathology in adolescence. Drugs (e.g., methamphetamines, LSD, cocaine) independently cause psychopathology, and gangs invariably result in problems related to interaction with the legal system, as well as disrupt the traditional family structure. To compound things, the impact of drugs and gangs are much more devastating and long-lasting compared to the usual *sturm und drang* conflicts we have come to expect and associate with the *normal* adolescent stage of development.

Case 3

A 14-year-old Filipino male was admitted to an inpatient pediatric unit because of withdrawal, isolation, auditory hallucinations that he claimed were coming from "the devil," and bizarre posturing and gesturing that seemed to mimic martial arts' movements.

The patient and his family migrated to the United States when he was eight years old and there were no remarkable medical or psychiatric problems reported until this current episode. The mother reported that he started exhibiting the symptoms a month after his return from the Philippines following a two-month vacation. Except for a circumcision that was performed on him, the trip was deemed uneventful from a medical or psychosocial standpoint. The mother was convinced that an evil curse had been cast on him by relatives or acquaintances in the Philippines who were jealous of his "good fortune (by virtue of being in the United States)" or who might have been offended by her son in some as yet unknown way. She initially sought the help of local indigenous healers (shamans). When the symptoms did not go away, she took him to his Filipina pediatrician, who hospitalized him. Initial differential diagnoses were Sydenham's chorea, psychoses secondary to illicit drug abuse, and psychotic disorder with catatonia.

An exhaustive workup that included EEGs, CAT scan with contrast, MRI, and HIV testing was unremarkable. The patient was started on an antipsychotic medication. This medication was discontinued after two weeks because there was no noticeable improvement in symptoms. Meanwhile, the family was more convinced than ever that the youngster was suffering from an evil spell cast on him, and they were now turning against the mother whom they now thought of as being "neglectful."

Four weeks into his hospitalization, the patient developed difficulties swallowing. The patient was transferred to the pediatric intensive care unit because of the high risk of aspiration. A myogram revealed that the posturing and gesturing were involuntary and the EMG patterns suggested a diagnosis of botulism. Benzodiazepines were given to counteract the posturing, gesturing, and dysphasia that were now thought to be due to botulism, but the symptoms persisted.

After eight weeks, the patient began exhibiting myoclonic jerks every three seconds that were bilateral in the upper and lower extremities. A repeat EEG was now abnormal, with a pattern that suggested subacute sclerosing panencephalitis (SSPE). A measles titre was obtained and confirmed the diagnosis. Despite explanation in laymen's terms as to the medical condition, the family still chose to believe that a curse was in effect, hence a shaman was allowed to perform his rituals with the youngster in the hospital.

Twelve weeks following hospitalization, the patient died due to SSPE complications. The family was gathered together and the consulting psychiatrists tried to effect a closure by processing the members' feelings, made it quite clear that the youth had died of SSPE, and absolved the mother of any "neglect." The family was relieved and quite grateful.

Discussion

This fascinating case shows the dramatic interplay of biological, psychological, and sociocultural factors in the differential diagnosis of psychopathology. Despite what eventually became a clear-cut "biological" etiology of the illness, the psychological and sociocultural factors had to be addressed as they were so intimately intertwined in dictating the clinical course of the patient.

INTRODUCTION

This chapter on Adolescent Psychopathology is one of only two chapters (the other is Geriatric Psychopathology) that makes the explicit assumption that each developmental stage is unique, hence requiring special consideration in discussing the influence of culture on psychopathology. The topic is unique in that the adolescent period and adolescents have *always* stirred controversies, and it is not easy to find consensus or unanimity when discussing *anything* pertaining to them. A brief statement of the ongoing controversies and an attempt to sort them out is therefore indicated before focusing on a specialized topic such as the impact of culture on adolescent psychopathology.

The first controversy strikes at the heart of the notion of adolescence itself: Does adolescence exist as a legitimate developmental age or stage or not? Throughout the ages there has been very little disagreement in multifarious societies regarding the onset of *puberty* as a neurophysiological phenomena (i.e., menarche, spermatogenesis, and secondary sexual characteristics) signifying the end of childhood, and the beginning of adulthood (GAP, 1968). The crux of the problem lies in the plethora of ways in which various cultures (even at different times in the same culture) have psychosocially dealt with the first few years immediately following the onset of puberty (roughly between the ages of 12 and 21)—what has now come to be known as becoming an *adolescent*, a *teenager*, or a *youth*. Historians are fond of reminding us that this period (henceforth called *adolescence* and the subjects, *adolescents*) is really just a social artifact, and a relative newcomer at that—arising as a socioeconomic strategy during the industrial period of the nineteenth century in Europe and North America to curb excess manpower and insure that adults did not get elbowed out of their industrial jobs (Aries, 1962; Demos & Demos, 1969). In nonindustrialized countries, on the other hand, where the need is the exact opposite (i.e., to have as many helping hands as possible to eke out daily subsistence), there is no equivalent of the adolescent period. There is only being a *child* and being an *adult*. In some southeast Asian countries, for example, young adolescent males become heads of households or get conscripted as soldiers early in their lives, and their female counterparts assume responsibilities for the care of their younger siblings while their parents are out all day, and sometimes all night, making a living.

The clash of cultures that held these opposing views regarding adolescents came to a head in the late 1970s and the 1980s with the exodus of countless refugees from war-torn southeast Asian countries like Vietnam, Cambodia, and Laos to Western countries. The youngsters from these countries, so used to assuming adult responsibilities, suffered from major acculturation problems, including significant clinical psychopathologies, from having to "regress" back to a more juvenile and dependent status in their host European or North American countries (Messer & Rasmussen, 1986; Nguyen & Williams, 1989).

Assuming that one gets past this first issue and is able to accept adolescence as a legitimate way-station in life, the second controversy is the continuing debate over whether adolescence is, in fact, the terrible but expected stage of *sturm und drang* as beleaguered parents, popular authors, and the movies portray it to be or whether, again, this is merely ranting by a minority of disaffected adults. The issue is not new. Hesiod, writing in the eight century B.C., and echoed by Socrates (who, in 500 B.C., wrote "Children now love luxury. They have bad manners and contempt for authority. They show disrespect to their elders and love to chatter in place of exercise") sounded very much like a contemporary parent when he said, "I see no hope for the future of our people if they are dependent on the frivolous youth of today, for certainly all youth are reckless beyond words." (GAP, 1968).

Despite a heroic and fairly convincing effort by Offer and Boxer (1991) to scientifically put the issue to rest by making large-scale, cross-cultural studies designed to show that the normative adolescent is a far cry from the sensationalized depiction of the adolescent as a perpetually rebellious, lost, anxious, sad, angry, young man or woman with a quicksilver temperament, owing no allegiance to anybody save himself or herself—the so-called "myth of the stormy period of adolescence" continues to persist and thrive, gaining currency with each successive generation. Holden Caulfield is the literary prototype of Hollywood's James Dean in the 1950s. Elvis prepared the way for the Beatles and the Rolling Stones in the 1960s, and they in turn provided role models for Janice Joplin and Jimi Hendrix in the 1970s. The "myth" continues, no less real, with today's "Generation X," with the late, lamented Kurt Cobain, and the much vilified "Gangsta Rappers."

The third issue, which is really a combination of both earlier issues, is the question of whether age/stage-specific psychopathology exists (which is implicit in the works of developmental theorists like Freud, Erikson, Piaget, Kohlberg, Bowlby, Mahler, etc.) or whether, as the *Diagnostic and Statistical Manual of Mental Disorders—Fourth Edition* (DSM-IV) (American Psychiatric Association, 1994) gingerly and delicately puts it, "The provision of a separate section for disorders that are usually first diagnosed in infancy, childhood, or adolescence is for *convenience only* and is not meant to suggest that there is any clear distinction between 'childhood' and 'adult' disorders (emphases added)" (p. 37). This is a very important consideration with profound and far-reaching clinical ramifications depending on which side one is on. For instance, to those practitioners who believe that the child/adolescent is "merely" a miniature adult, psychopathology, like depression, bipolar disorder, schizophrenia, and so forth, not only exists during these times, but for all intents and purposes *ought* to be treated as it is in adults. Hence, there are no second thoughts regarding the administration of such "proven" pharmaceuticals as neuroleptics, antidepressants, beta-blockers, anticonvulsants, lithium, oftentimes in mega-doses, "like in adults," to children and adolescents. Needless to say, proponents of the opposing view, that each age or stage requires different treatment, are of course horrified by what they consider egregious and wanton pill-pushing by their "dangerously misguided" colleagues.

By now it should be evident that discussing adolescence is certainly not an easy task. On the positive side, however, despite what may look on the surface to be a hopelessly muddled state of affairs (perhaps not unlike a "typical" adolescent, if such a person exists), things are not really all that bad. On closer scrutiny, we find that these controversies owe their continuing existence (and perhaps their insolubility) from confusing *puberty* with *adolescence*. Both puberty and adolescence are *transition periods*, and as such, are inherently imbued with a lot of ambivalence, contradiction, and paradox—where, as some pundits would put it, opposites coincide. It is quite helpful to remind ourselves, however, that although both are facets of a bigger whole (i.e., the developing and maturing person) they are separate and distinct phenomena. One is biologically driven (puberty), the other psychossocioculturally determined (adolescence). Biological maturity (puberty) does not necessarily confer or bring with it automatic psychosociocultural maturity (adulthood) as adolescent parents have shown us time and again. There is indeed a "coincidence of opposites" in adolescence in that the youngster is both a child *and* an adult, or, to be more precise, *no longer* a child but *not yet* an adult. This peculiar relationship between puberty, adolescence, and culture requires further explanation.

PUBERTY, ADOLESCENCE, AND CULTURE

"Culture," according to McDermott (1991) is ". . . not simply a layer on top of a biological core. Rather, cultural influences are woven into personality like a tapestry" (p. 408). The relationship between puberty as a biological phenomenon, and adolescence as a psychosociocultural phenomenon—what Marsella (1988) calls "internal" and "external or environmental" factors, and what Watzlawick (1993) designates as "first-order" and "second-order" realities, respectively—is best viewed as complementary, and not, as most reductionists would have it, an either/or, or a linear/causal one. That is to say, it is a mistake to think that one "causes" the other (e.g., "testosterone causes masculine, aggressive behaviors"). Rather, the relationship is more like what occurs when we speak of *genotypes* interacting with *environments* resulting in manifest behaviors or *phenotypes*. Puberty is the equivalent of the genotypes in providing the endocrinological substrates of behavior, which will interact with the prevailing psychosociocultural milieu (environment), resulting in adolescent behaviors (phenotypes). Adolescence and a particular adolescent behavior then is the "dance" that results between the "dancing" of puberty as a biological phenomenon and a particular environment. To put it more poetically, adolescence is the *music* (or noise, depending) created by the flautist (environment), playing the flute (puberty). As described in Chapter 1, "culture" in this model is a very significant part of the environment representing the sum total of beliefs, values, and assumptions of a given society (more about culture later).

Marsella (1988) hypothesizes that there is an inverse relationship between the *internal*, that is, the biological, and in our specific case, the puberty-based factors, and the *external*, that is, the psychosocio-cultural or environmentally based factors. This means that there is less cross-cultural variability when psychopathology can be traced quite obviously to biological factors, for example, "cerebro–vascular accidents." The inverse is that the more psychopathology can be traced to psychosociocultural factors and less to biological factors, the more the cross-cultural variability, as in "dissociative disorders." Similarly, Watzlawick (1993) talks about "first-order realities" as the relatively invariant, objective, essence of things "out-there," like the molecular composition of gold as a metal. "Second-order realities," on the other hand, are the result of our "opinions" or "values" regarding first-order realities. The day-to-day fluctuation of the value of gold in the stock market is an example of second-order reality. In this context, culture could be construed as a group of people's commonly shared second-order realities and, as in Marsella's dictum, one finds more variability the farther away one gets from first-order realities.

Case three is a good illustration of decidedly biological factors (subacute sclerosing panencephalitis) accounting for psychopathology in the 14-year-old young man despite the patient himself and his family wanting, or trying to impose cultural beliefs/practices onto the clinical process, in the hopes of influencing the clinical course and the outcome. Unfortunately, in the end the biological substrate eventually prevailed and the family had no recourse but to accept the alternative hypothesis (i.e., that the "cause" of the young man's psychopathology was biological). Small consolation as it may be, the positive aspect of the shift in the family's cultural perception from the etiology being an "evil curse" to a biologically based one ("virus") exonerated the mother from the guilt in her family's eyes of being a neglectful mother "for having allowed her son to be a victim of an evil curse."

On the opposite end of the spectrum is case one, the 15-year-old young woman who "lost face" and was "shamed" into refusing to go to school. She was diagnosed with almost all of the "biologically based" DSM-IV diagnoses (major depression, schizophrenia, psychotic disorder, agoraphobia), treated with antidepressants and neuroleptics, and eventually hospitalized. The biologically based reason that started the whole episode—the chronic middle ear infection—was really incidental to the case. The main issue was the potency of the cultural dynamics of "shame" (*hiya*) and "losing face" (*amor propio*) in the Filipino culture, which are capable of producing and perpetuating what in the West could be construed as "major psychopathology" (Ponce and Foreman, 1980).

Marsella's and Watzlawick's models of talking about the biological–psychosociocultural continuum was demonstrated by Mann et al. (1992) and his associates in a cleverly designed study involving cross-cultural differences in establishing the presence of attention-deficit hyperactivity disorder and disruptive behaviors in 8-year-old boys. Mental health professionals from China, Indonesia, Japan, and the United States rated the presence of hyperactive–disruptive behaviors in standardized videotape vignettes of these boys participating in individual and group activities. The results showed that the Chinese and Indonesian clinicians gave consistently higher scores than their other colleagues, suggesting rather strongly that psychosociocultural perceptions vary significantly across various cultures despite standardization of rating criteria.

When both biological (internal, first-order reality) and environmental (external, second-order reality) factors are equivocal, then there is a "borderline" quality to the clinical presentation and a moderate degree of cross-cultural variability. Adolescence fits right into this "middle ground" category, with both biological (puberty) and psychosociocultural (environment) factors equally strong in their influence, thereby accounting for the "borderline" quality of behaviors described earlier as the *sturm und drang* of adolescence.

CONTEMPORARY CULTURAL DEVELOPMENTS AND ADOLESCENT PSYCHOPATHOLOGY

Illicit Drugs and Other Mind-Altering Substances

Mind-altering drugs or substances, especially those that create and/or mimic psychopathology, such as LSD, methamphetamines, and cocaine, have drastically changed the cultural "rules" regarding adolescence. For one thing, drugs are biologically based and therefore not as susceptible to cultural influences, hence no amount of cultural suppression will prevent the appearance of psychopathology for the user. Another powerful alteration of the "rules" is the distinct probability of long-lasting negative sequelae (e.g., flashbacks) from use of these drugs, despite discontinuation of their use. The hope that sprung eternal in previous, relatively drug-free eras that, despite several turbulent years, "these too shall pass away," may no longer be warranted with early and extensive drug abuse. In addition, drug use often goes hand in hand with membership in youth gangs.

Youth Gangs

The phenomenon of youth gangs is of course not at all new. In fact in earlier times, they were quite beneficial in providing the adolescent with an opportunity to rehearse and master social behavior in groups, which is crucial in adult life. What is new is the current ominous association of youth gangs with very deadly and criminal activities such as law violations, drug use, guns, and killing.

Case three illustrates the typical disorientation and helplessness of traditional cultures (in this case, Laotian) in coping with the drug and youth gang phenomena.

Technological Advances

Advances in technology have grown exponentially, especially in the so-called "information autobahn." Computers, faxes, modems, satellite/cable television, and pagers are relentlessly and inexorably making the world into the virtual "global village" predicted by McLuhan (1968) 27 years ago. Needless to say, "pure" cultures are probably a thing of the past as a result of geographic and cultural boundaries becoming more and more blurred with increased abilities to travel and instantaneous and accessible communication with anybody anywhere in the world.

Disintegration of the Traditional Family

Quite paradoxically, as the world is consolidating into a homogenous, global village, the concept and even the composition of the traditional family is disintegrating in a majority of cultures. Ironically, technological advances that are creating this global village are also transforming the concept of "family." Husbands and fathers (or even lovers), are no longer essential with the perfection of artificial insemination and in-vitro fertilization. Half of all Western marriages now end in divorce, and the single-parent family (usually mother), with the parent working sometimes two jobs and "latchkey" children, is fast becoming the norm. The tradition of marriage itself is undergoing extensive modifications as a result of intense pressures from gay and lesbian couples. The net result of all this buffeting is that the family can no longer be relied upon to be the societal unit that will insure the transmission and perpetuation of culture. Technology and its dazzling array of wonders (e.g., video games, virtual reality, Internet) is now the arbiter, creator, instiller, maintainer, and transformer of culture. Quite simply, we have even gone beyond being *multicultural* (Time, 1993), and are now *techno-cultural*.

Discussion

Puberty then is the *biological* facet of adolescence. As such, it is more universal, ubiquitous, and less susceptible to randomness, variations, or differences in terms of cross-cultural norms or pathology. So far, only three factors have been mentioned in reference to the *environmental* aspect of adolescence—the psychological, societal, and cultural (contracted into "psychosociocultural"). A fourth dimension is spiritual. The *psychological* factor consists of the personality aspects of the individual adolescent. Personality is included with the "external" (environmental) factors, since "personality" (literally *personal* or mask) is really a social or interpersonal definition closely aligned with roles, rules, and relationships, hence "outside" the individual. The *societal* aspect of the environment consists of the system of social relationships of a particular group of human beings. The *cultural* aspect, as mentioned earlier, is that particular society's *entire way of living*—their beliefs, assumptions, expectations, standards, rules, practices, and so on (Griffith and Gonzalez, 1994). The fourth dimension, *spirituality*, refers to the intangible dimensions of human existence, such as the *meaning* or *purpose* of one's life (Newsweek, 1994), and not necessarily religion or religiosity, although it could include both. The clinical importance of meaning and purpose is nowhere more urgently and dramatically demonstrated than in adolescence and the elderly. As a concession to the growing acceptance of clinicians to talk about this dimension in their practice, the DSM-IV (American Psychiatric Association, 1994) has designated a new code, "Religious or Spiritual Problem."

To summarize, culture impacts on adolescent psychopathology by (1) suppressing or facilitating the appearance of psychopathology; (2) determining the content of psychopathology and the form(s) it will take; (3) influencing the duration and clinical course of the psychopathology; and (4) sorting out the effective from the ineffective intervention in dealing with psychopathology.

Case one very nicely illustrates all four of these points. In some other culture (e.g., Western), in some other stage of human development (e.g., childhood), a teacher yelling at a student would not have been a "big deal," and even if the yelling had led to a sense of shame and embarrassment, the outcome would probably not have been as intense or as psychopathological. Being an adolescent Filipino female, the patient exhibited the culturally correct reaction to being shamed and losing face which was to inwardly withdraw, passively suffer, and *in extremis* commit (or at least attempt) suicide. Had she been an adolescent male, the Filipino "prescription" to restore face would have been more outwardly directed—an aggressive, even violent assault on the perceived perpetrator of the "crime." Of course, these different prescriptions lead to different outcomes—in females it would usually become a health problem (i.e., depression or suicide) and have a long, protracted course (in this case, 2½ years); in males it becomes a legal or a criminal problem (i.e., assault or homicide) with an expeditious denouement.

Culture also significantly influences which interventions will work and which will not. The protracted clinical course in this case led to the psychopathology developing a life of its own, becoming functionally autonomous from the original precipitating factors. Somewhat related to, but quite independent of her being "shamed" and her subsequent "vow" not to go to school ever again, the young lady was now caught in a power struggle with members of her family and the array of agency workers involved in her case. On one hand, she could not afford to relinquish the secondary gains she had made by breaking her "vow" and giving in to parental and agency entreaties to get out of the house and go back to school. On the other hand, she could not forever resist the powerful pressures to which she was being subjected. Again, the cultural factor of "face" becomes crucial in determining a reasonably satisfactory outcome. A Filipino family caught in a similar impasse will wittingly or unwittingly look for a *deus ex machina*—a perceived, powerful outside force that will impose a solution, albeit contrived, and take matters out of the hands of the patient and/or all the key players. This has the salutary effect of preserving the integrity of everyone involved (i.e., nobody has won or lost, hence no "lost face"), and everybody can blame the outsider if things do not work out. In this case, the *deus ex machina* was the hospitalization and the male Filipino doctor, both powerful cultural icons of competence and authority. Though the solution was quite serendipitous and unplanned, in retrospect it was syntonic with the Filipino culture's belief in deference to authority (Ponce and Foreman, 1980). It *had* to be syntonic to explain the almost "miraculous" resolution of the psychopathology that had been festering for 2½ years.

SUGGESTED CLINICAL GUIDELINES

When we think of culture and adolescent psychopathology in a clinical context, we are probably going through a mental drill where, in an algorithmic fashion, we are asking ourselves the following questions: Is what I am observing in this adolescent patient psychopathological or merely a normal variant of his age? If it is psychopathological, what is the role of culture in terms of etiology, treatment, prognosis, and outcome? If there are significant cultural factors, what do I do next? With the above considerations in mind, the following guidelines recapitulate some of the points made earlier and elaborate other helpful points:

1. Setting aside biologically based psychopathology for the moment (e.g., drug or "organically" induced psychopathology), in adults the diagnosis of psychopathology is often made more or less independent of *context*, for example, the DSM-IV criteria are collections of symptoms. In contrast, with adolescents one needs to bring in a lot of *contextual* considerations. These include duration (How long has it been going on?); intensity (Has it become disruptive enough?); scope and magnitude (Is it now spilling over to school and the community?); peer influence (Is this merely an emotional contagion like an epidemic of suicide attempts?); family influence (Is this merely a *folie à deux* with mom?). The guideline is not to be too quick to find and label psychopathology based on adult norms.

2. If psychopathology is established reliably and validly in the adolescent, culture *can* influence its expression or suppression in terms of form or content. For instance, in cultures

that are more "visual and religious" (e.g., Tibetan) one would expect psychopathology to be expressed in preponderantly visual and religious terms. The same is true with cultures that have a preference for auditory or kinesthetic modes of communication and expression. Culture can also influence differences in the way psychopathology is expressed in terms of gender roles. Finally, knowing cultural "rules" and "meta rules" (e.g., "How can an outsider be effective in dealing with members of this particular culture?") will greatly enhance the clinician's effectiveness. The guideline here is to make every attempt to get key members of the adolescent's life to share their views of what the problem(s) is (i.e., their "diagnoses"), their notions of how to go about solving the problem (i.e., their "treatment plans"), and their ideas of how things would be if the problem were solved to everyone's satisfaction (i.e., their "ideal outcomes"). A master treatment plan can then be put together that incorporates elements of everybody's clinical perspective of the problem(s)—including that of the clinician, of course.

3. If culture is indeed playing a significant clinical role in a case, and the clinician is *not* a member of the adolescent patient's culture, the first thing to remember is *not* to automatically "cop out" and make a referral to "more culturally relevant resources." This is a common mistake made by relatively insecure clinicians, because "like" does not necessarily cure "like." By going through the exploration of the "clinical world view" of each of the significant members of the adolescent's life as described above, the clinician should have a fairly reliable estimate of whether his or her views are compatible with a majority of the influential members regardless of cultural affiliations. If discrepancies are minor (e.g., the clinician believes the youngster has attention deficit disorder and could benefit from a trial with methylphenidate; a father believes his son suffers from disrespect of his elders), these can be skillfully negotiated and resolved. If, however, the clinician's views are widely discrepant with a majority of the influential members in the adolescent's life (e.g., the clinician believes that the youngster has bipolar disorder and needs to be placed on lithium, carbamazepine, and clonidine, but the family believes in

the power of prayer and no medication) then perhaps it is best for the clinician to refer to somebody else. The final guideline is that a clinician can be effective even if he or she is not a member of the adolescent patient's culture by assessing compatibility between the clinician's clinical values and those of the adolescent and significant members of his life.

REFERENCES

American Psychiatric Association. (1994). *Diagnostic and statistical manual of mental disorders—fourth edition*. (DSM-IV). Washington, D.C.: American Psychiatric Association.

Aries, P. (1962). *Centuries of childhood: A social history of family life*. London: Jonathan Cape.

Demos, J. & Demos, V. (1969). Adolescence in historical perspective. *Journal of Marriage and the Family, 31*, 632–638.

Griffith, E. & Gonzalez, C. (1994). Essentials of cultural psychiatry. In R.E. Hales, S.C. Yudofsky, & J.A. Talbott (Eds.), *Textbook of psychiatry, second edition* (pp. 1379–1404). Washington, D.C.: American Psychiatric Press, Inc.

Group for the Advancement of Psychiatry (GAP) (1968). *Normal adolescence*. New York: Charles Scribner's Sons.

Mann, E., Ikeda, Y., Mueller, C., Takahashi, A., Tao, K.T., Humris, E., Li, B.L., & Chen, D. (1992). Cross-cultural differences in rating hyperactive–disruptive behaviors in children. *American Journal of Psychiatry, 149*, 1539–1542.

Marsella, A. (1988). Cross-cultural research on severe mental disorders: issues and findings. *Acta Psychiatrica Scandinavia*, Suppl 78, *344*, 7–22.

McDermott, J. (1991). The effects of ethnicity on child and adolescent development. In M. Lewis (Ed.), *Child and adolescent psychiatry: A comprehensive textbook* (pp. 408–412). Maryland: Williams and Wilkins.

McLuhan, M. (1968). *War and peace in the global village*. New York: McGraw–Hill.

Messer, M. & Rasmussen, N. (1986). Southeast Asian children in America: The impact of change. *Pediatrics, 78*, 323–329.

The new face of America: How immigrants are shaping the world's first multicultural society. (1993). *Time, 142*, no. 21.

Nguyen, N.A. & Williams, H.L. (1989). Transition from East to West: Vietnamese adolescents and their parents. *Journal of the American Academy of Child and Adolescent Psychiatry, 28*, 505–515.

Offer, O. & Boxer, A. (1991). Normal adolescent development: Empirical research findings. In M. Lewis (Ed.), *Child and adolescent psychiatry: A comprehensive textbook* (pp. 266–278). Maryland: Williams and Wilkins.

Ponce, D. & Foreman, S. (1980). The Filipinos. In J.F. McDermott, W.S. Tseng, & T. Maretzki (Eds.). *People and cultures of Hawaii: A psychocultural profile* (pp.155–183). Honolulu: University Press of Hawaii.

The search for the sacred: America's quest for spiritual meaning. (1994). *Newsweek*, November 28, 1994.

Watzlawick, P. (1993). *The language of change.* New York: WW Norton & Co.

CHAPTER THIRTEEN

Geriatric Psychopathology

Iqbal Ahmed, M.D.

CASE VIGNETTES

Case 1

A 70-year-old woman was brought for an evaluation of depression by her son. She was from a small town in Punjab, India but had been living with her son in the United States for the past year, since the death of her husband of 52 years. Four years prior to her husband's demise, her mother-in-law, whom she had nursed for 9 years, died. The patient had always been an anxious woman, who felt obligated to care for her mother-in-law even though it was very stressful. After her mother-in-law's death, she started spending more time with her three daughters in India. She was afraid that her children would abandon her. She was also concerned about the well-being of her only son, who had resided in the United States for many years with his Indian wife. Finally, her son brought her to the United States to live with him.

The patient considered her son and daughter-in-law to be too "Westernized." In turn, they expected the mother, for her own happiness, to be active and develop a social life independent of them. She refused to go to the market—she expected her daughter-in-law to do this chore, as she had dutifully done for her own mother-in-law for many, many years. She also refused to go out socially, unless accompanied by her son, because she did not believe it was proper. The patient's behaviors, unhappy mood, and her constant preoccupation with her son's well-being caused tension in the couple's relationship. The son felt guilty, but believed he had no choice but to send his mother back to India. After a family meeting, it was agreed that she would go back to India to live with her daughters, and that she and her son would visit each other.

Case 2

A 65-year-old African-American woman in declining health, which included worsening of her childhood asthma, was referred to a psychosomatic clinic for evaluation of depression. Her physician thought that her physical symptoms were worse than would be expected due to her medical condition. The patient, while acknowledging that she felt "down" and "blue," denied being "depressed." She said she could not understand what was meant by being "depressed" and she suggested that her therapist use a different term to communicate with her. The patient had been raised by her grandmother, an overprotective woman who lived in rural Georgia. The patient's mother had gotten pregnant as a teenager and had given her daughter over to her own mother. The patient grew up believing that her grandmother was her mother and that her mother was her sister.

The patient described a history of talking to various imaginary companions since her childhood. While she reported that she actually saw them and heard them, she did not believe that they were real, but instead thought they were friends she had conjured up in her imagination. She said that they had been part of her life since she became sick as a child with asthma. Her imaginary companions were not viewed by her family as pathological, but as adaptive. To this day, she has projected a childlike quality and has played with her granddaughter in a manner of much concern to her "sophisticated," college-educated son, who is a professor at a prestigious university.

Case 3

A 74-year-old first-generation immigrant Filipino male is currently hospitalized with a diagnosis of schizophrenia. He repeatedly leaves the psychiatric ward and waits for a plane to come and take him away. He believes that General Douglas MacArthur, of World War II fame, is coming by plane to rescue him from his current confinement and return him to the Philippines. He insists that the general is still alive and if he stays in the building he might miss his arrival.

Case 4

A Nisei (second-generation Japanese American) male in his 70s would hoard objects such as kitchen utensils, towels, clothes, and pencils after foraging for them on the psychiatric hospital premises. He said he needed these objects and would get upset when they were taken from him by his children and the hospital staff. This symptom seemed to worsen as he became demented. He had lived through World War II and had experienced severe hardship during that time.

DEFINITION OF AGING

Aging is an ongoing process and can be defined in chronological terms or in terms of biological, psychological, and social terms. Chronological age as a marker of growth and development is imprecise. It is an arbitrary measure of aging, perhaps particularly so among older minority adults (Jackson et al., 1990). The focus of this chapter will be on *social aging*.

Social Aging

This term refers to changes in roles and social functioning with increasing chronological age.

Definition of Aged (Old Age)

This definition generally refers to a chronological age of 65 years or more, or a point in the lifespan when there are 10 more years left in the life expectancy (Siegel & Taeuber, 1986). In certain countries such as China and Japan, people as old as 50, 55, or 60, would be considered old or aged depending on gender and legal age of retirement (Freed, 1992).

Definition of Age–Period–Cohort

This definition would be a cohort or a large group of elderly people who have grown old during the same period of history and have lived through similar historical events, such as wars, migrations, and economic and social changes, for example, *Issei* (first-generation) and *Nisei* (second-generation) Japanese Americans in the United States (Sakauye, 1992).

DEMOGRAPHY

Demographics of aging across the globe are evolving and differ in developing versus developed countries. There has been a greater proportional rise in the elderly population compared to the younger population in the developed and industrialized countries, as compared to developing countries (Hauser, 1986). This rise may be due to a number of factors, such as increased longevity from improved public health, nutrition, and medical care, and increased resources. Of similar significance may be differences in birth rates among these countries.

In the United States, there are four major groups that have been classified as ethnic minorities: African Americans; Asian Americans and Pacific Islanders; Native Americans, including Alaska natives; and Hispanic Americans. The number of ethnic elderly in the United States has doubled with each census since 1960, a pattern expected to continue well into the next century. Among Asian Americans, for example, the Chinese and Japanese populations are aging particularly rapidly as children are bringing older parents to the United States in increasing numbers. By the year 2030, ethnic elderly minority groups may constitute a majority of the elderly, particularly in certain regions and urban areas (Advisory Panel on Alzheimer's Disease, 1992).

Another demographic trend of significance for the elderly is the increased rate of modernization across the world due to increased technology, telecommunications, and travel. Consequently, the population's mobility has increased, which has led to increased urbanization, greater immigration, and less stable societies. These demographic changes have important social and economic consequences and have relevance to the understanding of the interaction of culture, ethnicity, and aging (Keith, 1990; Markides et al., 1990).

As people age, their differences increase based on life experiences, which are shaped to a significant degree by culture and ethnicity. It is important to understand concepts of normal and abnormal aging and the effects of culture and ethnicity on this developmental process, as well as epidemiologic differences in the incidence of psychopathology and diseases in the elderly, such as suicide, depression, and dementia. The interaction of age factors and cultural factors shapes our understanding of the influence of culture on psychopathology, especially as it relates to the elderly. *Age factors* include aging, period–cohort issues, generational issues, and gender effects. *Cultural factors* include culture, ethnicity, race, religion, language, country of origin, urban versus rural society, mobile versus stable society, modernization, immigration, assimilation, minority issues, and socioeconomic status.

CULTURE, ETHNICITY, AND AGING

Sociological studies of normal aging are much more prevalent than studies of the psychopathology of aging. Most literature focuses on ethnic groups and different countries as compared to different cultures.

There may be several ways in which ethnicity influences the process of aging (Markides et al., 1990). One possible influence is the cultural factors traced to the country of origin or to the particular racial or religious groups. Cultural factors may provide norms and values and other resources that make the experience of aging different from that of the dominant culture. Some of the cultural patterns seen in minorities may have emerged in response to challenges faced in the host culture. Ethnicity, for example, may have different meanings as people age. Cohort effects may reflect socialization to the host culture, and period effects are reflective of the historical experiences of that particular ethnic cohort. A particular issue is the minority status and possible discrimination and subordination within society. Specific aspects of the aging process itself may be affected by these variables. These include the life course, gender roles, esteem, and intergenerational issues.

Life Course

The course of life from birth to death could be conceptualized as a cultural unit. There are cultural effects on life course such as: age norms; roles (e.g., reproductive and family responsibility); age grading (whether it is formal or informal); life stage rituals (which have cultural meanings and act as social markers of the stages); the concept of unity of life course (Hindu culture); uniformity (in rural societies) or multiplicity (in urban societies) of life course; life stage parameters and differentiation; transitions (abrupt versus gradual); and evaluation of life stages (Fry, 1988). Concepts such as Freudian or Ericksonian stages of development might be unique to Western culture. Other cultures might have different concepts of discrete stages in the life course or may have less defined stages of development.

Universality of the Aging Process

While cultural factors clearly affect the aging process, leading to differences among the aged in different cultures, there is some universality to the aging process. Factors affecting the *esteem* in which older people are held are: (1) control by the elderly of resources, including information, technology, and the environment; (2) continuity in role shifts; (3) ongoing responsibility and continued involvement in valued activities; (4) the presence of extended families; and (5) socioeconomic homogeneity (Silverman & Maxwell, 1983; Lee & Kezis, 1981). However, deference to the elderly is not distributed uniformly—women receive less of it (Silverman & Maxwell, 1978). Older people who are "intact" are accorded high status and are treated well (Glascock & Feinman, 1986).

Cross-cultural studies show that the experience of aging is different for men and women. This is particularly noted in *gender roles*, with a male/female reversal in late life in many unrelated cultures (Guttman, 1975). Men move from a position of active to passive mastery while women move from passive to active mastery. This has been related to "the emergency of parenting." Women have functioned primarily in the domestic domain and surrendered aggressive tendencies to provide emotional support to the family. Men have functioned in the public domain and have given up dependency needs that would interfere with physical and instrumental support. Once children mature and assume responsibility for themselves, each gender recaptures the characteristics that were repressed (Fry, 1988).

Intergenerational Issues

Issues of filial responsibility, filial piety, familism, and dependency shape intergenerational relationships (Fry, 1988). Filial piety requires children to be obedient, to fulfill obligations, and to show respect for their parents with near religious devotion during and after their lifetimes (Ikels, 1980). Familism is the viewing of the family as the center of the lives of its members, young and old alike (Johnson, 1983). These values tend to benefit the older generations, and are affected by culture and ethnicity.

There are also differences between the generations in the degree of acculturation, especially in immigrant families, as well as in the expectations one generation may have of the others regarding these values in the context of the modern American reality. There has to be negotiation and accommodation between the generations to work through feelings of disappointment, avoid ongoing conflict, and have protective influences on the mental health of the elderly as well as their children (Markides, 1990).

ETHNICITY, MINORITY STATUS, AND PSYCHOPATHOLOGY IN THE AGED

Interactional Mechanisms

The life satisfaction, morale, and mental and physical health status of the elderly are affected by adaptation or adjustment to old age. One theoretical perspective in understanding the relationship between ethnic elderly and psychopathology has been the *double-jeopardy hypothesis*, which states that being old and a member of a minority constitutes a double disadvantage (Dowd & Bengston, 1978). However, research actually suggests that while differences in various indicators are still found in elderly populations, age levels rather than accentuates cultural and behavioral differences (Rosenthal, 1986).

Other theoretical perspectives suggest that the stress of modernization and acculturation on immigrant elderly may also affect the mental health of the ethnic elderly—*the acculturation stress hypothesis*. Acculturation of younger generations may have negative influences on the psychological well-being of their older parents (Markides, 1990). The ethnic elders may find that the values of the dominant culture of their adopted country might be very different from their points of origin and early life experiences (Freed, 1992). They might come from cultures in which children were expected not only to care for their aged parents, but also to live together with them.

While modern American society does maintain family responsibility in terms of care for aged parents, it does not stress their living together. The elderly who expected to be cared for in their old age but find that they have to live independently, may end up being disappointed. They get caught in a conflict between dependence and independence, activity and passivity. They might find that only illness allows them to be dependent. Some ethnic families, such as the Japanese, might feel so responsible for the care of sick elders that they encourage excessive dependence and passivity (Sakauye, 1992).

Reviews of the relationship between ethnicity and mental illness suggest that this is a complex relationship (Wong & Reker, 1985; Markides, 1986; Sakauye, 1992; Stanford & Du Bois, 1992; Browne et al., 1994). There appears to be support for the double-jeopardy hypothesis with the stress of acculturation, discrimination, language barriers, and lower socioeconomic status a result from being a ethnic minority. The elderly may also have diminished physical and psychological resources, as well as fewer opportunities for educational, occupational, or social involvement.

However, there may also be protective factors for ethnic elderly. For example, ethnic identity may function as a buffer in reducing the stress related to identity loss that often occurs in old age. The ability of ethnic elders to adjust to aging was heightened by congruence of their values with those of their peer groups, not of their children (Browne et al., 1994). In addition, intergenerational solidarity, familism or family closeness, the continued role of the three-generational family, and emotional and economic support as a result of filial piety lead to increased life satisfaction, decreased depression and suicide, and increased functional capacity.

Factors that affect the incidence of mental disorders or their presentation among the ethnic elderly include overall incidence in the country of origin, cohort factors such as immigrant status, gender, age, and time since immigration, mental health prior to immigration, and evaluative methods used, including psychological tests and rating scales.

Mental Illness in Different Countries

Comparing the rates of mental illness in various countries, there is a lower incidence of Alzheimer's dementia in non-Western countries, but a similar incidence of vascular dementia and behavioral symptoms in patients with dementia (Homma, 1994). The incidence of depression was found to be low in Japan. The differences may have been due to true cultural differences or to methodological differences related to diagnostic criteria and measurement tools.

In the Taiwan Psychiatric Epidemiologic Project (TPEP), using methodology similar to the National Institute of Mental Health Epidemiologic Catchment Area Study (NIMH ECA) Program, six disorders, including manic episodes, schizophrenia, drug dependence, panic disorder, antisocial personality, and transsexualism were not identified in the elderly age group in either six-month or lifetime periods across the three study sites (Yeh et al., 1994). In comparison with the NIMH ECA Yale study, which used almost identical methodology, the most conspicuous differences in the six month prevalence of mental disorders between these two studies was the finding of 0.3% schizophrenia and 0.1% bipolar disorder among the elderly in New Haven versus no such case identified in the TPEP. In view of the fact that these disorders were identified in the life-time period among younger age groups, but not in the elderly age groups, it was suggested that patients with these disorders have poor survival rates, and do not live long enough to reach the age of 65 in the Taiwan community. Further cohort studies may be needed to confirm this speculation.

COHORT FACTORS AMONG UNITED STATES ETHNIC MINORITIES

The historical experience and cultural context of ethnic elders is also important, because these factors influence their definition of illness (medical and psychiatric), their expectation of the health care delivery system, the time at which they choose to enter into treatment, and the person and/or system from which treatment is sought (Baker & Lightfoot, 1993). Ethnic minority elderly frequently have experienced adversity and prejudicial treatment in their relationship with the majority culture. Legalized segregation (African Americans), exclusionary immigration laws (Chinese), internment during World War II (Japanese), backlash against immigration (Hispanics), genocidal acts before and after the United States Indian Wars (Native Americans), and the overthrow of a sovereign government (Hawaiians) are parts of American history that ethnic elders recall.

There are differential patterns of adaptation and coping among the immigrant elderly that are a function of length of residency in the United States, historical events that led up to migration, degree of familiarity with the larger culture, and presence of kin, cultural and religious institutions. In addition to the stigma of mental illness, which is more prevalent in the elderly, the ethnic elders and their families may not define mental disorders as "illnesses" to be treated by Western medicine, but as conditions that bring shame upon the family (Sakauye, 1992; Baker & Lightfoot, 1993). This definition would affect the rates of incidence of mental disorders reported in the different studies.

African Americans have significantly higher levels of general life satisfaction after age 65 in addition to greater happiness, although the latter was a nonsignificant trend (Stanford & Du Bois, 1992). Hispanic-American mental health data support the notion that the Hispanic elderly who are most vulnerable to mental illness are those who suffer from more social and economic deprivation. There also appears to be evidence of protective effects from the Hispanic family and kin networks. While there were lower levels of life satisfaction in Native Americans compared to Whites and Blacks, these were lower still among their younger generation. There was also a positive correlation between life satisfaction and mental health among older Native Americans.

Studies of mental health among Asian Americans (such as Chinese, Japanese, Koreans, and Indochinese) and Pacific Islanders (such as Hawaiians, Samoans, and Micronesians) are few, but suggest that the prevalence of psychopathology is similar to the larger population and appears to be affected by both acculturation stress and socioeconomic stress (Sakauye, 1992; Stanford & DuBois, 1992; Browne et al., 1994). While both males and females are affected by these factors, females tend to have higher rates of impairment in the areas of affective, anxiety, and somatoform disorders, while males tend to have higher rates of substance abuse/dependence and suicide.

An epidemiological study of Asian Americans found higher rates of depression compared to Whites (Kuo, 1984). Koreans (the most recent immigrant group) had the highest rate of depression among all the ethnic groups. Among those over 60 years of age, those with the lowest depression scores were the Chinese. The aged were not the most depressed within the ethnic groups except among the Koreans. Among the different ethnic groups, only the Koreans over age 40 had greater depression scores than those below 30 years of age.

Most Korean elders immigrate to the United States to join younger family members who preceded them. Their families tend to be geographically dispersed, however, so that community networks are difficult to access without transportation. Studies of Korean and Indochinese elderly suggest that the elderly immigrants and refugees have poorer social adjustment in their new country than their younger counterparts (Browne et al., 1994). This appeared to be related to a number of factors such as education, knowledge of English, preparation for adjustment to life in America, socioeconomic status, and absence of close family and ethnic ties.

The issue of the cohort experience of immigration, acculturation, and discrimination as related to psychopathology is illustrated in studies of the different Japanese generations: Issei (first), Nisei (second), and Sansei (third) (Sakauye, 1992). Many Nisei seen in psychiatric treatment show hoarding behavior and paranoid trends related to insecurity about further losses based on their experiences of internment during World War II.

Little is known about the mental health of Hawaiian elders (*kupuna*), but they might be at increasing risk for mental health problems with the changing role of the *kupuna*.

SPECIFIC GERIATRIC PSYCHOPATHOLOGY IN THE UNITED STATES

Suicide

The rates of completed suicide by older African Americans, Native Americans and Alaskan Natives, Asian Americans and Pacific Islanders, and Hispanic Americans are lower than for older Whites, but there are exceptions (Baker, 1992). The rates of completed suicide for Whites ages 75–84 and 85 and older are exceeded by Chinese and Japanese Americans of similar ages. The highest rates of completed suicide among the ethnic minority elders were observed in older Japanese and Chinese men.

A possible explanation is that cultural attitudes toward suicide in Japan may be carried over into the Japanese-American context. The Japanese may commit suicide as a way to resolve a difficult situation or to atone for an inappropriate act and resolve an interpersonal conflict. The older Chinese men are a "bachelor cohort." Chinese male immigrants were prohibited from bringing their wives from China or intermarrying. They were alone with marginal resources. They experienced acculturation stress without the traditional cultural context, and did not establish a positive relationship with the dominant culture. They have higher rates of completed suicides.

Dementia

A number of authors have reviewed the incidence and prevalence of mental disorders in specific ethnic elderly cohort groups (Markides, 1986; Stanford & Du Bois, 1992; Sakauye, 1992; Baker & Lightfoot, 1993; Browne et al., 1994). Inadequate data have been collected to provide precise delineation of the incidence and prevalence of dementia especially *Alzheimer's dementia* (AD) among the four major ethnic minority groups in the United States (Advisory Panel on AD, 1992). Data from a number of studies have suggested that cognitive impairment, a possible indicator of dementia, is more frequent in ethnic populations. Epidemiologic catchment area studies reported relatively higher levels of cognitive impairment among adult African-American and Hispanic populations, almost double that in the general population. Other than an actual increase in cognitive impairment, an alternative hypothesis to explain the differences has been that the instruments used in the study were not culture sensitive.

Studies also indicate that Black elderly may be more prone to multi-infarct and alcoholic dementias due to the prevalence of obesity, diabetes, hypertension, and earlier and heavier use of alcohol among alcoholics (Baker, 1994). Studies of AD in China show similar prevalence to the United States and a possible lower prevalence in Japan (Advisory Panel on AD, 1992; Homma, 1994). However, these findings cannot be extrapolated to Asian Americans.

EVALUATIVE TOOLS

In addition to the effect of cultural factors on the process of clinical evaluation as described in Chapter 1, the potential cultural bias of psychological tests and rating scales has to be considered. This has been of particular concern with regard to instruments used to evaluate cognitive function (Advisory Panel on AD, 1992; Lowenstein, 1994, 1995). Efforts to develop culturally appropriate tests involve proper translation into the different languages as well as modifying content. These tests have to be evaluated with the different ethnic groups for validity and reliability. Once appropriate tests are developed and used, epidemiological studies will provide a clearer picture of the true incidence and prevalence of disorders such as dementia and depression in the elderly.

Kua (1994), studying the Chinese population in Singapore, adapted the Geriatric Mental State of Copeland for cultural differences. For example, many Chinese elderly remember their birth dates according to the Chinese calender and tend to add one more year to their age. Similarly, in the assessment of orientation, the elderly may very often give the Chinese date. In this study, using the *International Statistical Classification of Diseases and Related Health Problems—Ninth Revision* (World Health Organization, 1978) (ICD-9) criteria, there was no case of manic-depressive psychosis, hysterical neurosis, phobic disorder, or obsessive-compulsive neurosis. Overall, compared to Western studies, there was a lower prevalence of mental disorder, with differences in prevalence rates being less marked in dementia but greater in depression. In patients with depression, there were no reports of guilt feelings, psychotic symptoms, or psychomotor symptoms. They were more likely to present somatic complaints such as headache and chest discomfort. The lower prevalence of depression was explained by the sociocultural influence on the perception of the elderly in Chinese society. Confucian principles of respect for the elderly, filial piety, and caring for the elderly may be crucial in minimizing stress in old age.

CONCLUSIONS

Culture and ethnicity affect both the aging process and the incidence, prevalence, and phenomenology of psychopathology in the aged. The relationship can be a direct but complex one, or an indirect one related to being a minority experiencing prejudice, socioeconomic disadvantage, language and communication barriers, and immigration issues. The effects of culture on psychopathology can only be understood in the context of the relationship among culture, ethnicity, and the aging process. This understanding reveals both the universality of the evolution of gender roles as well as the unique effects of culture on different aspects of aging. These include definitions of aging, age norms, roles, age grading, life stages with their rituals, transitions between stages (gradual or abrupt), the concept of life course as a cultural unit, the status of the elderly, and intergenerational issues.

To evaluate the psychopathology of an elderly patient, the mental health professional needs to be culturally sensitive to the macrohistory (ethnic cohort history) of the patient while empathically obtaining the microhistory (personal psychiatric history) (Baker & Lightfoot, 1993).

DISCUSSION OF CASE VIGNETTES

The case vignettes from the beginning of the chapter may now be understood in light of what has been described so far.

Case 1

The woman from India assumed she would experience the reverence for the elderly that was consistent with the values of her country, culture, and ethnic group. As the oldest woman in the household and the matriarch of the family, she expected a prominent and central role in all decisions made by the family. When she moved to live with her only son and did not experience this, she felt left out and alienated. She had no network of friends or social supports outside the family. Her disappointment led to depression and a decrease in self-esteem. This case is an example of intergenerational conflict around the issue of filial piety as a result of differences in acculturation.

Case 2

The African-American woman grew up in the deep South of the United States in a rural community where extended families lived together and it was common for a child to be taken care of by grandparents or other family members, particularly if the parents did not have the financial or emotional resources to do so. In this woman's culture it was quite common to deal with emotional conflict through somatic symptoms (including conversion) or through dissociation. Her more sophisticated son had a hard time coming to terms with her symptoms and clearly felt she needed psychiatric treatment.

Case 3

This patient was part of the cohort of elderly Filipino men who had lived under Japanese occupation and had been liberated by General MacArthur. He had problems adapting to life in the United States, and his psychosis focused around the delusion that General MacArthur would rescue him from the psychiatric ward. The content of his delusion was shaped by his life experience.

Case 4

As the Nisei man became more cognitively impaired, he demonstrated more hoarding behavior and fought to keep objects he found. This might have been related to his experience, common to his cohort group during World War II, of being removed from his home and losing his possessions.

SUGGESTED CLINICAL GUIDELINES

1. Involve family members in the evaluation of an elderly patient whenever possible. This is particularly relevant to the ethnic minority elderly when they are living with their family as issues related to dependency, filial piety, roles in the family, and family loyalty are important to assess.

2. If family is involved in the life of the elder, search for differences among family members in the degree of acculturation and in expectations about age roles, dependency, and intergenerational obligations. Evaluate the issue of stigma and attitudes toward mental illness and its treatment.

3. Obtain a cultural history. This includes information about country of origin, ethnicity, and migration history, including recency of migration, age at migration, reasons for migration, presence of family and support systems in the adopted country, the migration experience, and acceptance and integration in the larger culture of the adopted country. Obtain occupational and socioeconomic history before and after migration to evaluate premorbid functioning as well as to determine if a significant change in status occurred that

might be an added stress in adaptation to the adopted country. Determine if psychopathology predates migration. Also consider the use of language, barriers to communication, and availability and accessibility of appropriate services.

4. Find out about cohort experiences, such as common historical experiences for ethnic groups of that particular age.

5. Evaluate the patient's cultural identity and sense of integration with the larger culture. Determine if there are conflicts between the patient's culture and the larger culture, especially as it relates to attitudes toward normal and abnormal aging, age norms, stages, roles, and intergenerational relations. If so, determine how the patient has dealt with these conflicts.

6. Use culture-specific or culture-sensitive tests, especially for cognitive evaluation, if available. Otherwise, interpret tests very cautiously, because of reduced reliability and validity across cultures.

7. Do not automatically assume that there are cultural explanations for behavior and psychopathology. Be aware that there are universal aspects of aging and psychopathology, such as the increasing incidence of dementia as people age.

REFERENCES

Advisory Panel on Alzheimer's Disease. (1992). *Fourth report of the advisory panel on Alzheimer's disease.* National Institute of Health Publication No. 93–3520. Washington, D.C.: Supt. of Docs; U.S. Govt. Print. Off., 1993.

Baker, F. M. (1992). Suicide among ethnic minority elderly: A statistical and social perspective. *Journal of Geriatric Psychiatry, 23,* 241–264.

Baker, F.M. (1994). Issues in the psychiatric care of African-American elders. In *Ethnic minority elderly—A task force report of the American Psychiatric Association* (pp. 21–62). Washington, D.C.: American Psychiatric Press, Inc.

Baker, F. M & Lightfoot, O. B. (1993). Psychiatric care of ethnic elders. In A.C. Gaw (Ed.), *Culture, ethnicity and mental illness* (pp. 517–552). Washington, D.C.: American Psychiatric Press, Inc.

Browne, C., Fong, R., & Mokuau, N. (1994). The mental health of Asian and Pacific Island elders: Implications for research and mental health administration. *The Journal of Mental Health Administration, 21,* 54–59.

Dowd, J. & Bengston, V. L. (1978). Aging in minority populations: An examination of the double jeopardy hypothesis. *Journal of Gerontology, 33,* 427–436.

Freed, A. O. (1992). Discussion: Minority elderly. *Journal of Geriatric Psychiatry, 23,* 105–111.

Fry, C. L. (1988). Theories of age and culture. In J.E. Birren & V.L. Bengston (Eds.), *Emerging theories of aging* (pp. 447–481). Berlin: Springer–Verlag.

Glascock, A. P. & Feinman, S. (1986). Toward a comparative framework: Propositions concerning the treatment of the aged in non-industrial societies. In C. L. Fry & J. Keith (Eds.), *New methods for old age research: Strategies for studying diversity* (pp. 281–296). South Hadley, MA: Bergin & Garvey.

Guttman, D. (1975). Parenthood: A key to the comparative study of the life cycle. In N. Data & L.H. Ginsberg (Eds.), *Life-span developmental psychology: Normative life crises* (pp. 167–184). New York: Academic Press.

Hauser, P. M. (1986). Ageing and increasing longevity of world population. In H. Hafner, G. Moschel, & N. Sartorius (Eds.), *Mental health in the elderly* (pp. 9–14). Berlin: Springer-Verlag.

Homma, A. (1994). Mental illness in elderly persons in Japan. In J.R.M. Copeland, M.T. Abou-Saleh, & D.G. Blazer (Eds.), *Principles and practice of geriatric psychiatry* (pp. 857–863). Chichester, England: John Wiley & Sons, Ltd.

Ikels, C. (1980). The coming of age in Chinese society: Traditional patterns and contemporary Hong Kong. In C.L. Fry (Ed.), *Aging in culture and society: comparative viewpoints and strategies* (pp. 80–100). New York: Springer Publishing Co.

Jackson, J.S., Antonucci, T.C., & Gibson R.C. (1990). Cultural, racial and ethnic minority influences on aging. In J.E. Birren & K.W. Schaie (Eds.), *Handbook of psychology of aging, third edition* (pp. 103–123). San Diego: Academic Press.

Johnson, C. L. (1983). Interdependence and aging in Italian families. In J. Sokolovsky (Ed.), *Growing old in different cultures* (pp. 92–103). Belmont, CA: Wadsworth.

Keith, J. (1990). Age in social and cultural context—anthropological perspectives. In R. H. Binstock & L.K. George (Eds.), *Handbook of aging and the social sciences* (pp. 91–111). San Diego: Academic Press.

Kua, E. H. (1994). Mental illness in elderly Chinese in Singapore. In J.R.M. Copeland, M.T. Abou-Saleh, & D.G. Blazer (Eds.), *Principles and practice of geriatric psychiatry* (pp. 851–855). Chichester, England: John Wiley & Sons, Ltd.

Kuo, W. H. (1984). Prevalence of depression among Asian Americans. *The Journal of Nervous and Mental Disease, 172,* 449–457.

Lee, G. R. & Kezis, M. (1981). Societal literacy and the aged. *International Journal of Aging and Human Development, 12,* 221–234.

Lowenstein, D. A. (1995). Culturally appropriate tests. *International Psychogeriatric Association Bulletin,* 31–32.

Lowenstein, D.A., Arguelles, T., Arguelles, S., & Linn-Fuentes, P. (1994). Potential cultural bias in the neuropsychological assessment of the older adult. *Journal of Clinical and Experimental Neuropsychology, 16*, 623–629.

Markides, K. S., Liang, J., & Jackson, J. S. (1990). Race, ethnicity, and aging: Conceptual and methodological issues. In R.H. Binstock & L.K. George (Eds.), *Handbook of aging and the social sciences* (pp. 112–125). San Diego: Academic Press.

Markides, K. S. (1986). Minority status, aging, and mental health. *International Journal of Aging and Human Development, 23*, 285–300.

Rosenthal, C. J. (1986). Family supports in later life: Does ethnicity make a difference? *The Gerontologist, 26*, 19–24.

Sakauye, K. (1992). The elderly Asian patient. *Journal of Geriatric Psychiatry, 23*, 85–104.

Siegel, J. S. & Taeuber, C. M. (1986). Demographic perspectives on the longlived society. *Daedalus, 115*, 77–118.

Silverman, P. & Maxwell, R.J. (1983). The significance of information and power in the comparative study of the aged. In J. Sokolovsky (Ed), *Growing old in different societies: Cross-cultural perspectives* (pp. 43–55). Belmont, CA: Wadsworth.

Silverman, P. & Maxwell, R. J. (1978). How do I respect thee? Let me count the ways: Deference towards elderly men and women. *Behavioral Science Research, 13*, 91–108.

Stanford, E. P. & Du Bois, B. C. (1992). Gender and ethnicity patterns. In J.E. Birren, R.B. Sloan, & G.D. Cohen (Eds.), *Handbook of mental health and aging, second edition* (pp. 99–117). San Diego: Academic Press.

WHO. (1978). Mental disorders: Glossary and guide to their classification in accordance with the ninth revision of the International Classification of Diseases. Geneva: World Health Organization.

Wong, P. T. & Reker, G. T. (1985). Stress, coping and well-being in Anglo and Chinese elderly. *Canadian Journal on Aging, 4*, 29–37.

Yeh, E., Hwu, H., Chang, L., & Yeh Y. (1994). Mental disorders and cognitive impairment among the elderly community population in Taiwan. In J.R.M. Copeland, M.T. Abou-Saleh, & D.G. Blazer (Eds.), *Principles and practice of geriatric psychiatry* (pp. 865–871). Chichester, England: John Wiley & Sons, Ltd.

CHAPTER FOURTEEN

Integration and Conclusions

Wen-Shing Tseng, M.D.
and Jon Streltzer, M.D.

The preceding chapters demonstrate quite clearly the wide-ranging influence of culture on various forms of psychopathology. The relationship between culture and psychopathology, however, is far from simple, and is often indirect and multifaceted. Our knowledge is limited by the paucity of well-designed research studies. Even descriptive and epidemiological studies are relatively scarce. These studies only allow a broad, general understanding of the field, enticing us to increase our knowledge base and our cultural sensitivity.

FACTORS LIMITING OUR UNDERSTANDING OF CULTURE AND PSYCHOPATHOLOGY

Culture is an abstract concept that defies measurement. As discussed in Chapter 1, culturally related behavior may be considered from alternative viewpoints, including: *stereotypical, actual, ideal,* and *deviant,* each of which may be substantially at variance with

241

any other, even though referring to the same cultural group. Psychopathology is also a highly complex concept that is subject to alternative definitions and categorizations, and is shaped by many factors other than culture, including: age, gender, individual life experiences, socioeconomic status, biological predisposition, and medical illnesses. Thus, it becomes exquisitely difficult to delineate the influence of culture on psychopathology.

Research in the area is automatically subject to limitations that interfere with our ability to form clear-cut conclusions. Defining the cultural group can be quite difficult. Most studies are done by comparing ethnic groups. This can be misleading, however, because ethnic groups may be composed of subcultures that differ markedly from each other. Socioeconomic status and minority status are commonly confounded with culture. Immigration status, including generation and cohort experiences, is also critical in modifying conclusions about culture. For example, a low socioeconomic class, immigrant Hispanic population in the United States would have substantial cultural differences from a related population in the home country.

Attempts to sort out these differences can be made by being aware of issues such as acculturation, ethnic identification, and heritage consistency. Being familiar with these concepts when considering the individual's personal cultural experience helps to overcome the difficulties these multiple factors introduce into an assessment of psychopathology. In a clinical situation, a good general rule is to assume that individuals more than likely will not conform to stereotypes.

UNIVERSALITY VERSUS CULTURAL SPECIFICITY

Psychopathology may be conceptualized as having different degrees of universality or cultural specificity. At one extreme are conditions with a predominantly universal core that are essentially free of cultural influence. Biologically driven conditions, in particular, are most likely to manifest similarly in all cultures. The dementias, involving the deterioration of the brain, have mostly universal characteristics. Culture does not influence the intellectual decline, memory loss, and disorientation that accompany dementia. Schizophrenia appears to be a universal disorder that is present in all societies with remarkably little variation in incidence. Although the etiology of schizophrenia is still not understood, there is a presumption of strong biological determinants. The apparent universality of schizo-phrenia supports this presumption.

At the other extreme are the culture-bound syndromes (CBSs). For example, *koro* is a syndrome that involves the fear that the penis will shrink into the abdomen and the person will die. From a clini-cal perspective, it could be considered an anxiety, or possibly a depersonalization disorder (Jilek, 1986; Tseng et al., 1992). Koro occurs only within certain cultural groups, sometimes in epidemic fashion affecting hundreds or even thousands of individuals. In other cultures, the condition is considered laughable and, thus, unimaginable.

Most syndromes, however, lie in between the extremes. They might be considered to have greater or lesser universal core, with more or less cultural elaboration or revision of the base psy-chopathology. Depression appears to be a universal human phe-nomenon, with some forms, particularly the melancholic subtype, that may be strongly biologically based. Other forms of depression appear to be more induced by "stress" and situational factors. Since culture profoundly influences the interpretation of events and pro-vides the context for life experiences, we believe that culture has a significant influence on many forms of depression (Kleinman & Good, 1985). Dissociative disorders would seem to have particularly prominent cultural influence, and many CBSs could be considered dissociative disorders. On the other hand, this class of disorders seems to be present in all cultures, and there may, indeed, be a bio-logical basis to the ability to dissociate. Pain would appear to be a universal experience caused by an external injury or disease, yet we have learned that culture strongly affects the reaction to pain, so much so that the experience of pain may actually be different because of cultural background.

We conclude that most psychopathological conditions have both universal and cultural aspects. The cultural influence may some-times be considered "core" or etiological. Most commonly, culture has secondary influences affecting the disorder at various levels.

From an epistemological standpoint, the determination of which portion of a pathological condition is core or "typical" and which is secondary cultural elaboration, may actually reflect the ethnocen-tric perspective of the person who is classifying or evaluating the condition. For example, American psychiatrists have considered the Japanese disorder *taijinkuofusho* as a "variation" of the social pho-bia defined in American classification. Japanese psychiatrists, how-ever, consider *taijinkuofusho* to be a typical social phobia, while social phobia as observed and described in the United States is a

"Western variation" (Kirmayer, 1991; Prince, 1991). One of the most common diagnoses in the world is "neurasthenia" (prominent in China, Japan, and other countries), yet American psychiatry (DSM-IV) considers the condition to be an "unclassified" somatic disorder. For disorders with predominantly psychological, and thus, socio-cultural determinants, it is necessary to be cautious in deciding the "core" condition.

LEVELS OF CULTURAL INFLUENCE ON PSYCHOPATHOLOGY

In addition to a primary role in etiology, as with the CBSs, culture secondarily affects psychopathology at various levels. These include the phenomenology or clinical presentation of the disorder, the reactions to and interpretations of the disorder by the patient and the family, including their help-seeking behavior, and, most importantly, the outcome or prognosis.

Symptom Presentation

The type of complaint presented to the examiner is frequently influenced by culture. The patient's understanding of illness, the meaning of symptoms, reasons for help-seeking, and culturally shaped "problem-presenting style" all affect the patient's pattern of symptom presentation to the clinician. There is a great deal of evidence that culture is highly influential when somatic complaints are the presenting symptoms of psychopathology. Somatic complaints may represent any of several underlying disorders, including somatoform, depressive, anxiety, and physical illness. There may also be more universality to this type of complaint than previously believed. In fact, there is evidence that, world-wide, the presentation of psychological complaints in these disorders is more unusual and culture specific.

Phenomenology

Culture clearly has substantial influence on the phenomenology of different disorders, including those considered to be universal. For example, dementia and schizophrenia tend to manifest different behavioral abnormalities in different cultures. In some cultures, the paranoid subtype of schizophrenia is most common, whereas, in others, paranoia is fairly rare while catatonia is quite common. Similarly, dementia varies in appearance depending upon the demands placed on the individual undergoing the dementing process. If an elderly demented patient is revered and well taken care of by a supportive family, the individual's limitations may not be recognized or problematic, compared to an individual subjected to ongoing environmental demands. Because culture has a strong influence on the attitude toward and care of the elderly, it can even influence the phenomenology of such a clearly biological condition as dementia.

Family Involvement

Families frequently play a critical role for the mentally ill person, including being the greatest potential source of support. Culture is a potent determinant of the family's response. The family may consider the patient's condition to be shameful and something to be hidden, or the family may be motivated to solve problems and provide resources. At another level, the family may foster or minimize psychopathology (Tseng & Hsu, 1991). For example, the family may be more or less facilitating of dependent, paranoid, or narcissistic traits on the part of the patient.

Community Response

Culture determines the community's degree of tolerance for deviant behavior. This includes the threshold for considering behavior "shameful." In a related fashion, culture influences the laws governing behavior that is disruptful to the community, such as violence. Cultural values are also demonstrated in the community's concern for the mentally ill, as reflected by provisions in the health care system for treatment and resources for rehabilitation.

Prognosis

Culture markedly influences the impact of illness and its prognosis. For example, schizophrenia seems to have a better prognosis in less developed countries, possibly because demands for complex behavior are less. Work-related emotional disorders tend to become more chronic and severe in societies where compensation and disability benefits are provided by the social system for such illnesses. Dissociative and conversion reactions tend to recover more rapidly in cultures where people do not take favorable attitudes toward the occurrence of such disorders.

INFLUENCE OF MEDICAL CULTURE ON THE ASSESSMENT OF PSYCHOPATHOLOGY

The examining clinician's values and beliefs critically influence his or her perceptions and understanding of a patient's psychopathology. These values and beliefs are primarily associated with the clinician's training and professional orientation. This "medical culture" is not fixed, but is continuously being modified. Historically, medicine has experienced many evolutionary changes. Within psychiatry, there have been alternating shifts in belief systems, whereby psychopathology has been considered to be either primarily biological or primarily psychological. Psychopathology has been evaluated from objective–descriptive, existential, and psychoanalytic orientations, among others. Diagnoses have been categorical (criteria-based), or dimensional (theory-based) on a spectrum of normal to abnormal. A dualistic approach to the mind–body problem remains prominent in clinical practice, despite the popularity of a holistic or biopsychosocial approach in medical teaching.

Currently, there is a tendency to "medicalize" psychiatric assessment. The needed information must be gathered efficiently in a limited time. A differential diagnosis is made by checking the presenting symptoms against less defined categories. Diagnostic trees are traced until the final diagnosis is made. This technique offers simplicity and clarity and appears quite scientific. There are risks associated with this approach, however, from a cultural point of view (Alarcon, 1995). Expediency may lead a clinician to accept the presenting complaints at face value. Undetected cultural factors may distort the gathering of clinical information, as well as its interpretation, leading to a less than optimal clinical assessment (Koss, 1987).

It is important to note that culture is not the same as ethnicity, and that even within a given culture, there is a range of beliefs, values, and attitudes. Thus, culture must be used as a guide to understand the individual, not as an excuse for stereotyping (Comas-Diaz

& Griffith, 1988). By exploring the patient's cultural background, the clinician may begin to understand the specific values and beliefs, as well as the meanings, that the patient gives to his or her complaints, as well as the patient's perceptions of the current impact of the illness and his or her expectations for the future (Favazza & Oman, 1980). For the assessment to be comprehensive and accurate, the clinician must understand not only the patient's cultural background, but also the potentially distorting effects of his or her "medical culture" on the evaluation process.

CLINICAL ASSESSMENT AS A DYNAMIC PROCESS

This section reemphasizes the information presented in the introductory chapter. The first step in the process leading to a clinical evaluation involves the patient's recognition of his or her difficulties. The patient's perception and insight into his or her problems will commonly have significant cultural roots. This may be the case even if the problem has a primarily biological etiology. Additional cultural factors may be present if the problem arose as the result of environmental stress or interpersonal interactions.

The patient's help-seeking behavior will be closely related to his or her understanding of the problems or disorder. Cultural and family factors determine when, how, and from whom help is sought.

When the patient presents the complaint to the clinician, the issue of the dynamic interaction between the patient and care provider becomes important. In the chapter on pain, for example, it was noted that, in some clinical situations, the assessment of severity of pain was more related to interaction between staff and patient, than it was a result of actual complaints of pain.

This interaction occurs on several levels. The patient has culturally influenced expectations of the clinician. The patient may modify the way complaints are presented, depending on his or her anticipation of the clinician's response. The patient's expectations of the clinician will be based on the patient's interpretation of the clinician as an individual with his or her own cultural background, and, more often, as a clinician who is part of the "medical culture." In turn, the manner in which the clinician asks questions or seeks information will also be influenced by his or her personal culture, as well as his or her clinical training. The "style" of gathering information will influence the patient, affecting the information which is forthcoming. The clinician is likely to only elicit information that he or she would be able to understand, and, thus, the clinician may be susceptible to finding only what has been sought. This would particularly be the case if the patient's cultural background is such that the patient wishes to please or accommodate the clinician. The "net" (see Chapter 1) that the clinician uses to capture information thus determines what information is given. The clinician who is insightful about these issues will be likely to obtain more information, and will have a broader ability to interpret the information received.

CLINICAL REQUIREMENTS FOR SKILLFUL TRANSCULTURAL ASSESSMENT

Cultural Sensitivity

The clinician should automatically assume that the patient's knowledge, values, and belief systems will differ from his or her own, until proven otherwise. If, indeed, there are significant differences in values and beliefs, the clinician must be careful to be non-judgmental, open to learning about these differences, and respectful of the patient's viewpoint.

Cultural History

Early in the process of evaluation, the clinician should take a cultural history. This would cover not just the patient's ethnic background, but information about the importance of cultural factors in the patient's upbringing, including his or her ethnocultural identity (Jacobsen, 1988). The clinician should explore basic values and life view, and look for relevant belief systems, especially having to do with the presenting symptoms and problems (Westermeyer, 1993). This latter issue is particularly elaborated in the chapters on dissociation, anxiety, and violence.

Understanding the Patient's Culture

It is highly desirable for the clinician to have basic knowledge about behavior patterns that are common within the patient's cultural system. This includes orientation to the world, attitudes toward life, patterns of personal development, family structure, religion, rituals, generally held beliefs, and so on. Based on "ordinary" patterns of behavior, and "usual" types of response, a clinician can make a more relevant assessment of the patient's behavior. This is particularly essential when the clinician is evaluating a personality disorder, or "unusual" behavior that is closely related to culturally observed rituals. Without knowledge of culturally acceptable ranges of behavior, cultural variations in development and life cycle, or culture-related rituals, judgments about psychopathology are fraught with danger. For example, it would be difficult for a clinician to make a diagnosis of pathological mourning without knowledge of typical grief reactions and mourning rituals in the patient's culture.

Of course, it is impossible for the clinician to have ample anthropological knowledge for very many cultures. Medical anthropological consultation can be of immense help, but may not be readily available. The clinician is thus advised to make use of the patient or family members as resources to provide cultural information. Needless to say, the objectivity of such information should be assessed carefully. On the other hand, the patient and his or her family's opinions about their culture is useful information in and of itself.

Knowledge of Cultural Variations in Psychopathology

It is, of course, desirable to know of culture-related specific psychiatric disorders, the CBSs, but from a practical point of view, it is rare to encounter such exotic cases, unless a clinician is practicing in a particular setting where an identified culture-related specific syndrome is prevalent. Furthermore, many so-called CBSs are rather loosely identified or labeled, and, in fact, are not necessarily culture-related specific psychiatric syndromes at all (Tseng & McDermott, 1981). They may merely reflect folk names (such as *susto* for "loss of soul"), that are used to address and interpret certain universal emotional conditions, and which, in turn, invite certain social responses, or they may refer to culturally reinforced behavior (such as *latah*, or "startle reaction"), which has specific social functions, but is not necessarily pathological (Simons, 1985). Thus, in most clinical settings, it is more important to recognize that common types of psychopathology may not always present in the "typical" fashion encountered in any particular country when they occur in a members of a different culture. Psychopathology tends to be influenced by culture, not necessarily in etiology, but most frequently in its manifestation. This appears to be true for almost any kind of psychopathology. Knowledge of the cultural modifications in presentation of common psychopathological conditions is important for the clinician treating patients of diverse cultural backgrounds (Gaviria & Arana, 1987; Gaw, 1993; Pfeiffer, 1994).

The Cultural Gap Between Clinician and Patient

From the beginning of a clinical evaluation, it is important to be aware of and to assess the extent of the "cultural gap" that may exist between clinician and patient. This cultural gap can potentially interfere with and sabotage the process of assessment and management. This is a particularly critical issue when the clinician is dealing with an adolescent patient.

It is recommended that early in the assessment process the clinician bring up for discussion the fact of the cultural difference when this is obvious. This discussion is particularly important if it addresses dominant and submissive, or majority and minority, differences in background. By putting the issue of the cultural gap up front, the clinician makes it subject to examination and can negotiate how to minimize possible ill-effects. The clinician should take the position of working with the patient on a fairly equal basis, avoiding any appearance of condescension or paternalism.

While there may be disadvantages in evaluating a patient where there is a significant cultural gap because of the potential for misunderstanding, there are also advantages. The patient may be more comfortable with an evaluator from a different culture, who might be considered less likely to critically judge the patient's condition or behavior. Just as most people would feel uncomfortable revealing difficulties, inadequacies, or conflicts to friends and relatives, they would be more comfortable revealing these to a neutral stranger, particularly one with professional qualifications to help them.

The clinician may also use the cultural gap to his or her advantage by openly acknowledging a lack of understanding of the patient's situation, that is, the context in which the symptoms occur. The patient should be asked to explain his or her beliefs, values, and expectations. This allows for a more in-depth assessment, and minimizes the chances of false assumptions. Indeed, with a patient of similar cultural background to the clinician, it may be dangerous to assume too quickly that the problems are understood, and that the patient has similar values, or would respond in the same ways as the clinician in a given situation.

CULTURE-ORIENTED TRAINING AND EXPERIENCE

Training for contemporary mental health workers should include a significant component that focuses on the influence of culture on behavior, mental illness, and mental health treatment. The incorporation of cultural sensitivity should always be an objective in the teaching of interviewing and diagnostic skills. Ideally, however, the contemporary mental health worker will have cultural experience that goes beyond the knowledge of cultural influences on behavior and psychopathology. It is extremely useful to have actual clinical experiences working in a multiethnic community, or a setting in which patients have distinctly varying cultural backgrounds. Such cross-cultural experiences allow knowlege to translate into meaningful application. It is also extremely desirable for a clinician to have experience living in a foreign society or with a group of people from a cultural background widely different than his or her own. Even if the experience is brief, it will enable a deeper appreciation of cultural differences, and (hopefully) foster an attitude of respect toward others. This attitude, involving cultural sensitivity and appreciation of individual differences, should enhance work with people of all backgrounds, including those who are culturally similar.

REFERENCES

Alarcon, R.D. (1995). Culture and psychiatric diagnosis: Impact on DSM-IV and ICD-10. In R.D. Alarcon (Ed.), *The psychiatric clinics of North America: Cultural psychiatry* (pp. 449–465). Philadelphia: W.B. Saunders Company.

Comas-Diaz, L. & Griffith, E.E.H. (Eds.) (1988). *Clinical guidelines in cross-cultural mental health*. New York: John Wiley & Sons.

Favazza, A.R. & Oman, M. (1980). Anthropology and Psychiatry. In H.I. Kaplan, A.M. Freedman, B.J. Sadock (Eds.), *Comprehensive textbook of psychiatry/III*. Baltimore: Williams & Wilkins.

Gaw, A.C. (1993). *Culture, ethnicity, and mental illness*. Washington, D.C.: American Psychiatric Press.

Gaviria, M. & Arana, J.D. (1987). *Health and behavior: Research agenda for Hispanics*. Chicago: Simon Bolivar Hispanic-American Psychiatric Research and Training Program.

Jacobsen, F.M. (1988). Ethnocultural assessment. In L. Comas-Diaz & E.E.H. Griffith (Eds.), *Clinical guidelines in cross-cultural mental health* (pp. 135–147). New York: John Wiley & Sons, Ltd.

Jilek, W.G. (1986). Epidemics of "genital shrinking" (*koro*): Historical review and report of a recent outbreak in South China. *Curare, 9,* 268–282.

Kirmayer, L.J. (1991). The place of culture in psychiatric nosology: Taijin kyofusho and DSM-III-R. *Journal of Nervous and Mental Disease, 179,* 19–22.

Kleinman, A. & Good, B. (1985). *Culture and depression: Studies in the anthropology and cross-cultural psychiatry of affect and disorder.* Berkeley: University of California Press.

Koss, J.D. (1987). Ethnomedical categories in the diagnosis and treatment of Hispanic patients: A review of the studies and implications for research. In M. Gaviria & J.D. Arana (Eds.), *Health and behavior: Research agenda for Hispanics* (pp. 187–206). Chicago: Simon-Bolivar Hispanic-American Psychiatric Research and Training Program.

Pfeiffer, W.M. (1994). *Transkulturelle psychiatrie: Ergebnisse und probleme.* New York: Georg Thieme Verlag Stuttgart.

Prince, R.H. (1991). Transcultural psychiatry's contribution to international classification system: The example of social phobias. *Transcultural Psychiatric Research Review, 28,* 124–132.

Simons, R.C. (1985). The resolution of the latah paradox. In R.C. Simons & C.C. Hughes (Eds.), *The culture-bound syndromes: Folk illnesses of psychiatric and anthropological interest* (pp. 43–62). Dordrecht: D. Reidel Publishing Company.

Tseng, W.S. & Hsu, J. (1991). *Culture and family: Problems and therapy.* New York: Haworth Press.

Tseng, W.S. & McDermott, J.F., Jr. (1981). *Culture, mind and therapy: An introduction to cultural psychiatry.* New York: Brunner/Mazel.

Tseng, W.S., Mo, K.M., Li, L.S., Chen, G.Q., Ou, L.W., & Zhen, H.B. (1992). Koro epidemics in Guangdong, China: A questionnaire survey. *Journal of Nervous and Mental Disease, 180,* 117–123.

Westermeyer, J.J. (1985). Psychiatric diagnosis across cultural boundaries. *American Journal of Psychiatry, 142,* 798–805.

Westermeyer, J.J. (1993). Cross-cultural psychiatric assessment. In A.C. Gaw (Ed.), *Culture, ethnicity, and mental illness* (pp. 125–144). Washington, D.C.: American Psychiatric Press.

NAME INDEX

SUBJECT INDEX